JOURNAL FOR THE STUDY OF THE OLD TESTAMENT
SUPPLEMENT SERIES
114

Editors
David J.A. Clines
Philip R. Davies

JSOT Press
Sheffield

Louis Jacobs

A
TRADITIONAL
QUEST

Essays in Honour of
Louis Jacobs

Edited by
Dan Cohn-Sherbok

Journal for the Study of the Old Testament
Supplement Series 114

Copyright © 1991 Sheffield Academic Press

Published by JSOT Press
JSOT Press is an imprint of
Sheffield Academic Press Ltd
The University of Sheffield
343 Fulwood Road
Sheffield S10 3BP
England

Typeset by Sheffield Academic Press
and
Printed on acid-free paper in Great Britain
by Billing & Sons Ltd
Worcester

British Library Cataloguing in Publication Data

A traditional quest.
  1. Judaism
  I. Cohn-Sherbok, Dan   II. Jacobs, Louis
  296

  ISSN 0309-0787
  ISBN 1-85075-279-6

CONTENTS

PREFACE

This collection of essays is presented to Rabbi Dr Louis Jacobs by a number of his many friends and admirers. Over the years he has made a monumental contribution to Jewish scholarship in a wide range of fields. In over thirty books and numerous articles he has engaged in pioneering research and has also provided illuminating introductions to various aspects of Jewish thought. In addition, he has provided spiritual leadership to members of his congregation, the New London Synagogue. The individual chapters in this Festschrift deal with subject areas in which Louis Jacobs has had an interest, and the contributors are drawn from a number of different spheres of his academic life. The volume is intended as a tribute both to him as a person and as one of the leading Jewish scholars of our time.

Dan Cohn-Sherbok

1

FROM PHILOSOPHY TO RELIGION

Jacob Neusner

It is with that certainty of its appropriateness that I present to Louis Jacobs this theoretical statement on the classification of Judaisms, or Judaic systems, with special interest in the movement from an essentially philosophical to an essentially religious Judaism. For Rabbi Jacobs is a formidable figure in contemporary Judaic theological discourse, and his combination of wit, perspicacity and learning—the counterpart to 'Torah and greatness' of another age—have won for him a well-earned position in the forefront of religious thought in the theological framework. He will therefore be the first to recognize that discourse in Judaism need not take, and frequently has not been given, the form of theological or even religious discourse. In two distinct ages, the first and second centuries, and the tenth through fourteenth centuries, it was an essentially philosophical Judaism, and not a fundamentally religious one, that occupied center-stage among the important intellects of Judaism. In this paper I offer a tribute to an honored and esteemed colleague and friend by setting forth a theory of the movement from a philosophical Judaism, fully set forth in the Mishnah, in the second century, to a religious Judaism laid out in the Yerushalmi, Genesis Rabbah, Leviticus Rabbah, and related writings, in the late fourth and fifth centuries. Subsequent research of mine will undertake to show the further transformation, from a religious to a theological Judaic system, emerging whole and complete from late antiquity.[1]

---

1. This paper summarizes the main thesis of my *Transformation of Judaism: From Philosophy to Religion* (Urbana: University of Illinois Press, 1991).

1. *The Canon and the System of the Judaism of the Dual Torah*

To gain access to the theory of the social order that a religious system wishes to set forth, we turn to its canon, since the canon recapitulates the system, not the system, the canon. In the case of the description of successive Judaic systems—theories of the social order made up of a new world view, a way of life, and a theory of the social entity, 'Israel'—we have therefore first of all to gain perspective upon the canon of the Judaism that emerged from ancient times and governed to our own day. When we have grasped the stages in the unfolding of the canonical writings of that single Judaism, we shall find it possible also to characterize the Judaic systems to which each subset among the group of documents attests. That canon, called 'the Torah', in two parts, written and oral, consisted of the Hebrew Scriptures of ancient Israel ('the Old Testament'), called in this Judaism 'the written Torah', and a set of writings later on accorded the status of Torah as well and assigned origin at Sinai through a process of oral formulation and oral transmission, hence, 'the oral Torah'.

The first of those writings that came to comprise the oral Torah, the single most important one, was the Mishnah, c. 200. That document carried in its wake two sustained amplifications and extensions called talmuds, the one produced in the Land of Israel, hence the Talmud of the Land of Israel, c. 400, the other in Babylonia, in the Iranian Empire, hence the Talmud of Babylonia, c. 600.

The other important part of the Torah, the written part, served analogously to define a framework for (formally) continuous discourse and so received a variety of sustained amplifications, called Midrash-compilations. These form three sets, corresponding to the Mishnah, the Talmud of the Land of Israel, and the Talmud of Babylonia.

1. *The Mishnah's counterparts in Midrash-compilations.* The first, within the orbit of the Mishnah, c. 200–300, addressed the books of Exodus, Leviticus, Numbers, and Deuteronomy, in *Mekhilta de R. Ishmael* for Exodus, *Sifra*, for Leviticus, one *Sifré* to Numbers, another *Sifré*, to Deuteronomy.

2. *The Yerushalmi's counterparts in Midrash-compilations.* The second, c. 400–500, associated with the first of the two Talmuds, took up the books of Genesis and Leviticus, in *Genesis*

Rabbah and *Leviticus Rabbah*, and the latter begat *Pesiqta deRab Kahana* in its model.

3. *The Bavli's counterparts in Midrash-compilations*: The third, c. 500–600, identified with the second Talmud, addressed a lectionary cycle of the synagogue, dealing with the books of Lamentations (read on the ninth of Ab), Esther (read on Purim), Ruth (read on Pentecost), and the Song of Songs (read on Passover), in *Lamentations Rabbah*, *Esther Rabbah* I (the first two chapters only), *Ruth Rabbah*, and *Song of Songs Rabbah*.

The first of the three groups presents marks of transition and mediation from one system to the next.[1] The second, *Genesis Rabbah* and *Leviticus Rabbah*, joined by *Pesiqta deRab Kahana*, with the Talmud of the Land of Israel, attest to that system that I classify as religious. The third, the final Rabbah-compilations, together with the Talmud of Babylonia, point to the one I classify as theological, and in a moment I shall define the indicative traits of each classification.

Now, as is clear, the documentary evidence set forth a system of a very particular kind: one that laid out the components of the social order and explained how they formed a cogent whole. From beginning to end, the Judaic systems attested by the successive parts of the canon defined as their problem the construction of a social world. The categorical structure of each, in succession, framed intelligible thought by appeal to the issues of the world framed, first of all, by a particular ethnos, the social entity (the most neutral language I can find), which was called (an) 'Israel'. Every Judaic system, moreover, would take as its task the definition of the shared life of (an) Israel: its way of life or (broadly speaking) ethics, its world view or ethos. So each set forth the account of the social entity or the 'Israel' that realized in its shared and corporate being the ethics (again, broadly construed), and explained that ethos by appeal to the ethos. As a matter of definition, it must follow, a Judaic system is a system that derives its generative categories from the (theoretical) requirements of framing a social order: who are 'we', what do we do together, and why are we the corporate body that we are, thus, ethnos, ethics, ethos. And that brings us back to

---

1. That is the thesis of my *The Canonical History of Ideas. The Place of the So-called Tannaite Midrashim, Mekhilta Attributed to R. Ishmael, Sifra, Sifré to Numbers, and Sifré to Deuteronomy* (Atlanta: Scholars Press for Brown Judaic Studies, 1990).

the first of the great Judaic systems that in the end formed Judaism, the system to which the authorship of the Mishnah refer in framing their writing.

The Mishnah set forth in the form of a law code a highly philosophical account of the world ('world view'), a pattern for everyday and material activities and relationships ('way of life'), and a definition of the social entity ('nation', 'people', 'us' as against 'outsiders', 'Israel') that realized that way of life and explained it by appeal to that world view. Then the successor-documents, closed roughly two centuries later, addressed the Mishnah's system and recast its categories into a connected, but also quite revised, one.

Why call them 'successors'? Because, in form, the writings of the late fourth and fifth centuries were organized and presented as commentaries on a received text, the Mishnah for the Talmud, Scripture for the Midrash-compilations. So the later authorships insisted, in their own behalf, that they (merely) explained and amplified the received Torah. When these documents attached themselves to the Mishnah, on the one side, and the Hebrew Scriptures, on the other, they gave literary form to the theory that the one stood for the oral, the other, the written, revelation, or Torah, that God gave to Moses at Mount Sinai.

Specifically, the Talmud of the Land of Israel, formed around thirty-nine of the Mishnah's sixty-two tractates, and *Genesis Rabbah* and *Leviticus Rabbah* (joined by *Pesiqta deRab Kahana*), addressed the first and third books of Moses, respectively, along with some other documents. The very act of choosing among the Mishnah's tractates only some and ignoring others, of course, represents an act of taste and judgment—hence system-building through tacit statement made by silence. But, as a matter of fact, much of the Talmud as well as of the principal Midrash-compilations do amplify and augment the base-documents to which they are attached.[1] In choosing some passages and

---

1. My estimate for the Talmud of the Land of Israel, in the tractates I probed, is that, in volume, as much as 90% of the Talmud serves to amplify passages of the Mishnah, and not much more than 10% contains intellectual initiatives that are fundamentally fresh and unrelated to anything in the Mishnah-passage under discussion, see my *Talmud of the Land of Israel, ch. XXXV. Introduction. Taxonomy* (Chicago: The University of Chicago Press, 1983). Then my *Judaism in Society. The Evidence of the Yerushalmi. Toward the Natural History of a Religion* (Chicago, 1983) aims to show that even the passages that (merely) clarify words or phrases of the Mishnah in fact set forth a considerable, autonomous program of their own, cf. especially pp. 73-112. But what is clearly distinct from the Mishnah is set forth on pp. 113-254.

neglecting others, and, more to the point, in working out their own questions and their own answers, in addition to those of the Mishnah, the authorships[1] attest to a system that did more than merely extend and recast the categorical structure of the system for which the Mishnah stands. They took over the way of life, world view, and social entity, defined in the Mishnah's system. And while they rather systematically amplified details, framed a program of exegesis around the requirements of clerks engaged in enforcing the rules of the Mishnah, they built their own system.

2. *The Mishnah: Judaism as a Philosophy in the First and Second Centuries*

The Mishnah set forth a Judaism that is to be classified as philosophical—both in method and also in message. The Judaism of the Mishnah portrayed an economics in the model of Aristotle's, and a politics closely akin to his. An economics in this context must likewise present a theory of the rational disposition of scarce resources that (other) philosophers of the same age will have recognized as familiar, therefore philosophical. A politics along these same lines must exhibit the traits of a philosophical politics as other philosophers of the age will have defined it. Since the Mishnah reached closure in c. 200, my definition of philosophy and what may be characterized as philosophical derives from that same age, the Greco-Roman one, and as a matter of fact, within the vast and varied Greco-Roman philosophical tradition, a specific figure emerges as paradigmatic.

Aristotle, for the present purpose, defines the model of philosophical method. As to a philosophical proposition of considerable weight, I appeal to an important proposition of Middle Platonism, coming to full expression, to be sure, only in the writings of Plotinus' neo-Platonism two generations after the closure of the Mishnah. If I can show that the method of the Mishnah corresponds to that of Aristotle, and

---

1. This term is meant to take account of the collective and social character of much of the literary enterprise. I have already underlined the anonymous character of the canonical evidence. Not a single authoritative book of Judaism in late antiquity bears the name of an identified author, and the literary traits of not a single piece of writing may securely be imputed to a private person. The means for gaining acceptance was anonymity, and the medium of authority lay in recapitulating collective conventions of rhetoric and logic, not to mention proposition. To speak of 'authors' in this context is confusing, and hence they resort to the word at hand.

that a fundamental message of the Mishnah restates within the appropriate idiom a proposition of Middle Platonism, I may fairly characterize the Mishnah's system as philosophical in context, that is, as a system that other philosophers could (with proper education) have recognized as philosophical. As to economics and politics, Aristotle likewise serves to set forth the standard for defining an economics that is philosophical and a philosophical politics as well. The Mishnah was philosophical both in its method, which is Aristotelian, and in its message, which is the one of Middle Platonism, and fully realized later on in Plotinus.[1]

3. *The Talmud of the Land of Israel, Genesis Rabbah, and Leviticus Rabbah: From Judaism as a Philosophy to Judaism as a Religion in the Fourth and Fifth Centuries*

We turn to the modes of thought of the successor-writings and ask principally about how, methodologically, the later documents compare with the rhetorical and logical modes of thought that, in the Mishnah, are to be classified as philosophical. What we see is that the literary evidence is consistent for both the Yerushalmi and the pertinent Midrash-compilations in pointing toward rhetoric and logic of an other-than-philosophical character. So as to modes of thought and argument expressed in rhetoric and logic (and, as a matter of fact, proposition as well) a philosophical system is set forth by the Mishnah and faithfully preserved but not replicated in the philosophical manner by the successor-documents. These writers make connections, draw conclusions and portray the result in a way vastly different from the way of the Mishnah. That sets the stage for the movement from worldview, expressed through philosophy, to way of life and

---

1. I substantiate the statements of this section in the following: *For philosophy*: *The Philosophical Mishnah, I. The Initial Probe* (Atlanta: Scholars Press for Brown Judaic Studies, 1989); *The Philosophical Mishnah, II, The Tractates' Agenda. From Abodah Zarah to Moed Qatan* (Atlanta: Scholars Press for Brown Judaic Studies, 1989); *The Philosophical Mishnah, III, The Tractates' Agenda, From Nazir to Zebahim* (Atlanta: Scholars Press for Brown Judaic Studies, 1989); *The Philosophical Mishnah, IV, The Repertoire* (Atlanta: Scholars Press for Brown Judaic Studies, 1989); *Judaism as Philosophy. The Method and Message of the Mishnah* (Columbia: University of South Carolina Press, 1991). *For Economics*: *The Economics of the Mishnah* (Chicago: The University of Chicago Press, 1989). *For Politics*: *Rabbinic Political Theory. Religion and Politics in the Mishnah* (Chicago: The University of Chicago Press, 1991).

definition of the social entity, that is, for the Mishnah, economics and politics, respectively.

Two questions clarify the issue of continuity in category-formation. What we want to know is simple: have the successor-authorships revised or redefined the received categories? Do we find in the Yerushalmi and its companions a considerable extension and reformation of the philosophical economics and politics set forth by the Mishnah? In fact the philosophers whose ideas are presented by the Mishnah will have been surprised and also informed by what they found in the Yerushalmi's re-presentation of the Mishnah. A continuing, philosophical reading of an essentially philosophical economics and politics was not underway. The Yerushalmi's reading of the Mishnah served purposes other than those of clarification, extension, and above all, practical application. That proves that the Yerushalmi and related writings have undertaken a considerable labor of category-reformation. Not philosophers but something else, they have given to the Mishnah a decent burial and gone on to other matters.

The criteria for knowing how the Mishnah's system has been received, then, are clear. On what problems do the successor-authorships concentrate—theoretical or exegetical? And whence do they derive their continuing intellectual program—the tasks of reconsideration and criticism, or the work of practical application? Exemplary discourses, time and again, show a range of questions deriving not from philosophers and theorists but from clerks and judges: people who have to know one thing from something else in material reality.

In the case of economics we find rules governing cases, not definitions of abstractions. In the case of politics we come up with not the extension and elaboration of the received structure but the portrayal of a quite different one. When speaking of the Mishnah, the successor-writers paraphrase and clarify its sentences. When moving beyond the limits of the Mishnah, they make matters their own and set forth, side by side with the Mishnah and its message, a quite different account of economics and politics.

In other-than-exegetical passages of the Yerushalmi scarce resources, so far as these are of a material order of being, for example, wealth defined as the Mishnah and Aristotle did, are systematically neutral. A definition of scarce resources emerges that explicitly involves a symbolic transformation, with the material definition of scarce resources set into contradiction with an other-than-material one. So we find side by side clarification of the details of the received category and adumbration of a symbolic revision, and hence a categorical transformation in the successor-writings. The representation of the political structure of the Mishnah undergoes clarification, but alongside, a quite separate and very different structure is also portrayed. The received structure presents three political classes, ordered in a hierarchy; the successor-structure, a single political class, corresponding on earth to a counterpart in Heaven. Here too a symbolic transaction has taken place, in which one set of symbols is replicated but also reversed, and a second set of symbols given instead.

I may express this in a simple way: a structure comprising a hierarchical composition of foci of power gives way to a structure made centered upon a single focus of power. That single focus, moreover, now draws boundaries between legitimate and illegitimate violence, boundaries not conceived in the initial system. So in all three components of the account of the social order—politics, economics, and philosophy—the philosophical system gives way to one of another classification. The worldview comes to expression in modes of thought and expression—the logic of making connections and drawn conclusions—that are different from the philosophical ones of the Mishnah. The way of life appeals to value expressed in other symbols than those of economics in the philosophical mode. The theory of the social entity comes to concrete expression in sanctions legitimately administered by a single class of persons (institution), rather than by a proportionate and balanced set of classes of persons in hierarchical order. Moreover, that same theory recognizes and defines both legitimate and also illegitimate violence, something beyond the ken of the initial system. So, it is clear, another system is adumbrated and attested in the successor-writings. And the classification of that other system is not within philosophy but within religion.[1]

---

1. Works of mine in which these matters are substantiated include the following: *The Talmud of the Land of Israel. A Preliminary Translation and Explanation* (Chicago: The University of Chicago Press, 1983), ch. XXXV, *Introduction, Taxonomy; The Integrity of Leviticus Rabbah. The Problem of the Autonomy of a Rabbinic Document* (Chicago: Scholars Press for Brown Judaic Studies, 1985); *Comparative Midrash: The Plan and Program of Genesis Rabbah and Leviticus Rabbah* (Atlanta: Scholars Press for Brown Judaic Studies, 1986); *From Tradition to Imitation. The Plan and Program of Pesiqta deRab Kahana and Pesiqta Rabbati* (Atlanta: Scholars Press for Brown Judaic Studies, 1987) [with a fresh translation of Pesiqta Rabbati *Pisqaot* 1-5, 15]; *Judaism in Society: The Evidence of the Yerushalmi. Toward the Natural History of a Religion* (Chicago: The University of Chicago Press, 1983); *Judaism and Scripture: The Evidence of Leviticus Rabbah* (Chicago:

4. *Counterpart Categories*

The social order by definition attends to the way of life, world view, and definition of the social entity, that a system puts forth. But by 'way of life' or 'world view' one system need not mean exactly the same category of data that another system adopts for itself, and, it goes without saying, we cannot claim functional equivalency, for obvious reasons as irrelevant as the judgment of relativism. A system selects its data to expose its systemic categories; defines its categories in accord with the systemic statement that it wishes to set forth; identifies the urgent question to which the systemic message compellingly responds. To understand a system, we begin with the whole and work our way inward toward the parts; the formation of categories then is governed by the system's requirements: the rationality of the whole dictates the structure of the categorical parts, and the structure of the parts then governs the selection of what fits into those categories:[1] the philosophical character of the initial system's world-view, way of life, and theory of the social entity, that is, its philosophy, economics, and politics. We have then to wonder how these same categories fared in the successor-system's documentary evidence. As a matter of simple fact, while sharing the goal of presenting a theory of the social order, as to their categorical formations and structures, the initial, philosophical Judaic system and the successor system differ in a fundamental way.

The University of Chicago Press, 1986) [fresh translation of Margulies' text and systematic analysis of problems of composition and redaction]; *The Foundations of Judaism. Method, Teleology, Doctrine* (Philadelphia: Fortress Press, 1983–85) I-III, I, *Midrash in Context; Exegesis in Formative Judaism* [second printing: Atlanta: Scholars Press for Brown Judaic Studies, 1988]; *The Foundations of Judaism. Method, Teleology, Doctrine* (Philadelphia: Fortress Press, 1983–85) I-III, II, *Messiah in Context. Israel's History and Destiny in Formative Judaism* [second printing: Studies in Judaism series, Lanham: University Press of America, 1988]; *The Foundations of Judaism. Method, Teleology, Doctrine* (Philadelphia: Fortress Press, 1983–85, I-III, III, *Torah: From Scroll to Symbol in Formative Judaism* [second printing: Scholars Press for Brown Judaic Studies, 1988]; *Judaism in the Matrix of Christianity* (Philadelphia: Fortress Press, 1986; British edition, Edinburgh: T. & T. Clark, 1988); *Judaism and Christianity in the Age of Constantine. Issues of the Initial Confrontation* (Chicago: University of Chicago Press, 1987).

1. None of these points intersects with either relativism or functionalism; the issues are wholly other. At stake in systemic description, analysis, and interpretation, after all, ultimately is the comparative study of rationalities. But this conclusion carries us far beyond the argument of this part of the book—and indeed of the book as a whole.

Stated very simply, the successor-system held up a mirror to the received categories and so redefined matters that everything was reversed, left becoming right, down becoming up, power turned into weakness, things of real value transformed into intangibles. A free-standing document, the Mishnah, reverently received for merely exegetical purposes by the authorship of the first Talmud, the Talmud of the Land of Israel, served to precipitate the transvaluation of all of the values of that document's initial statement.

The categorical transformation that was underway, signaling the movement from philosophy to religion, comes to the surface when we ask a simple question: precisely what authorships of the successor-documents speaking not about the Mishnah but on their own, mean by economics, politics, and philosophy? That is to say, to what kinds of data do they refer when they speak of scarce resources and legitimate violence, and exactly how—as to the received philosophical method—do they define correct modes of thought and expression, logic and rhetoric, and even the topical program worthy of sustained inquiry? The questions arise because in consequence of the results of Part 1, we now know that the received categories were in no way subjected to redefinition.

The components of the initial formation of categories were examined thoughtfully and carefully, paraphrased and augmented and clarified. But the received categories were not continued, not expanded, not renewed. Preserved merely intact, as they had been handed on, the received categories hardly encompass all of the points of emphasis and sustained development that characterize the successor-documents—or, as a matter of fact, any of them. On the contrary, when the framers of the Yerushalmi, for one example, moved out from the exegesis of Mishnah-passages, they also left behind the topics of paramount interest in the Mishnah and developed other categories altogether.[1] In these other categories, the framers of the successor-system defined their own counterparts. These counterpart-categories, moreover, redefined matters, following the main outlines of the structure of the social order manifest in the initial system. The coun-

---

1. That fact is demonstrated in my *Talmud of the Land of Israel. A Preliminary Translation and Explanation* (Chicago: The University of Chicago Press, 1983), p. 35, *Introduction. Taxonomy*. There I show that when Mishnah-exegesis is concluded, a quite separate agendum takes centerstage, the emphases of which find no counterpart in the Mishnah. That seems to me to justify the consideration of counterpart-categories, such as I introduce here.

terpart-categories set forth an account of the social order just as did the ones of the Mishnah's framers. But they defined the social order in very different terms altogether. In that redefinition we discern the transformation of the received system, and the traits of the new one fall into the classification of not philosophy but religion.

For what the successor-thinkers did was not continue and expand the categorical repertoire but set forth a categorically-fresh vision of the social order—a way of life, world view, and definition of the social entity—within appropriate counterpart-categories. And what is decisive is that these served, as did the initial categories, within the generative categorical structure definitive for all Judaic systems. So there was a category corresponding to the generative component of worldview, but it was not philosophical; another category corresponding to the required component setting forth a way of life, but in the conventional and accepted definition of economics it was not an economics; and, finally, a category to define the social entity, 'Israel', that any Judaic system must explain, but in the accepted sense of politics it was not a politics.

Addressing the issues ordinarily treated by the method and message of philosophy, economics, or politics, the counterpart categories nonetheless supplied for the social order a worldview, way of life, and definition of the social entity. And, as a matter of fact, the Judaism that emerged from late antiquity adopted as its categorical structure the counterpart categories we are going to define and explore, and recast the Mishnah within them. The formation of Judaism that took place through its transformation from an account of the social order that was essentially philosophical to one that was fundamentally religious was accomplished by the system-builders whose conceptions came to literary expression in the Talmud of the Land of Israel, Genesis Rabbah, Leviticus Rabbah, and Pesiqta deRab Kahana.

5. The Foundations of Systemic Reformation

Exactly how was this categorical reformation accomplished? To state matters first in the most abstract way, it was done by reversing the flow of language, specifically taking the predicate of a sentence and moving it to the position of the subject, that is, commencing not from subject but from predicate. From '[1] economics is [2] the rational disposition of scarce resources', the category of way of life was rephrased into, '[2] the rational disposition of scarce resources is [1] (their, in context, systemic) economics'. The reverse reading therefore yields the counterpart category, defined by this sentence: '*a (any) theory of rational action with regard to scarcity. . .* , then: is (for the system at hand) its economics'. The same procedure serves, too— *mutatis mutandis*—for discerning system's politics and science or learning or philosophy. Precisely what the framers worked out as their economics, politics, and philosophy is laid out in this part of the book, and the result, the third part of this book will show, was a quite new system. This transvaluation of values, through not merely the reformation but the utter transformation of categories, set forth an essentially fresh answer to a fundamentally new urgent question. But here, the answer is the main point of interest.

Let me make more concrete this matter of the reverse-definition of economics, placing the predicate as the subject. The Judaism of the Mishnah presents a theory of economics. The Mishnaic system addresses the definition of rational action with regard both to the allocation of scarce resources, on the one side, and to the increase and disposition of wealth, on the other. It was a specifically philosophical economics because, in structure and in doctrine, it conformed with that of Aristotle. Now in the successor-system, can we identify what is meant by scarce resources and can we define the rationality required for the disposition, in the systemic context at hand, of such resources? When we say, '*a* (or any) theory of rational action with regard to scarcity *is* (an) economics', we mean, any account of what is deemed scarce and therefore to require rational action as to allocation, increase, and disposition, functions to define the category that is the counterpart, in the philosophical system of the Mishnah, to economics. It answers the same question, but it utterly recasts the terms of the question.

In the Mishnah, as in other philosophical systems, the way of life finds definition in economics, the worldview in philosophy (both as to method and as to proposition), and the account of the social entity in a politics. But that is simply not the case in the successor-documents, and what serves as way of life, world view, and definition of the social entity in no way conforms to what had defined these same categories. That fact is hardly surprising, for there are quite elaborate and well-composed systems of the social order, fully spelling out the way of life, worldview, and definition of the social entity, in which—to concentrate on the case at hand—in the received and accepted sense of economics as a theory of the rational disposition of scarce resources, we simply have no economics at all. Augustine's design and account of the City of God, for example, introduces its own categories in response to the same requirements of definition and articulation of the social order. The history of salvation, deriving from the Christians' great creation, the Bible, for instance, forms the critical center, and philosophy, while profoundly influential on his thought, hardly generates the primary categorical structures. The first twelve hundred years of Christian system-builders found it entirely possible to set forth the Christian social order's way of life without defining an economics for themselves.[1]

It follows that for failing to present an economics, accounts of the social order do not define a way of life. To the contrary, the simple fact is that, when they do define a way of life in terms of scarce resources, what they mean is not what we ordinarily mean by economics. True, such systems omit all reference to, or treat as systemically inert and inconsequential, such topics as wealth and money, production and distribution, work and wage, ownership and conduct of economic entities. The entire repertoire of subjects comprising economic action in all its forms are simply lacking. But the issues of tangible wealth and material goods do emerge—must emerge, and, it follows, the systems will have to identify for themselves something other than real wealth (real estate, capital, for instance) when they design those societies that express the respective systems' messages: urgent question, self-evidently valid answer, integrating the whole and rendering the system cogent and coherent.

But how to deal with such accounts of the social order that lack an economics or a politics or a philosophy in the familiar senses of these categories? To answer that question of method in the analysis of category-formation, I have to discover and define what serves, in such a system, the task of economics in a philosophical system. To do so—as stated in abstract form just now—I propose the notion that, '[2] a (any) theory of rational action with regard to scarcity *is* [1] economics'. Matters that hardly fall into the category of economic theory at all may yield points of congruency. As a matter of fact they may also

---

1. As with the sages of Judaism, so with the first important Christian economics, it was the encounter with Aristotle (and not with Scripture) that made urgent the formation of a Christianity encompassing, for the way of life of its social order, elaborate attention to the expression of theological truth in economics and rules for the Christian management and preservation of scarce resources, defined in the conventional sense of philosophical economics.

validate those systemic comparisons and contrasts that permit us to trace the history of an on-going system from its philosophical to its religious formulation.

Let me now spell out why I find critical this two-directional reading—first, '*economics is* (or, encompasses) the theory of rational action with regard to scarcity', second, 'a theory of rational action with regard to scarcity *is encompassed by economics*'. To state matters negatively, if one system presents a conventional economics and another does not, then I cannot compare the one to the other (beyond the observation that one has, the other does not have, an economics). But—on the positive side—if I can show how one body of coherent thought in one system addresses the same question that another body of equally coherent thought takes up in the other, then the comparability—at the point not of detail but of the main beams of structure—of the two systems becomes possible. The sole undemonstrated premise of argument is that any system must explain in its account of the social order what people are to think and do and how they are to define themselves as a social entity. But in the very language, social order, are embedded these three components: society and order in both intellect and practice. So at stake is the comparison of systems.

6. *The Comparison of Systems, the Contrast of Rationalities*

In this context, by the comparison of systems, I mean the contrast of one rationality to another.[1] The comparison of rationalities, then, is made possible by the dual and reciprocal definition of [1] economics as the theory of rational action with regard to scarcity, and of [2] the theory of rational action with regard to scarcity as economics. The same is so, of course, for philosophy and politics.[2] When we under-

---

1. I allude, of course, to the great conception of M. Weber in his studies of China, India, and ancient Israel. In asking why capitalism here, not there, he founded the comparative study of rationalities. Many present themselves as his successors, some with more reason than others, but, in the aggregate, I have not found a rich theoretical literature to revise Weber's definition of issues. In this regard philosophy has gone far beyond the limits of theory in social science.

2. Would I extend the matter to, let us say, medicine, technology, city-planning, mathematics, the provision of a water-supply, a department of defense, or any of the other diverse components of the social order and its culture, whether intellectual or institutional? At this moment, I should have to decline an invitation to descend into such unbounded relativism, for then everything is the equivalent of something, and

stand the particular rationality of the economics of—to take the case at hand—the Judaism of the Mishnah, we find the way to translate into categories of rationality that we can grasp that Judaism's (to us) familiar category with the (to us) alien and odd rationality of the Yerushalmi's counterpart, which, as we shall see, covers matters we do not conceive to fall into the rubric of economics at all but that answered the same questions to which, for us and for the philosophical economics of the Mishnah, economics attends.

That is to say, when we see that a category for an alien system and its rationality constitutes *its* economics and therefore forms a counterpart to economics as we understand that subject within our rationality, we learn how, in a critical component, to translate system to system. We may then make the statement, 'In that system, within their rationality, that category of activity forms a component of economic theory, while in our system, within our rationality, we do not think of that category of activity as a component of economic theory at all'. And this we do without assuming a posture of relativism, for example claiming that their economics, and, with it, their rationality, is pretty much the same, or as at least as valid, as ours. Framing the relativist judgment in that way, we see that relativism is simply not relevant to what is at stake. That kind of interpretation of matters is not pertinent to my exercise in translation and comparison carried out through the definition and examination of counterpart-categories in this larger analysis of the formation of Judaisms, seen as statements of social systems.

---

nothing is to be defined in itself. So for the moment I leave matters at the basic components of any and all social orders, as I have identified them.

2

A THEOLOGICAL RESPONSE TO ORTHODOXIES

Eugene Borowitz

I deem it a high privilege to participate in a project honoring Louis Jacobs. He has by his great range of publications been my teacher in many aspects of Judaism and I have regularly been enlightened by his loving honesty in reading the Jewish tradition and our modern condition. *Dayenu*. But ever since our first meeting nearly thirty years ago I have been equally instructed by him as person and rabbi. He has set an example of quiet integrity and gentle authority which has ennobled our generation and enriched my life. In the essay which follows I have sought to take up in my own way a topic which has been of the greatest significance to his life and thought, what is popularly called religious fundamentalism. Though I respond to it with a measure of freedom he will surely find uncongenial, I hope that its total effect will nonetheless indicate one reason I continue to be his admirer.

Permit me to begin with a personal experience still fresh in my mind though it took place in March 1950. The Reform rabbis' association in the United States, the Central Conference of American Rabbis, perturbed by the changing religious mood of the post-war world, held an unprecedented assembly for its members then, an Institute on Theology. I attended one of its several discussion sections, that on revelation, and recall that despite two days of rewarding discussion we could not compose a consensus statement for the plenum. Our report merely indicated the eight problems which engaged the group, many of them related to God's role in revelation.

This notion so startled the Chairman of the Institute, Ferdinand Isserman, that he broke into the proceedings with a personal response. He was astonished that we had made no reference to the Documentary Hypothesis and its conclusions about the creation of the Torah. As far as he was concerned it had settled the matter of revelation. Like most other American religious progressives—a term I shall use here for all the non-Orthodox—he considered the Bible a thoroughly human document, though an endlessly relevant one because of its incomparable account of humankind's spiritual quest.

Progressive religious thinkers often added that it was inspired by God but this seemed more a deference to traditional usage than a living sense of God's partnership in the process. They had little doubt about the truth of their radically modern view for it was supported by university research and organic to the *Zeitgeist*, the social optimism that expected cultural enlightenment to power steady human progress. The rabbis attending the Institute would no doubt have hooted down a suggestion that in a few decades fundamentalism—or, its less terminologically troublesome Jewish equivalent, orthodoxies—would claim best to express the *Zeitgeist* and win the willing allegiance of many university graduates.

The totally unanticipated resurgence of orthodoxies in the nearly four decades since then has surely had little to do with new findings concerning the Biblical text. Rather, it has come as a reaction to the failure of the cultural messianism espoused by progressive religion. With all its many benefits modernity has also traumatically increased human misery in ways as local as the threat of drugs or the loss of meaning, and as global as unchecked pollution or nuclear destruction. Individuals, institutions and ideologies so regularly disillusion us that cynicism and depression abound while hope is uncertain and escapist fantasies appealing. We call this a postmodern time for we no longer share the modernists' confidence in humankind's capabilities. In this context orthodoxies have had great appeal, either to those seeking to replace anarchy with psychic stability or to those who believe that a good God gave us Divine instruction to save us from the vagaries of our too free wills.

The modern ethos lost its cultural hegemony largely because of the demythologization of its allies, university rationalism and science. Once we thought them our finest sources of truth and our surest means to ennoblement. Today the sophisticated know they deal only in possible constructions of reality and the masses sense they commend ethical relativism more than necessary values and compelling duties. For, having brilliantly unmasked all the ethical cant around us, they abandon us to the free promptings of the self. Progressive religion has fallen on such hard times because many believe it has abetted this

modernist gutting of standards. By turning God's revelation into mere
human growth and self-determination, it helped destroy our faith in
stable human values and made us prey to moral anarchy. Conscience
alone, which for so long seemed to mandate a turn from orthodoxies,
should now rather prompt our return to the old religious paradigms of
reality with their strong, clear teaching of what a person, a family, a
community and a nation ought to be.

The uncertain status today of progressivism's former academic
cornerstone, the Higher Criticism of the Torah, amplified the ethical
bankruptcy of progressivism. My seminary teachers said they were
teaching us 'Biblical Science', a method so reliable that one professor
regularly assigned a numerical probability to his emendations of our
printed Bibles so as to restore the original biblical text. They all
espoused the Documentary Hypothesis but confidently, perhaps even
arrogantly taught it as 'the facts'.

Today, the theory is a shambles, used largely for want of a better
explanation of the messily discordant data. No one can specify an
empirically verifiable description of the distinctive language of the
Torah's alleged documents, or resolve the doubts as to their century or
sequence or clarify their relation to the redaction process or to the
local traditions present in the text, or satisfactorily explain how the
oral became the written, or the role of literary coherence in all of this,
much less how the unique religious vision of the Torah, its most
significant characteristic, utterly transforms the cultural images it
employs. The older critical work on the Bible seems, for all its academic hermeneutic, essentially another *midrash*, one which tells us
more about the author's trendy professional suppositions than about
the text's own apparent concerns. Surely one ought not urge the perplexed of our day to stake their lives on such flimsy grounds. Rather
than trim our religion to what one generation or another's celebrated
professors teach, should we not rather live by what our religious tradition tells us a good God has graciously made available to us?

Some such case, I believe, grounds the conservative religious *Zeitgeist* of our day. Hence my response to it focuses primarily on the
issue of the consequences of our theory of God's revelation and only
secondarily on how we can best understand the Biblical text.

To facilitate the central discussion, I shall shortly grant this conservative statement of the case. But I should like to be quite explicit that,
in fact, I consider it false when stated so unconditionally and, even
when properly nuanced, so altered in meaning as to lose its decisive

effect. Permit me, then, a few counter-comments before I turn to the central argument.

I know of no major progressive religion that advocates drugs, child abuse, family violence, robbery, hard core pornography, graft, cheating the government or other niceties of the nightly news. Progressives often get tarred with the brush of every social pathology because they think it morally responsible to confront and talk about the human realities in our midst, from mental retardation to wife abuse. The orthodoxies generally prefer another strategy. First they deny that their communities have such problems or simply exclude such sinners and defectives from the community of the faithful; later they admit that such problems do occur among them but suggest greater faith and devotion as the best therapy; and finally, when humanistic treatments have long been established elsewhere and prove themselves efficacious, the orthodoxies co-opt them with the guidance of a suddenly more accommodating Scripture and tradition.

Orthodoxies do present a legitimate challenge to progressivism, that its emphasis on individual freedom leads to an impoverished sense of duty and a virtual abandonment of limits, of what in one's freedom a progressive believer must *not* do. I shall be speaking to that charge toward the end of this paper because I should like to devote my major attention to comparing the problems orthodoxies can engender as contrasted to progressive religion's approach to the same issues. That should clarify why the non-orthodox know their faith to be truer.

Let us begin historically. Had traditional religions not behaved so badly when they had effective power, progressive religion would most likely not have come into being. The rationalists of the Enlightenment scornfully charged that religion—by separating people into the saved and the damned, by its persecutions, inquisitions, crusades and wars— has created more evil than good. Religions which proclaim that they seek to bring peace into the world stand doubly damned by such iniquity. More important, this divisiveness and controversy arise from fundamental, not peripheral, claims of the orthodoxies. Insofar as a faith claims to know in some detail what God wants of all humankind, then loving one's neighbors like oneself can mean hating the one who is not like you and lovingly forcing them to be like you. Thus, Jewish law—and not merely its moralizing homiletics—restricts the neighbor I am commanded to love like myself to the one who is like me in religious observance. It classically grounds this negativity in texts like Ps. 139.21-22. 'O Lord, You know I hate those who hate you, and loathe

Your adversaries. I feel a perfect hatred toward them; I count them my enemies.'

By internal standards one cannot logically impeach the theology of such orthodoxies. Their founding faith avers that God, who alone has every right to do so, has made perfectly plain how human beings ought to live. To spurn God's holy law not only contravenes the highest good but personally affronts God. When the pious do nothing about this perversity they become deeply implicated in it, for by appeasing evil they teach humankind to accept evil and thereby do the devil's work. Moreover, they also retard the coming of God's rule and draw forth God's punishment on the righteous as well as the sinful. So for God's sake and their own, those who love God should fight and uproot sin.

This limited tolerance or intolerance arises precisely from what the orthodoxies claim to be their great strength: against moral flabbiness and uncontrolled freedom, their faith and discipline are certain. And because that knowledge is unqualified and absolute, no argument can logically challenge or refute it. One cannot range human understanding against what God has ordained since God, who set these standards, is the ultimate ground of all human existence and dignity. One hears this same understanding in the Talmudic retort, 'The words of the master and the words of the disciple: to which should one listen?'

Indeed, a special horror must greet any serious challenge to God's behests. With absolute good at stake, what normally would be a sin can now become a virtue; one kills flagrant sinners to save their souls. Given full social power, or access to it, orthodoxies have been known to utilize it against those demonic souls who deny God. Thus, in the Spanish Inquisition, Jews who had converted to Catholicism but, under torture, confessed that they had reverted to Jewish ways, still received capital punishment but of a somewhat more humane kind.

I am not arguing that orthodoxies *necessarily* or *inevitably* lead to these harsh consequences and I am not saying that the orthodoxies have learned nothing since the middle ages. All the traditional faiths I know have beliefs which could counteract such absolutism, God's love for every creature and God's desire for their genuine repentance being the most notable among them. And there have always been leaders in our religions who have been revered for their compassionate embrace of everyone, even vile sinners. Orthodoxies *can* be tolerant. That is not the issue between us. Nor is it one of determining which approach to faith is wholly correct and which wholly wrong. Progressive and orthodox faiths share too much of their views of God and humankind for such simplistic judgments. I think it irresponsible to charge that the orthodox ignore human self-determination or that the progressives forget that God, not the human mind, ultimately grounds our values and being. Both affirm the transcendent pre-eminence of God and ascribe some independent dignity to humankind. We radically diverge, however, over the issue of the proper balance or relative significance we ascribe to God's sovereignty and to human will.

Progressives reject orthodoxy not because, given the power, orthodoxies *will be* intolerant, but that, because of their basic faith, they can generate extremism, zealotry and fanaticism—something they have often done in the past and still do today. These, simple human experience has taught us, desecrate God's name while claiming to exalt it and therefore are among the foulest of human sins.

By contrast, progressive religion intrinsically affirms religious pluralism. It does so because its experience of closeness to God emphasizes the human side of the relationship and thus the limited though commanding nature of our human comprehension of God. Hence progressivism affirms each individual's and each generation's right to find a better approach to God. Few of us are wiser at this than our inherited religious traditions. But, in principle, with none of us able to affirm that ours is the only, the absolute way to God, we are led to affirm the rights of others to go to God in their own way, even if it differs from ours. Such pluralism as the orthodoxies know is limited to groups and movements that are loyal to their revelation though odd interpreters of it. But to those who differ radically, even in their own communities, no such positive pluralism applies; the orthodoxies draw the circle of tolerance relatively closely to them while progressivism seeks to make it ever more inclusive. Traditional Jewish law, for example, tolerantly teaches that one need not be a 'Jew to know God and gain the life of the world to come. But it also asserts, in Maimonides' famous ruling, that in a Jewish state gentiles must accept this universal religion as a matter of Jewish revelation or be put to death— and that from the greatest of medieval Jewish rationalists.

Sensitive to this problem, many spokesmen [*sic*] of contemporary orthodoxies have indicated their spiritual unease with extremism and used their influence to oppose it. In the Jewish community no one has more eloquently and consistently undertaken this task (and the pains it brings) than Emanuel Rackman, though he has been joined in it by such other North American immigrants to the State of Israel as Eliezer

Berkovits, David Hartman and Shlomo Riskin. While admiring such leadership greatly, I cannot help but see their struggle with their own community growing from a recognition of the genuine merit of the progressives' moral-religious passion for pluralism. Human nature being what it is, we cannot be asked long to rely on compassionate leaders regularly arising to offset the exclusivist thrust of orthodox religious belief. Consider, for example, how the years continue to go by and all the theory that the halakhic process can do something about just complaints of feminists still has led to little significant authoritative action. I must also add that if proper leadership can satisfactorily be relied on to offset a religion's shortcomings, then that should also apply to progressive as to orthodox leadership.

Besides, prudence suggests to progressives that the present more positive attitude of the orthodoxies toward pluralism derives more from their lack of effective power than from their principled commitment to pluralism. Were there not so many orthodoxies fighting for pre-eminence in the United States, for example, were one of them able radically to influence our country's leaders, their view of how much sin they should be asked to tolerate would most likely narrow. This assessment of the orthodoxies' political potential lies behind the deep distress most American Jews, including spokesmen of American Orthodoxy, feel at the power wielded by the Israeli Orthodox political parties. Knowing many of the Israeli Orthodox have never lived in a truly pluralistic society and how many others believe the Torah militates against its modern expression, most American Jews devoutly hope the Orthodox never become a majority in the State of Israel.

Orthodoxies have a principled problem with democracy. One sees it most easily in the functioning of their communities but it also carries over to what they tend to find most desirable in a government. As to the former, God being one, indeed incomparably so, any institution properly representing God will speak with hierarchical authority to its members. The will of the community may still have an important role in orthodoxies. At Sinai, for all that God spoke directly to the Jewish people and summoned them into Covenant, their willing assent was solicited and memorably gained. (One *midrash* explains the purpose of the first 'commandment' of the Decalogue, God's self-identification as the people's redeemer, as the data they needed to know with whom they were being asked to join in partnership). Nonetheless, by ethos and formalities orthodoxies strictly limit the functioning of the individual conscience to that alone which God's own law and institutions permits.

Consider, for example, the logic of the traditional Jewish laws regarding menstruation. To begin with, no other body of Biblical ritual purity laws continue in operation after the destruction of the Temple (the focus of all the practices related to ritual purity). In post-Biblical times the menstrual laws gained a somewhat surprising addition. Though the Torah prescribes a separation of husband and wife only during the period of the menstrual flow, the later law added a further seven days to the period of ritual impurity. The sages do not agree about the basis of this ruling but most came to ascribe it to a custom Jewish women voluntarily adopted. To the extent that custom can occasionally make law in Judaism, something like democracy has a place in it. Nonetheless, wherever Jews have modernized, Jewish women have overwhelmingly abandoned the practice of the menstrual laws; they would thus seem to have retracted their previous decision. Only they apparently cannot do so. The sages of each era, all male, retain the exclusive authority to determine not only the law but which customs can become law and which must be opposed.

Perhaps that issue agitates only a small number of the pious among us. What, then, shall we say of the issues raised by feminism generally? Setting aside for the moment the merits of one specific issue or another, Jewish feminists appear to care most fundamentally about the critical issue in democracy: participation in the power to make binding decisions. Little touches the modern spirit more than self-determination, having a realistic role in determining the rules by which one is expected to live. In the established orthodoxies I know, God has commanded, or God's appointed authorities have long decreed, that religious authority is reserved to males. Progressives will surely agree with the orthodoxies that the content of a religion should not be determined simply by ballot. Nonetheless, progressives esteem autonomy in principle because they believe the human self always mediates what we know of God. Hence each individual's quest for God concerns progressives as much as does what the past or the present community discerns as God's reach toward humankind. This alliance of self and communal spiritual experience becomes the foundation of a religious life that enshrines democracy because it fundamentally esteems individuality.

By extension, the same contrast in attitude toward democracy may be seen with regard to government generally. In the Bible, God can be pictured as considering the Hebrews' call for a king a rejection of God's own rule over the people, obviously the most desired state of affairs. Historically, then, governmental structures which provide the stability of enforcing or at least encouraging what the orthodoxies know God requires of all people, have been most congenial to them. By contrast, democracies, with their shifting determinations of how people ought to act, with everyone equally entitled to a say in what ought to be done, can easily be far more problematic to them. Consider, for example, how much easier it would be to resolve our continuing American religious tensions over abortion with less democracy. Were our governmental leaders more independent of the people and congenial to a given orthodoxy, or were one or another of the orthodox faiths decisively in power, the issue would move decisively toward a conclusion. Surely one reason why no constitutional amendment on abortion has thus far been approved by the Congress of the United States has been that our orthodoxies could not agree on a specific delineation of God's own truth about abortion.

This brings us to an important qualification of the orthodoxies' claim that they would bring order into our anarchic society. This could happen if one orthodoxy dominated our nation or the several orthodoxies could agree on a policy. But orthodoxies often disagree as to what constitutes God's own will and when they do they can generate intense social conflict—and do so today as in the past. Traditional Jewish law, for instance, does not consider an abortion performed by a Jew murder but rather mandates an abortion when the mother's life, or according to some, even her basic mental health is at stake. At the same time, it rules, for reasons which are obscure at best, that Gentile abortions are murder.

I quickly add that progressives need not necessarily be pro-abortion, though their high regard for the individual leads them here as elsewhere to make the decision of the person immediately involved, in this case, the mother, their primary concern. And this religious appreciation of the individual will makes them, in principle, enthusiastic about democratic governance despite its occasional vagaries.

In some orthodoxies thinkers have sought to make room in their midst for 'the rights of conscience' though only uncommon exegesis might find the equivalent of this modern notion in Hebrew Scripture, the New Testament or the Koran. I see such orthodox efforts at accomodation as another silent acknowledgment of the religious truth that more centrally engages progressive spirituality. Obviously, orthodoxies which have greater regard for individual spirituality find it easier to work out a reconciliation with democracy but the difficulty of harmonizing God's own truth with individual self-determination should not be underestimated. Thus, I see no institutional acceptance of the rights of conscience in traditional Islam and only a limited measure of it among traditionalistic Christians. In the latter case, where American Roman Catholics and Southern Baptists in their diverse ways have honored individuality, those who conscientiously seek new ways these days often find themselves forcefully reminded that in an orthodoxy obedience has precedence over autonomy.

I know of only one Orthodox Jewish thinker, Michael Wyschogrod, who has sought to legitimate democracy in a Jewish polity. He acknowledges that classic Jewish tradition, despite some hints of a similar notion, has no fully self-conscious concept of conscience. With our primal Jewish certainty that our people possesses God's highly contentful revelation we must reject the autonomous conscience in its common, humanistic form. That, as Heidegger penetratingly argued, radically destroys obedience to anything other than ourselves. To replace this faulty concept of conscience, Wyschogrod carefully elaborates one he believes would be acceptable to Judaism. He describes the individual's sense of right as a faculty given humans by God so that they might discern and respond to God's will. This formulation avoids two philosophic evils. By linking individual autonomy with God—theonomy—he has maintained individuality but limited arbitrariness. And with God the ground of human and thus individual value, linking conscience to God prevents a clash between the autonomous demands of the self and those of our religious community that some might deem heteronomous.

Wyschogrod then seeks to situate conscience in contemporary Orthodoxy by arguing that the willingness to remain Orthodox today must be made against the crowd and thus may be said to arise out of a significant exercise of autonomy. To be sure, should the promptings of the *halakhah* and one's will conflict, one must sacrifice one's self-determination, our personal version of the binding of Isaac. Since this overcoming of self can occasionally be sensed taking place, one has a phenomenological indication of autonomy's reality within Orthodoxy.

He admits that the concept of autonomy correctly points us to a critical locus of human dignity. Without some such self-actualization, we would be less the creatures that God formed us to be. Hence Orthodox Judaism needs to make room for the concept of conscience, a theoretical amplification his unique intellectual enterprise seeks to accomplish. But I believe a practical consideration, though unstated, can be deduced from a consequence he derives from his argument. He boldly inquires, if conscience legitimately commands, do we deny its validity when someone utilizes it against God-given standards? Catholic teaching once specified that error has no rights. Wyschogrod daringly asserts the opposite, that as long as one has come to a whole-hearted decision after reverential study of God's revelation, Hebrew Scripture, we must grant individual conscience rights even when we know it to be in error. To say otherwise would allow a heteronomous revelation to override our God-given right to think and judge for ourselves, thus negating the very essence of conscience.

I believe Wyschogrod's unique Orthodox appreciation of conscience has a high moral purpose: to provide an Orthodox theological justification for allowing Christians to be Christians. He does this not by a relativism which would sacrifice the absoluteness of God's revelation but by carefully providing room for individual conscience within it. Consequently those who cannot read its message as others do may still claim the right to go their deviant way. Some years back, John Courtney Murray, the noted Roman Catholic theoretician of democracy, mounted a similar argument which Vatican Council II made official church teaching.

To the best of my knowledge, Wyschogrod's sophisticated argument has had no echo even in the centrist American Orthodox Jewish community. This may, of course, change but I find it more an indication of the resistance of orthodoxies to the concept of conscience and its entailments than of the weakness of his argument.

The general discomfort of orthodoxies with sinners and evildoers creates another of its problematic manifestations: the limited moral horizon we call ethnocentrism. Their characteristic high self-esteem comes from knowing their community, having uniquely received God's truth, now alone lives in full loyalty to it while others do not know, or ignore, or pervert, or even reject it. As a result, the orthodoxies tend to tilt heavily in their own direction the balance between the love of all God's creatures and of those in their community. When the common human preference for the known and the familiar over the strange and alien co-opts this sense of cosmic group worth, others can easily appear to be uncanny, unnatural and perhaps even inhuman. At the extreme, pietists seclude themselves from a defiling world so that they may live as exclusively as possible with their sacred kin. Yet even in less self-ghettoized settings the orthodox appreciation of the universal can highly constrict and charity, most broadly construed, not only begins at home but tends to stay there.

Modern Jews are often startled to learn about the *halakhah's* interpretation of neighbor love, the commandment Rabbi Akiba called the most inclusive generalization in the Torah. Over the centuries our authoritative sages said it applied only to fellow Jews (and, essentially, to righteous ones). The law requires Jews not only to have regard for a fellow Jew's honor and body but for his money. This led some authorities to rule that Jews should give preference in their business dealings to other Jews, a principle we would find most disturbing if enunciated by leaders of other faiths.

No religious community which hopes long to maintain itself, indeed which believes that, for all its humanity, it contains a true insight into the Divine, can do without some separatism and self-differentiation. In recent years many Jews have reasserted their Jewish particularity and some have even built a cultural ghetto to do so. But modernized Jews, though they have participated in this same cultural development, believe that traditional Jewish law engenders a restrictive ethos which underestimates the sacred quality of the common humanity they encounter wherever democracy truly functions.

All these unhappy consequences of orthodox theories of revelation come to a climax in their necessary subordination of persons to text, interpretation, structure and precedent. God stands behind just these words and no others, behind just these interpretations of the words and no others, behind just this institution by which proper interpretations are mediated, and behind just this inherited wisdom which largely fixed what is and what is not God's will. Let individuals testify that to serve God most responsibly they believe they must significantly depart from these dicta, their spiritual leaders will tell them that their 'conscience' must defer to what their religious heritage knows to be God's will. God knows best, they will be told, and so, as a consequence, do the leaders of one's faith.

To progressives, an alternative explanation seems very much more probable. Rather than function as the privileged channel of God's instruction, religious institutions behave very much more like other human structures. All we have learned about the history of groups, of their transition from charismatic beginnings to institutionalization to bureaucratization, for good and for ill, seems to explain much better than does God's revelation or providence why they act as they do. Few orthodoxies today will deny their institutional humanity but as God's own legatees, they regularly claim to be exempt from the same sort of correction we think appropriate for other human structures. Progressives, too, hope that God's will manifests itself in their activities. But putting the balance on the human partner in our faiths, they deem it a duty, in principle, to be open to those new human experiences which, while deviating from the past, now appear to express its contemporary meaning.

Classic Jewish law, like that of other orthodoxies, contains many rulings where text and precedent are reinterpreted by the law's own means to permit what moderns see as greater personal fulfillment. Thus, the *lex talionis* remains God's immutable law but the rabbis so interpreted it that it calls for monetary compensation, not physical retribution. To make possible a second marriage, one witness instead of two may be acceptable to the rabbinic court, and that one may be a woman as well as a man. And, perhaps most tenderly of all, though Jewish husbands should divorce wives who do not bear children after ten years of marriage, we have no record of that law being enforced, only waived. Only a caricature would depict religious orthodoxies as without heart.

For all that, the principle of tradition over person substantially maintains itself. The classic Jewish cases have long been the *agunah* and the *mamzer*. In the former instance, a woman cannot remarry because she cannot legally prove that her husband has died or divorced her. The latter case covers the Jew born of adulterous or incestuous intercourse. That Jew may never marry a *kosher* Jew. Progressives cannot understand how such rulings can be understood to be God's will for us today. They also do not understand how those traditional Jews who agree that these laws should be made inoperable continue to be appeased by authorities who say the *halakhah* can remedy these inequities when the authoritative figures have not significantly modifed them.

Permit me a further example, not any the less interesting because the public furor over it was initiated by a hoax in the State of Israel. One of the humane considerations articulated in the Mishnah concerns a structure that collapsed on the Sabbath and buried someone in the ruins. Though breaking Sabbath law makes one technically subject to capital punishment, in this emergency we immediately set aside all the usual prohibitions of labor on the Sabbath and work as hard as we can to dig the person out. Saving a life supersedes every law in Judaism except the prohibitions of murder, idol worship and sexual offense. To this extent, the *halakhah* gives the personal priority over the customary law. But the Mishnah further specifies that, should we discover that the buried person is a gentile, the Sabbath laws immediately go back into effect and we stop digging. No progressive Jew I know can face such a law without a protest and at least one Orthodox Jewish legal authority has by some similar sentiment been led to reinterpret the Mishnah rule—but precedent having the weight it does in orthodoxies we cannot say what proportion of observant Jews would follow this liberalized ruling. Pious progressives have little doubt that whether in or out of communities, persons as such have a major claim on received religious law and precedent, and that this case from the Mishnah involves an old human understanding, not God's own will.

Thus far I have sought to show how the deleterious social consequences fundamentalists associate with religious progressivism must be balanced against the evils which can and have arisen from orthodoxies. For progressives these humane, ethical considerations are generally decisive. But since this dispute arose, at least on the surface, in relation to Scripture, I wish to return now to the debate over our sacred texts.

In principle, orthodoxies avow God's authorship of the explicit verbal form in which, all things being equal, we have Scripture. Thus, should we, reading it, be surprised that God stated what seems contrary to presently established fact, or that God enjoined or condoned what seems an inhumane act, then our understanding of it must be faulty. As Rabbi Mana said, it is we, not the verse, which is empty. Thus, Abraham, Isaac and Jacob cannot be charged with what, from the stories in the text, we would otherwise consider lying or deceit. So, too, the command to the invading Israelites to kill every Canaanite man, woman and child of the seven local nations, must have religious validity despite its ethical abhorrence. And the apparent duplication of stories in the text, the close parallels the Bible sometimes has to other Near Eastern texts, the statements of the Torah which seem post-Mosaic, the shifting chronology of the narrative, the odd orthography, all must be there to serve a Divine purpose. In perhaps the most popular contemporary traditional American Jewish commentary to the five *megillot*, that in the Artscroll series, the author deems it heresy to suggest that the Song of Songs celebrates human sexuality rather than, as tradition teaches, allegorically describing God's love for the people of Israel. To the progressive eye, these and other such exegetical strategies seem a defense against what contemporary common sense suggests, that the text is very much more human than Divine, though surely a mixture of both.

Progressives hold to their divergent, more humanistic theory of revelation because it gives us a more fully integrated view of the data before us and accords much better with all else we know and have experienced. Once one concedes a considerable role to the human partner in revelation, most of the ordinary difficulties we have in reading the Bible fall away. Few today will be shocked that human beings, even ones with rare human sensitivity to God's will, would express themselves in terms of the worldview and values of their day. However, it is awe-inspiring, literally so, that these same authors often completely transcend their time and culture and speak of ultimate truth and sanctifying duty in words in which we can still hear God addressing us.

Orthodoxies have so full a sense of God's own truth that they often insist that if one does not accept Scripture as entirely God's word then, by making it largely human, one renders it insignificant. Progressives find that dichotomy utterly distorts their religious experience. For them, precisely because rejecting Scripture as God's own truth liberates them from the burden of explaining away the innumerable problems in the text, it frees them to appreciate fully the spiritual genius that produced it.

The critical choice between progressivism and the orthodoxies centers upon their different approach to religious truth. For the progressives, faith in God needs to be understood as but one aspect, if the crucial one, of the seamless whole of human existence. The orthodoxies rather assert that their Scripture is unique in human experience, something God never fully did before and now will never supersede. Its proper meaning, then, cannot be ascertained by our customary methods of reasoning. Occasionally, orthodox religious philosophers try to demonstrate the coherence of common reason and the unique revelation of their faiths. But there are so many radical discontinuities between sacred texts and scientific data, to give one critical instance, that they presently prefer compartmentalizing truth. One assigns one's religious truth to one mental chamber while segregating one's clashing modern knowledge in another. And some few true believers seek to resolve the tension by rejecting modern knowledge altogether.

Progressives can appreciate the respect for God's uniqueness that lies behind this schizoid existence but they find it distorted by its lack of a balancing appreciation of every human being's ability to know

God. They would agree that God's incomparable indwelling presence must be accorded proper respect and dignity rather than being debased by being reduced to people's ordinary, workaday sense of things. At the same time, progressives reject a compartmentalized spirituality because they believe that the human soul, created in God's image, ought to strive to be one even as God is one. And that means, coordinating the discordant elements of one's personality into an ever expanding whole, integrating one's spiritual experience with that of one's faith community and, reaching beyond them, seeking to relate it to the experience of all God's children.

Hence progressive spirituality ideally knows no barrier between what we learn from every other human discipline and from religion's teaching. Explicating that unified sense of human existence has turned out to be a more difficult task than early progressive religious thinkers estimated. Not the least reason for this has been the unexpected shifts our modern worldview has taken as people have studied humankind and pondered its recent sorry behavior. Nonetheless, progressives know that their distinctive way of serving God centers on this pursuit of the integrated soul.

This dedication arises from a compelling sense of what the human spirit can achieve when empowered to use its gifts of intelligence and creativity freely in God's service. In youthful exuberance, American progressives grandly proclaimed the doctrine of human perfectibility and practiced social action as messianism. Today that soaring self-esteem appears naive and destructive but not so much as to refute two precious progressive truths. One, that in significant if limited ways human beings can substantially transform the world and make it more just and loving. And two, that God's mandates may still be heard, directing each present generation in new as well as in old ways.

Simple realism requires us to acknowledge immediately that even the supposedly mature self can easily collapse into willfulness or idiosyncrasy. On this score the challenge of the orthodoxies to progressive religion has considerable merit and postmodern progressives need to respond to it. Having dealt with this issue in some detail elsewhere here let me simply sketch in my response. I believe what I have called 'the Jewish self' ought never think of its existence as merely individual—hence the modifier 'Jewish'—but also as existence in Covenant. It will then exercise its autonomy in partnership with God, with the Jewish community of the present, with the community of the past through its tradition and with the Messianic Time through working for the Jewish people's future. Living the Covenant in this post-modern fashion will surely not enjoin the stated limits on human freedom that often makes the orthodoxies attractive today. But it also cannot, for all its emphasis on human self-determination, be called anarchic, libertine or uncommanded. In its devoutness it finds the imperatives arising from our people's Covenant with God more directly through the self than through any text or tradition.

The division between progressive religion and the orthodoxies arises, finally, from the different balance of faith and consequence we find most true to what God wants of us. Orthodoxies know the power of God's own word and the warmth of God's own communities but these strengths engender what progressives see as their problems with the rights and integrity of persons. Progressive religion's genius lies in its appreciation of the personal and the universal, but it creates the problems of relativism, indecisiveness and the proper limits of personal freedom. In the backlash against modernity which has swept across western culture, the orthodoxies have shown how deeply they still appeal to the human spirit. But despite their continuing power, most people who have tasted the personal dignity modernity has conferred upon them have rejected orthodoxy. I see this judgment arising from their quiet conviction that the secular movement to individualism, pluralism and democracy has a lasting spiritual validity that cannot be denied. Or, more rhetorically, that God has spoken to us through the personal freedom modernity has conferred upon us so that, for all that we may have abused it, only in its affirmation and responsible use we can truly serve God.

I have conducted this analysis in the broad context of our western religious experience so as to correct what seems to me a widespread misconception in the Jewish community. People often feel that our inner struggle over the contemporary meaning of Torah hinges essentially on our Jewish loyalty or willingness to sacrifice some measure of selfhood for our Judaism. I think that may be partially true but it overlooks the greater human spiritual/social development of which we have been a part. Our problems are not specifically Jewish but historical. Little that we argue among ourselves cannot be paralleled in other religious communities challenged by modernization and secularization, by disillusionment with these processes, and now by the possibilities of a postmodern non-orthodoxy. We, like them, must decide on the mix of modernity and tradition we believe to be faithful to what God demands of us. That, more than any other issue, will determine what we mean by Torah and how we envision its substance.

3

DEFINING THE UNIQUENESS OF THE HOLOCAUST

Steven T. Katz

Rabbi Louis Jacobs has been one of the most important contributors to the ongoing development of Jewish thought in our time. A master of nearly all phases of classical and modern Jewish learning, his work has set high standards for others in the field to emulate. Among his most notable and consistent contributions has been his insistence on clarity and precision in the decipherment of philosophical issues. It is therefore a special pleasure to include the present essay that seeks to investigate some of the preliminary conceptual issues that are apposite to any and all efforts to clarify the provocative issue of the historical and phenomenological *uniqueness* of the Holocaust in this *Festschrift* in his honor.

Given the confusion, crossed purposes, and misunderstandings that have accumulated around the evidently contentious question of the 'uniqueness' of the *Sho'ah* I should like to clarify six elemental issues that must be understood aright if any real philosophical advance is to be made in the analysis of this matter.

1. In advancing and supporting the position that the destruction of European Jewry between 1933 and 1945 is phenomenologically unique I am not proposing or endorsing any particular theological conclusion(s). It is not at all clear to me that there is a direct, and preferred, theological meaning to be drawn from the exceptionality of this event, at least not as I interpret this singularity. As I understand the multiple epistemological and metaphysical issues that are raised by this issue both the theological radicals, for example, Richard Rubenstein, Arthur Cohen, Emil Fackenheim, Yitzchak Greenberg, and on the Christian side, for example, A. Roy Eckardt and Alice Eckardt, to a degree Jurgen Moltmann, Franklin Littell, Franklin Sherman, Paul Van

Buren, Karl Thieme, Clemens Thoma, and to some degree John Pawli-kowski, as well as the theological conservatives, for example, Eliezer Berkovitz, Jacob Neusner, and the Lubavitcher Rebbe, and on the Christian side, for example, the Protestant Karl Barth, and the Catholic theologians D. Judant and Charles Journet, have all run ahead of the available evidence and the extant philosophical-theological argumentation to posit conclusions that are not epistemically or intel-lectually persuasive. Neither Rubenstein's endorsement of the 'death of God' nor the Lubavitcher's Rebbe's conservative kabbalistic pro-nouncements on the *Sho'ah* as a *tikkun* flow necessarily from the event itself. Both these, and other denominational expositions, are premature and inconclusive. They represent, in essence, *a priori* impositions that are extrinsic to the Death Camps and rooted in deeply held prior theo-logical positions.[1]

Any theological position, at present, is compatible with the singu-larity of the *Sho'ah*. Religious conservatives who 'intuitively' reject the uniqueness of the Holocaust on the, usually implicit, grounds that such an unequivocal conclusion would *necessarily* entail ominous alterations in the inherited normative *Weltanschauung* are simply mistaken. That is, one can, without self-contradiction, adopt an unex-ceptional conservative theological posture (either Jewish or Christian) while, at the same time, accepting the discrete contention that the destruction of European Jewry was an historical *novum*, given a dis-ciplined understanding of the concept of historical *novum*. Conversely, the theological radicals who hold that the singularity of the *Sho'ah* necessarily entails religious transformations, and within Jewish parameters halachic changes, have not shown this to be the case. They have merely assumed it to be so, positing the 'required changes' they take to be obligatory without providing either halachic or philosophi-cal justification for such innovation. It may be that one or other of these alternative positions is true, but so far none has made a convinc-ing case for itself. Therefore, the investigation of the question of the uniqueness of the *Sho'ah* needs to be separated from theologizing.

2. In defending uniqueness one must completely avoid simultane-ously endorsing the injudicious claim that the Holocaust is *more evil*

---

1. For further analysis of many of these recent Jewish theological views see my *Post-Holocaust Dialogues: Critical Studies in Contemporary Jewish Thought* (New York, 1983). I, however, do not discuss the argument of R.M. Schneerson, the Lubavitcher Rebbe, in this work.

than alternative occurrences of extensive and systematic persecution, organized violence, and mass death. The character of that historical and phenomenological uniqueness which can be defended is not tied to a scale, a hierarchy, of evil, that is, of an event X being more or less malevolent than another event Y, or all previous events E_1 to E_N. This, of course, is not to deny the compelling fact that the *Sho'ah* was a monumental crime, an astonishing act of cruelty, comprised of millions of acts of cruelty, as great as any that has ever taken place. But in acknowledging this one must at the same time avoid incorrectly asserting that the *Sho'ah* is *more* evil than certain other specific events, for instance, the centuries-long brutality and dehumanization represented by Greco-Roman and New World slavery, the mass-murder of Armenians in 1915–1917, the vast depopulation of the indigenous peoples of North and South America, the monumental violation of human dignity, the millions of dead, that is the Gulag, or the monstrous transgression that is Cambodia. These other happenings are also morally outrageous, and arguably as morally outrageous as the *Sho'ah*. The insuperable epistemological dilemma that arises here is that there is no argument, no method, that will allow for the quantification of evil beyond the simple mathematical—counting corpses. But this, I take it, is not what is meant when the Holocaust is said to be more evil than other incidents, at least not when this formidable proposition is defended by competent authors and speakers possessed of even minimal philosophical sophistication Moreover, on this measure, that is, numbers alone, the *Sho'ah*, as an empirical matter, is far from the 'most evil' event in history. In the absence of convincing criteria for making such absolute comparative judgments all such judgments become indefensible.[1]

1. In light of this I want explicitly to distance my defense of the uniqueness of the *Sho'ah* from Pierre Papazian's charge that: 'To claim that the Holocaust was unique can only imply that attempts to annihilate other national or cultural groups are not to be considered genocide, thus diminishing the gravity and moral implications of any genocide anywhere, any time. It also implies that the Jews have a monopoly on genocide, that no matter what misfortune befalls another people, it cannot be as serious or even in the same category as the Holocaust' ('A Unique Uniqueness?', *Midstream* 30, 4 [April, 1984], p. 18). Papazian commits the logical error we are here rejecting, if in an inverted way. He holds that Jews in denying the comparability of the Holocaust are advancing a moral claim and diminishing, if only by indirection, the 'misfortunes [that] befall another people'. That is, he too equates uniqueness with morality and again uniqueness with 'types' or 'degrees' of evil. Thus the Armenian tragedy can only be *as evil* as the Holocaust if the Holocaust is not unique. But if we

Here I demur from Yehuda Bauer's contention that there:

> may be no difference between Holocaust and genocide for the victim of either. But there are gradations of evil, unfortunately. Holocaust was the policy of total, sacral Nazi act of mass murder of all Jews they could lay their hands on. Genocide was horrible enough, but it did not entail *total* murder.[1]

The categorical distinction that Bauer draws between *some* and *all*, between Holocaust and Genocide, is not best, or even properly, understood as a moral distinction but rather as a phenomenological and logical one. Seeking to kill all of a group is descriptively, even ontologically, different from seeking to kill part of a group, but it is not *necessarily*, morally worse. For example, the killing of some X may be a greater evil, assuming one could measure such things, than killing all Y, where there are more X than Y and the absolute number of X killed exceeds the total number Y even though the killing of X is not, using a form of Bauer's nomenclature, 'Holocaustal'. To repeat: This is not to deny that non-Holocaust X *is* different from Holocaust Y but, rather, to assert that the *nature* of this difference is logical and structural not moral. To impute less evil, for example, to Stalin than Hitler because of the categorical distinction between Holocaust and genocide (Stalin, on Bauer's definition being guilty of perpetrating the latter but not the former crime while Hitler perpetrated the former crime), appears unwarranted on its face and undecidable, except by stipulation, in both theory and practice. Again, to judge the young Turks or the Khmer Rouge less evil than Hitler because they failed to want to kill all Armenians or Cambodians respectively is logically and ethically unconvincing.

Kenneth Seeskin, in commenting on an earlier and related argument of mine for what I called 'the intentionality of the Holocaust',[2] has

do not commit the basic error of equating uniqueness with levels of moral evil then we can assert, without either logical contradiction or offensive moral chauvinism, the uniqueness of the Holocaust while at the same time resisting any comparison (or judgment) of the amount of evil represented by, in this case, the comparison of the Armenian massacres and the destruction of European Jewry. As Papazian employs the unsatisfactory and ambiguous notion of 'implication' ('implies') twice in the few lines quoted above I here state my position directly so no one will take it, erroneously, as 'implying' its converse.

1. Yehuda Bauer, *The Holocaust in Historical Perspective* (Seattle, 1978), p. 36.
2. He is referring to the essay entitled 'The Unique Intentionality of the Holocaust' (*Post-Holocaust Dialogues*), pp. 287-317.

given voice to the elementary confusion we wish to disclaim, as follows:

> To his credit, Katz tries to avoid ethical or theological conclusions. He admits that numbers alone do not tell the full story. In his survey of mass murder, he refrains from judgments of better or worse. Unlike Maier and Aron, he does not get tangled in distinctions between an ideology and its interpretation. His thesis is simply that the uniqueness of the Holocaust consists in its 'genocidal intent against the Jewish people'. The question is whether he can employ a concept like genocidal intent without falling victim to moral comparisons he does not want to make. If the Nazi extermination of Jews is the first and only case of genocidal intent in history, how can we not conclude that it unleashed a new and previously unimagined form of evil? One cannot refer to a term like genocidal intent without expecting the audience to draw moral inferences for itself—particularly when writing on the Holocaust. So while Katz is anxious to stay clear of these inferences, his language gives him away. This is more than a verbal dispute. Even if Katz were to replace a charged word like intentionality with a neutral one like policy, the same problems would arise.[1]

But this criticism is unpersuasive for it rests on a logical error. There is no logical reason, that is, it is not a logical error, to maintain the distinction between G, the presence of genocidal intent, in event E, and G', the absence of genocidal intent, in event E_1, and again in every other event E_2 to E_N, while at the same time insisting that this phenomenological difference, between G and G', does not necessarily entail any hierarchy of immoral acts or events. It is true that the *Sho'ah* represents a 'new form of evil', but this is not logically or ontologically equivalent to the claim that the *Sho'ah* represents a 'new *and higher* level of evil'. The separable notions of form and degree, structure and quantity, intent and ethical valence, are not synonymous and should not be employed as if they were. Moreover, there is no incoherence or contradiction in entertaining the possibility that one could produce the same degree of evil through two alternate historic-systemic forms, assuming we could calibrate degrees of evil. *Contra* Seeskin, there does not appear to be any authentic reason why, given the careful disjunctive conditions here indicated, one cannot avoid 'falling victim to moral comparisons one does not want to make', indeed which one explicitly repudiates, and why intelligent readers, if

---

1. K. Seeskin, 'What Philosophy Can and Cannot Say about Evil', in A. Rosenberg and G. Myers (eds.), *Echoes from the Holocaust* (Philadelphia, 1988), p. 98.

requested to do so, cannot distinguish between different *forms* of evil 'without drawing [incorrect] moral inferences'.

In this connection it is also required, especially given the prominence of his work,[1] to reject the criticism of Irving Louis Horowitz. Horowitz writes: 'Those who take an exclusive position on the Holocaust [and argue for its uniqueness] are engaging in moral bookkeeping, in which only those who suffer very large numbers of deaths qualify'.[2] *Contra* Horowitz, however, it is an error to equate uniqueness with numbers. That is, the defense of singularity is unrelated to 'moral bookkeeping'. The two determinate categories that Horowitz erroneously equates, 'moral bookkeeping' and 'claims for exclusiveness', are in actuality distinct and can, and ought, to be separated. An admirable and supportable desire to empathize with all victims of oppression does not justify a fallacious argument.

3. The phenomenological character properly associated with the notion of historical incommensurability is to be wholly distinguished from more dramatic metaphysical claims sometimes associated with the concept of uniqueness. Though sympathetic to claims that 'The Holocaust has meant an ontological redirecting of the course and fate of history',[3] and agreeing with Emil Fackenheim that 'The Holocaust. . . was indeed a world, and it was dominated by the "logic of destruction" that left untouched neither God nor man, neither hope nor will, neither faith nor thought',[4] no one, in my view, has produced *arguments* that demonstrate the transcendental uniqueness of the *Sho'ah*. A. Roy Eckardt is right to note that the murder of European Jewry 'raises the question of *Heilsgeschichte* ("salvation history"), perhaps even the total eclipse of 'salvation history', and again that 'if it is comparable at all, [it] can only be compared with a very small number of other "incomparable" events, such as the Exodus and the giving of the Torah or the Crucifixion and the Resurrection'.[5] However, it is just the unsettling accuracy of this observation that entails caution for the Exodus, the giving of the Torah, the Crucifixion and the Resurrection, insofar as one enters into and reclaims their theological or

1. See especially his *Taking Lives: Genocide and State Power* (3rd edn, New Brunswick, 1982).
2. I.L. Horowitz, 'Many Genocides, One Holocaust? The Limits of the Rights of States and the Obligations of Individuals', *Modern Judaism* 1/1 (May, 1981), p. 75.
3. A. Roy Eckardt, *Long Night's Journey into Day* (Detroit, 1982), p. 54.
4. E. Fackenheim, *To Mend the World* (New York, 1982), p. 24.
5. Eckardt, *Long Night's Journey into Day*, p. 54.

metaphysical meaning, are not givens whose singularity is *proven* and incontrovertable, but rather *realia* whose overpowering mysterious presence is assumed by the believer and affirmed by the transforming experience of faith. The immediate significance of this unremarkable observation in the present context, however, is exacting for it reminds us that, for example, Jews do not affirm the transhistorical reality of the Resurrection, the essential dogma of Christianity, and no appeal seems able to convince them to abandon this skepticism. Though we must be open to the philosophical possibility that the *Sho'ah* is transcendentally unique, that it may transcend all inherited and established philosophical categories, categories that are unashamedly constructed to deny uniqueness by their categoricality, no one has so far made a convincing philosophical case for this position.

In particular, I would urge that the claim for the Holocaust's historical and phenomenological incomparability not be equated with Alice and A. Roy Eckardt's intriguing contention that among the various meanings of the term uniqueness there is one beyond others, 'transcending uniqueness',[1] that peculiarly applies to and individuates the *Sho'ah*. This exceptional category they define as follows:

> The concept of transcending uniqueness refers to events that are held to be essentially different from not only ordinary uniqueness but even unique uniqueness. With transcending uniqueness the quality of difference raises itself to the level of absoluteness.[2]

And they go on:

> One way to situate the qualitative shift to transcending uniqueness is to speak of a radical leap from objectness to subjectness, a total existential crisis and involvement for the party who makes one or another affirmation of transcending uniqueness. This extraordinary about face is accompanied by a marked transformation in modes of language.[3]

One recognizes that in this odd language the Eckardts are wrestling with the limits of the sayable, are striving to identify a distinctive ontic circumstance whose conceptualization may point to something philosophically fertile, but given the ambiguities of their formulation, the

---

1. Alice Eckardt and A. Roy Eckardt, 'The Holocaust and the Enigma of Uniqueness: A Philosophical Effort at Practical Clarification', *The Annals of the American Academy of Political and Social Science* 45 (1980), p. 168.
2. Eckardt and Eckardt, 'The Holocaust and the Enigma of Uniqueness', p. 169.
3. Eckardt and Eckardt, 'The Holocaust and the Enigma of Uniqueness', p. 168.

notion of 'transcending uniqueness' is unendorsable. To the degree that I understand their meaning, the shifts and modifications they introduce, especially insofar as these involve highly subjective factors—'a total existential crisis'—apply to many collective tragedies and do not provide compelling grounds for historical and metaphysical individuation. The Eckardts are correct to note that:

> Antisemitism, as it has manifested itself within the entire history of the West, is itself a markedly unique phenomenon. This phenomenon is radically discontinuous with ordinary forms of 'prejudice', such as is race and religion, forms that have their occasions and their locales and then atrophy or are superseded. Antisemitism is the one perennial malady of its kind within the history of the Western World, and it is spread universally within the entire geography of the West. Distinctively, it is pervasive in time as in space. Thus is the peculiar generality of antisemitism wedded indissolubly to the peculiar peculiarity of the Holocaust.[1]

But this penetrating judgment, even while being unimpeachable, does not serve to make their larger historiosophical and hermeneutical claim convincing. The authentic anomalousness of antisemitism, as well as its disquieting endurance over place and time, entails no transcendental correlates. It is true that the antisemitism of the West is rooted primordially in Christian theology, that on Christian grounds Judaeophobia is generated and warranted by meta-historic oppositions, but this intra-Christian dogma is not to be misunderstood, and extrapolated, *per se*, into a genuine transcendental reality or analysis. Thus we remain satisfied with a more modest phenomenological, *contra* transcendental, definition of the historical *novum* that is the *Sho'ah*.

4. In a recent work that attracted considerable scholarly notice, George Kren and Leon Rappaport attempt to define the uniqueness of the Holocaust in terms of the notion of 'historical crisis'. According to Kren and Rappaport an 'historical crisis' is to be understood as

> a crisis has occurred when events make such a profound impact on the way people think about themselves and the world around them that the apparent continuity of their history seems drastically and permanently changed. In the lives of individuals, such events are usually called life crisis; when they happen to whole societies or civilizations, they must be recognized as historical crisis. Moreover, like a personal life crisis, a historical crisis is compounded of events or situations which render accumulated past experi-

---

1. Eckardt and Eckardt, 'The Holocaust and the Enigma of Uniqueness', pp. 170-71.

ence or learning quite irrelevant. In many respects, the effect of historical crisis is to turn the world upside down, as Dwight MacDonald indicated when he suggested that in post-Holocaust society, it was not those who break the law but those most obedient to the law who would be the greatest threat to humanity.

Societies facing historical crises are usually thrown into a period of chaos until they can replace their traditional but now ineffective modes of conduct with new, more appropriate modes. It is, therefore, possible to define a historical crisis as involving any new situation of sufficient impact or magnitude to require serious, wide, and comparatively rapid changes in the normative behavior of a society. If these normative changes are at least minimally effective, they tend to become institutionalized as relatively fixed patterns of thought and action which resist serious change until another crisis situation occurs.[1]

Now while this proposal does not lack suggestiveness it is finally unsatisfactory for rigorous purposes of definition. As Kren and Rappaport themselves note:

> Applied to the Holocaust, the concept of historical crisis can as yet only be suggested rather than demonstrated, although the main thrust of the succeeding chapters is to show how the relevant cultural, historical, and psychosocial dimensions converge to require a crisis interpretation. Our thesis is that the Holocaust has been the major historical crisis of the twentieth century—a crisis of human behavior and values. If this has not yet been widely acknowledged, it is because the consequences of such a crisis—unlike economic, political, and ecological crises—tend to be impalpable, especially when they are masked by a language that seems unable to express them and a public rhetoric that seems unwilling to try. But these are matters that must await discussion in the concluding chapter, after diverse substantive material has been exposed to critical examination.[2]

And again:

> Yet the Holocaust may be hard to grasp as a historical crisis because the breakdowns of consensus and culturally defined meanings consequent to it are not easily perceived. There were no great changes in ideas concerning government and political power, for example, because the Holocaust was not a revolution. Economic systems and practices were not influenced, for it was not a financial or economic collapse. Furthermore, the Holocaust itself led to no startling changes in national boundaries; it did not generate

1. G. Kren and L. Rappaport, *The Holocaust and the Crisis of Human Behavior* (New York, 1980), p. 13.
2. Kren and Rappaport, *The Holocaust and the Crisis of Human Behavior*, p. 15.

any sweeping new religious forms or views of human nature; and it had no
discernible impact on modern science.[1]

That is, on their criterion the *Sho'ah* is not, except as an article of
faith and in conradistinction to their own definition, an 'historical crisis'. As an empirical matter the world appears little changed morally
or otherwise by Auschwitz. As Elie Wiesel has complained: 'Nothing
has been learned: Auschwitz has not served as a warning. For details
consult your daily newspaper',[2] viz. the tragedies of Ethiopia, Nigeria,
Sudan, Cambodia, Vietnam, Botswana, Burundi, Indonesia and various
parts of South America (to name only a few of the scores of deadly
happenings that have occurred since the end of World War II).[3]
Reflecting upon this abyssmal aggregate historical evidence ought we
not to conclude that the notion of 'historical crisis' is just a well-
intentioned 'wish', a pious hope that the *Sho'ah*, given its monumental
depravity, does mean something after all. And this recognized, the
category of 'historical crisis'[4] appears to offer little, if any, genuine
help in explicating and defending the claim for the Holocaust's
uniqueness.

5. Ismar Schorsch criticizes those who are 'obsessed' with uniqueness because such a claim 'impedes genuine dialogue, because it introduces an extraneous, contentious issue that alienates potential allies
from among other victims of organized human depravity. Similarly,
our fixation on uniqueness has prevented us from reaching out by universalizing the lessons of the Holocaust'.[5] But such apologetics, however well intended, however ecumenical, are misplaced. The question
'Is the Holocaust Unique?' is a legitimate question, a meaningful question, and perhaps even an important question in a variety of ways. To
rule it out because of some extraneous political, or even ethical,

---

1. Kren and Rappaport, *The Holocaust and the Crisis of Human Behavior*,
p. 129.
2. *One Generation After* (New York, 1970), p. 15.
3. Over 100 wars have been fought worldwide since 1945.
4. Kren and Rappaport's description, already quoted, of the Holocaust as an
'impalpable' crisis raises the elementary logical question: can a crisis that is *impalpable* be a crisis given the definition of the terms 'crisis' and 'impalpable'. *Webster's
New World Dictionary of the American Language* (Cleveland, 1956) defines the latter
term as: '1. not perceptible to the touch, that cannot be felt; 2. too slight or subtle to
be grasped easily by the mind; inappreciable' (p. 727).
5. I. Schorsch, 'The Holocaust and Human Survival', *Midstream* 17/1 (January,
1981), p. 39.

agenda, no matter how virtuous, is to confuse scholarship and homiletics, the often lonely search for truth with the altogether different effort to build practical coalitions or to win popularity contests. Even if the claim of incommensurability makes enemies, which if properly understood it should not, this conclusion is neither to be avoided nor denied. One could keep silent on this cardinal issue, exercising strict self-censorship, or even lie about one's hard-won conclusions to satisfy, at what high cost, those who object to the implications of the defense of uniqueness, but such behavior would hardly negate the truth of the claim. Moreover, and not inconsequentially, it would introduce undesirable elements of 'bad faith' into the serious, already difficult, discussion of the *Sho'ah* and its meaning, contravening thereby the very effort to create *genuine* dialogue between Jews and non-Jews that Schorsch advocates. Half truths and purposeful evasions are bad foundations for authentic cross-cultural, inter-communal, encounter. Then, too, the interpretive disjunction that Schorsch makes, the distinction that underwrites his entire polemic, between concluding for uniqueness and 'universalizing the lessons of the Holocaust' is neither necessary nor necessarily correct. There is no logical or normative reason why the maintenance of the notion of uniqueness *must* 'prevent us from reaching out [to other victims]'. Knowing that X is not Y does not entail that those who know phenomenological U about X cannot empathize and be *practically* concerned with the victims of Y, even if Y lacks U. There is nothing in warranting phenomenological U that makes a universal care and sympathy, a trans-X activism and involvement, impossible. Conversely, knowing X may make one more, not less, concerned with others, if only so as to deny the possibility of the repetition of X.[1]

6. In defining and defending uniqueness it is important that we repudiate the mystification of the *Sho'ah*, and this in at least four senses.

First, all efforts at *linguistic* mystification according to which the *Sho'ah* is said to transcend all language are to be rejected. If any event 'X' is described as being 'unique' in this *absolute* sense, in the strict form that: 'for X no predicates apply', then 'X' effectively drops out of our language and with its departure any coherent discussion of or reference to 'X' becomes logically impossible. Entailed by such a self-

---

1. Note: On my definition of 'uniqueness' the notion means not that X cannot happen again but that to this point it has only happened once.

sacrificing logical scenario is the elimination of the notion of 'uniqueness' for what is incomprehensible, 'that X to which no predicates apply', logically cannot be said to be 'unique'. The incomprehensible, the unintelligible, are not 'unique'—they are merely incomprehensible and unintelligible.

Though this apophatic status, this numinous being beyond language, would appear to be exactly what proponents of such a radical *via negativa* intend, even they, upon reflection, must reject this linguistic gambit. And this because it makes the Nazi terror unimaginable and unintelligible as well as irrelevant. Unimaginable and unintelligible because this is the logical consequence of such obliterative negations, irrelevant because what can post-Nazi generations understand of and learn from, not least in the arena of morality, an event that, by definition, transcends all language, all appraisals, all normative matrices, and is thus unavailable for transmission from one generation to the next. Apophatic claims deny efforts at both historical understanding and moral evaluation and, on these compelling grounds, are unacceptable.

In truth, rhetoric aside, no one *really* holds to the non-predicative form of the term 'uniqueness', because this sense of the term is actually meaningless. To summarize a highly complex philosophical argument, one could not even make sense to oneself regarding the concept of uniqueness or the reality of the Holocaust if one actually employed the concepts 'unique' and 'uniqueness' in accordance with the rule 'For any predicate Y, X is not Y'. This is because the present apophatic claim is another, if special, instance of what Wittgenstein labeled the search for 'the beetle in the box',[1]—the search for that elusive 'private language' that retains its intelligibility even though it is, by definition, uncommunicable.[2] But such a 'language' is self-devouring; the absence of public communicability negating private intelligibility.

Secondly, one must reject the metaphysical mystification of the *Sho'ah*. For this reason one should oppose, for example, the language

---

1. L. Wittgenstein, *Philosophical Investigations* (ed. G.E.M. Anscombe and R. Rhees; Oxford, 1967), sec. 293.

2. I have explored some of the peculiar and unintended consequences of this linguistic claim in the context of mystical reports and the study of mysticism in my essay, 'Language, Epistemology and Mysticism', in S. T. Katz (ed.), *Mysticism and Philosophical Analysis* (New York, 1978), pp. 22-74; see also my 'Utterance and Ineffability in Jewish Neoplatonism', L. Goodman (ed.), *Jewish Neoplatonism* (Albany, 1991), pp. 247-63.

(and approach) employed by the Eckardts that would draw an analogy between the *Sho'ah* and religious experience as such experience is described by Rudolf Otto:

> The response that finds in the Holocaust a transcendent, crushing mystery incarnates the dimension of the numinous, as described by Rudolf Otto in *Das Heilige*. The mental state called the numinous by Otto presents itself as *ganz andere*, wholly other, a condition absolutely *sui generis* and incomparable whereby the human being finds himself utterly abashed. There is a feeling of terror before an awe-inspiring mystery, but a mystery that also fascinates infinitely.[1]

But this is to confuse the issue not to clarify it. It must be shown, not merely asserted, that the *Sho'ah* is, in the mystical sense, *ganz andere*. Despite their well-intentioned efforts, the Eckardts have not been able to do this because the assumed analogy between the *Sho'ah* and God, the *ganz andere*, is misconceived. Whatever else the Holocaust is or is not, it is *not* beyond space-time nor does it stand in the same oblique relation to the categories of human understanding and meaning as does the *Eyn Sof*,[2] the Ineffable One, of the mystics.

The *Sho'ah* is not an ontological reality that is necessarily incomprehensible, except when it is so defined, as it often is. But creating incomprehensibility by stipulation does not make for convincing philosophical argument. Conversely, this is not to claim that we who were not there can 'know' the *Sho'ah* like those who were,[3] but this salient epistemological disparity obtains with regard to all historical experiences, indeed it is inherent in the difference between first and third person experience as such. It is, of course, in its actuality, made far more complex when we are dealing with a multi-dimensional, many person, event like the *Sho'ah*, but the epistemological problem of how

1. 'The Holocaust and the Enigma of Uniqueness', p. 169.
2. The term applied by Kabbalists to God as He is in Himself and beyond all human comprehension.
3. This epistemological dilemma is further complicated as a consequence of E. Fackenheim's salient methodological caution regarding survivor reports: 'It is normally assumed that, with all due allowance for bias of perception and memory, the eyewitness is the most reliable source of "what actually happened". When the eyewitness is caught in a scheme of things systematically calculated to deceive him, subsequent reflection is necessary if truth is to be given to his testimony' (*The Jewish Return into History*, p. 58). Fackenheim's remark is cited from A. Rosenberg, 'The Crisis in Knowing and Understanding the Holocaust', in A. Rosenberg and G. E. Myers (eds.), *Echoes from the Holocaust*, p. 388, wherein Rosenberg offers some pertinent glosses on this point.

we may know that past of which we were not a part is in no way unique to the experience of the *Sho'ah*.

Thirdly, I reject the *psychological* mystification of the *Sho'ah* according to which the Holocaust was *irrational per se* and thus is beyond discussion and analysis—except by psychoanalysts or psycho-historians—and beyond morality 'by virtue of insanity'.

Whatever the real contribution of the irrational, the pathological, the insane, to the murder of European Jewry, these psychological ele-ments have to be placed within the larger, encompassing, metaphysi-cal, historical and socio-political context of the event itself lest the Holocaust be understood as little more than a Rorschach test. In so contextualizing the psychological one comes to recognize that Nazism had a logic of its own, its own way of organizing the world, that, once its premises were accepted, most especially its racial theory, made its program, however evil on alternative moral and ontological criteria, 'reasonable'. This is to acknowledge that *racial theory, per se*, is not inherently irrational, even if it is false, and even though its fallacious imperatives led to genocidal enactments. Similarly, Nazism's, romantic embrace of Volkisch 'feeling' is not deranged, but rather a rational, if unacceptable, theory of what is fundamental, decisive, in individual and group behavior. One may disagree or despair at this conclusion, but it does not violate any canon of reason *per se*.

Saul Friedlander, a sophisticated practitioner of the psychoanalytic analysis of Nazism, has made an important methodological remark about the balance that must exist between the psychoanalytic and other factors whose consideration is vital for understanding Nazism aright:

> during crises in which existing interests, norms and certainties collapsed or seemed threatened, the emotional regression experienced by masses of people, the weakening of rational controls, offered vast opportunities to the extreme antisemitic minority. In German society extreme antisemitism, including Hitler's own obsessions, expanded against such a background after World War I. Yet while this very general analysis identifies condi-tions permitting the rise of Nazi anti-semitism, it leaves open the question of the specific relationship between the antisemitic obsessions of the Nazi leadership and the huge bureaucracy industriously implementing the Final Solution. Here our starting point should be, it seems to me, a re-examina-tion of the myth of the Jew in the Nazi world view, and particularly in Hitler's world view.[1]

1. S. Friedlander, 'On the Possibility of the Holocaust', in Y. Bauer and N. Rotenstreich (eds.), *The Holocaust as Historical Experience*, p. 7.

This embedding of the psychological in the larger historic and ideological context renders psychoanalytic mystification impossible. For it reminds us that to understand why the pathological was let loose cannot be explained by recourse to the pathological. And here it must be remembered that Hitler and his circle were not 'insane' in any ordinary sense. They threaten us precisely because while *unique*, their uniqueness comes from their merciless willingness to pursue a logic, however unconventional, that is recognizably intelligible to others,[1] even though others dared not dream it before they made it real. Having been manifest, it is now conceivable. What makes Nazism dreadful is not its contended irrationality, but its unlimited rationality, a rationality that devoured all opposition, all morality, all values other than its own and which, because rational, can be replicated. It was a case in which the *Idea* was supreme and would brook no exceptions, no compromises, no limits as a consequence of existing social norms and inherited fellow-feelings. Given the incontrovertible assumption that Jews are bacilli, Auschwitz was the logical conclusion: if one's home is infected, one calls the exterminator.

Fourth, one must reject the historiographical mystification of the *Sho'ah* according to which the confused and erroneous claim is made that because we cannot know everything about this event, or because we cannot know it like those who lived it knew it, we can know nothing at all about it. Post-Holocaust scholars can, despite their indirect relationship to the horrors, know about the *Sho'ah* even while acknowledging the real epistemological and existential limits and difficulties involved in their ability to know. Conversely, given their 'distance' from the event, such observers may actually be at an advantage at least as regards certain non-existential types of historical and philosophical knowledge.[2]

A similar, acute, epistemic sensitivity illuminates the discussion, the search, for *causes* in regard to the *Sho'ah*. Insofar as there were

1. 'The trouble with Eichmann', Hannah Arendt suggested in one of her few correct observations on the Eichmann trial, 'was precisely that so many were like him and that the many were neither perverted nor sadistic, that they were and still are terribly and terrifyingly normal . . . This normality was much more terrifying than all the atrocities put together' (*Eichmann in Jerusalem: A Report on the Banality of Evil* [New York, 1964], p. 276).
2. Here the philosophical distinction between 'knowledge by acquaintance' and 'knowledge by description', that is, existential versus propositional knowing, should be recalled and applied.

undoubtedly multiple causes at work in creating the *Sho'ah* their complete specification is difficult, in practice even impossible. However, this fact does not justify the argument that because we can only supply a partial and incomplete causal explanation we should resist offering any causal explanation whatsoever. The often-made presumption underpinning this false contention, that causal explanations must be complete explanations is merely a prejudice. That is, if we can offer partial and incremental explanations that cumulatively build a clearer and clearer account of the Holocaust we should not, on the grounds of some dubious *a priori* principle, reject these explanations or this approach to explanations. It may well be that the logical confusion that reigns in this area stems, at least in part, from the erroneous notion that a unique event E cannot be subjected to causal decipherment of the sort, 'Why is it the case that P?' without reducing its uniqueness. But this assumption, for it is only that, is indefensible and unwarranted.

The related misconception that insofar as the *Sho'ah* was not predictable[1] it transcends causal explanation is likewise to be rejected. Predictability and causal explanation are two distinct conceptual operations. So, for example, no one could predict the outbreak of AIDS but no biologist or physician would construe this as entailing that AIDS is not subject to causality and not open to causal explanation.

All these subtle ways of obscuring the study of the Holocaust, these multiple methods and forms of mystification, must be rejected. And they must be rejected precisely because we want to maintain, and retain, the singularity of the *Sho'ah* as a meaningful claim. The mystifiers by contrast, and contrary to their intentions, make this objective impossible.

The avoidance of the philosophical, methodological and logical errors here analyzed will not yet produce, in itself, a convincing argument for the incommensurability of the *Sho'ah*. However, if these confusions are not repeated it will at least make it possible to open up the conceptual space in which an exploration of uniqueness might reasonably take place—and even succeed.

---

1.   Jacob Katz has written very wisely on some of the historiographical and moral issues related to this difficult question, 'Was the Holocaust Predictable?', in Y. Bauer and N. Rotenstreich (eds.), *The Holocaust as Historical Experience*, pp. 23-42.

4

LEO BAECK: NEW DIMENSIONS AND EXPLORATIONS

Albert Friedlander

A Festschrift takes on a very particular character mirroring the person honoured. Students, scholars who seek the same approach, and scholars who differ, surround a very special person with products of their religions. In the case of Louis Jacobs this should be a rich harvest since he is the personification of the Jewish teacher of Anglo-Jewry. There is a profound emphasis in his work which reaches not only to the rabbis of the Talmud but also opens itself to the philosophers throughout the centuries. It is therefore logical, and indeed a foregone conclusion, that my contribution to the text should try to bring some new insights to the life and teachings of Leo Baeck. Just as Louis Jacobs founded the Society for Jewish Study so Baeck created the same shared pattern of encouraging a thoughtful approach to Jewish studies when he came to Great Britain. There was a great respect between the two of them and, indeed, the fact that Louis Jacobs has given so much of himself to the Leo Baeck College underscores a common quest and shared achievements.

The many books written by Louis Jacobs are not only part of the library of the Leo Baeck College but are also very much a part of the study of our rabbinic students. I would like to think that this volume written in honour of Louis Jacobs will not be the least of the texts studied by us. In the meantime we continue to sit at his feet and to move with him through the millennia in search of a theology which ever renews itself. That, of course, could also be said of Leo Baeck's 'Religion of Polarity'. With this in mind we return to a text which I recently presented in somewhat different fashion to a Conference of Scholars.

I

The life and work of Leo Baeck, one of the founders of contemporary Jewish thought, is part of the common domain of the study of religion. In order to avoid unnecessary exposition, I note the article I wrote for the Encyclopedia Britannica in 1974. I find it curious how little seems to need change—and how much should be added. Research on Leo Baeck has continued, and a new interest in Baeck has prompted both American and German publishers to prepare a paperback edition of the one full length study on Baeck's teachings available in German and English. Regular seminars on Leo Baeck appear as part of the curriculum of universities in Great Britain, the United States, and Germany. Frequently, in scholarly and in popular journals, contemporary questions are related to Baeck's teachings, with Baeck viewed as a representative figure of Jewish life whose insights can clarify issues particularly related to the new dialogue between Judaism and Christianity. In this paper, I would like to add to the growing literature in the field by re-examining Baeck's view on suffering; his response to Germany after his release from the concentration camp after the war; and the response to Baeck from friends who survived to build on his teachings.

II

An earlier work of mine (*Leo Baeck and the Concept of Suffering: the Claude Montefiore Memorial Lecture*, London, 1973) began with one of his rare statements dealing with the darkness through which European Jewry had just passed, and was given in 1946. However, there is an earlier text dealing with his own experiences in Theresienstadt, written on the 1st of August 1945, barely three months after his return from that camp.[1]

Baeck was a very private person. In his sermons, and in this text, the word 'I' does not appear. He describes one of the deepest experiences of suffering known to a people or, indeed, to a person. He does not dwell upon the horror, and does not show it graphically by taking an individual experience, or a person caught in a web of evil and

---

1. The now extinct 'Jewish Forum', London, published an English translation, 'Life in a Concentration Camp in March 1946; and the Leo Baeck Institute Bulletin, 18/19 reprinted the German text from the manuscript in the possession of S. Aller-Rudel. Here, I will use the German text in my translation.

responding to it. Instead, his vision of the *individuum ineffabile*—the human being touched by God—emerges in a quiet discussion of the qualities residing in humanity when encountering the darkest experience of suffering—the Maimonidean category of evil inflicted by humans upon humans:

> One of the individual traits of Jewish existence and of the Jewish Genius is the connection between phantasy and patience. Many possess phantasy and everywhere there are people with patience, but the living interconnection between the two, the mutual interpenetration of creative tension and vision is a particularity of the Jewish soul. Here is one of the reasons why this people has survived and why it can continue to survive.
>
> Whether or not survival took place in one of the concentration camps and in Theresienstadt depended upon outer circumstances: sickness, torture, annihilation could pass by or exterminate. But inner survival in its essence needed the continuance of both phantasy and patience. Patience— the tensile strength to resist which did not permit inner vitality to cease: perhaps a man does not die until he no longer wants anything; and phantasy—this imagination which always and despite everything keeps showing a future: perhaps a person only ceases to be when he can only see the past and the present moment. Both phantasy and patience must be there. Patience comes to stand erect through phantasy; without it it could sink into simple slavery. And phantasy has its connection to everyday life through patience; without it, it would be a dream, lost in a world of slumber within the day.

This is so *typically* Baeck: the erection of polarities in which the dynamic tension of human experience is depicted; the establishing of a foundation for survival which can be applied to almost any situation; the setting up of essence versus existence. But then, so rare for Baeck, he brings a graphic picture of the experience of moving through the gate into the camp, asking himself: 'What was the first thing experienced by one who entered?' The gate of the camp becomes the gate of fate. The experience of imprisonment, of being massed together, 45,000 pushed into a space too small for 3,000; dust; mud; and

> the vermin, from every place and any corner, the great army of the crawling, jumping, flying against that army of sufferers walking, sitting, lying; the voracious ones against the starving: a daily battle by day and by night. This was the world; month after month, year after year. And the mass swallowed up the individual. He was enclosed in it, just as he was surrounded by lack of space, by dust and dirt, by the swarming insects—by unending hunger—in the camp of the concentrated, never alone for a moment.

In theory, Theresienstadt was a 'model' concentration camp for the 'Prominent'. At times, Red Cross delegates would be seen, taken on tours where they could not see. And it was not an extermination camp. But then, it did not have to be one. Death came on its own. The daily fight against death, in the midst of suffering, is here internalized by Baeck: vision and patience, the outreach of imagination necessary to endure suffering, comes to be stated with great clarity.

How does one escape this suffering? Baeck lists various stations. There was the daily caravan of death. He describes the deep dark corridor of the fortress, where the long row of coffins appeared each day—often, over a hundred on the day. Heaped on top of one another, the dead listened to the psalms—up to the final 'I will let them see my help'—and then the coffins gained their freedom. The officiant was permitted fifty steps out of the darkness; then he returned. The coffins continued to their place of burning, free at last.

There was the other way of 'escape' from the camp: the transports to the East. Month after month; often day after day. The question of what was known and what was guessed arises again here. In this text, three months after leaving Theresienstadt, Baeck again stresses the terrible suspicion set against the principle of hope, of a phantasy needed to survive each day and the next day:

> No one knew for certain (where the transports would go). One only knew: they went to the East. A cloud of sorrow, of fear, and of horror kept enveloping the camp. That, of course, was the password of the master-jailers: keep the Jews uncertain. Give them no rest.

Baeck describes how those assigned to the transports were given new numbers, were isolated. 'As the lot came upon them' he says. But he had removed himself from the areas of power where the lots were determined. Others describe in great detail how Baeck came to be the pastor, rabbi and teacher of the community in the midst of their extreme suffering. Baeck does not mention himself. In the text which follows, Baeck clearly describes his own work, but without mentioning himself. The conceptual structure of vision and patience as a bulwark against surrendering to the darkness turns into a description of the way in which the darkness was held back: again, the ideational structure and the experience of existence come to join together:

> The battle between the 'mass' and the 'community' continued unabatingly. Humans who had not known one another tried to help one another physically and spiritually. They gave one another from their possessions, from

their spirit. Humans found one another, here and there. In the early morning hours and late at night they came together for divine worship, wherever a room was available. Out of windows, out of the hallways of the houses, the voices of those at prayer, the sounds of the Torah reading entered the streets. Or, they came together in the darkness of a long evening in the loft of a barracks, immediately under the roof. Pressed tightly together, they stood there to listen to a lecture on Plato, Aristotle, Maimonides, Descartes and Spinoza. They listened to talks on Locke, Hume, and Kant, or on the eras and issues of history, on music and the creative arts and poetry; on Palestine then and now, on commandments, prophecy, and messianic ideas. These were hours, hours belonging to all, where a community rose up out of the mass, where narrowness became wide. They were hours of freedom.

It was Baeck's prescription against the ultimate surrender to the suffering they were enduring. Here, he saw fantasy and patience reasserting themselves as individuals and a community realized their inner capacities. The fact that it was Baeck who gave these lectures was not considered important by him, not worth mentioning. But it mattered to the group, who saw their faith vindicated by their rabbi and teacher. They might still recite their prayers 'for our sins are we punished', might still be aware of a tradition equating suffering with punishment for all who have done evil. But, perhaps, Baeck's teachings about the Jewish response to suffering could realize themselves in the way Baeck envisaged in the closing peroration in which he summarizes his own belief in the confrontation with the darkness he had left behind so short a time ago:

> (These hours of freedom) nourished phantasy and the creative tension of patience. Many were given the strength to walk upright through the uncertainties and into the uncertain. All had to learn that they could carry an ultimate certainty within themselves, the certainty of truth, justice, and peace. Something of this deep conviction, something from this patience and this vision is now presented as a gift through this picture of these people and of those days.

At the very moment of giving his testimony of suffering—and Baeck did not become this personal again in his public utterances—the 'teacher of Theresienstadt' already began to instruct the next generation. He did not want to stress the details of the suffering, but rather the Jewish response. He did not want to stress evil and acts of persecution, but rather the response of the persecuted, the nobility of the human soul, the essence and existence of the Jewish people. While in

Theresienstadt, he continued to write the book in which in some ways became his testament: *This People Israel: the Meaning of Jewish Existence*. But at that point, one has to recognize that the very experience of suffering for Israel and for the individual Jew had to become part of his Judaism. The Baeck who had emerged out of the camp was no longer the irenic, neo-Kantian, distant and unemotional person (outwardly; the inner fires were always there) who had entered the camp.

III

We must come back to the basic concept of suffering as seen in Baeck's early writings (much of it, as indicated, is available in the Montefiore Lecture of 1973). Yet it is intriguing to see that he does, in some ways, come to the confrontation with those who had been responsible for the untold suffering which branded and effectually destroyed Europe during the dark decade. What is most notable here is that it is not a wild tirade against the Nazi leaders and the their henchmen who had actually committed the murders and the unspeakable acts of brutality. Baeck's sensitive vision reaches out to include the silent bystanders, the passive participants—and not only in Germany itself. In his presidential address to the World Union for Progressive Judaism, July 28, London 1946 'The Task of Progressive Judaism in the Post War World' Baeck apparently speaks to the victors more than to the defeated criminals. He is not concerned with evoking repentance within the German community now facing the wrath of the nations. He is more concerned with the establishing of a world in which there will be less suffering, in which compliance with evil will be less likely. Addressing the leaders of Progressive Judaism in the world, and noting the presence of the non-Jewish community, Baeck says,

> Since the last Conference. . . a terrible ordeal has swept over the Jewish people and over humanity. It has once again proved that the Jewish people and humanity are inseparable from one another. This ordeal has been so terrible, it has become such a torment. . . because men who were responsible for parts of the world, for the leadership of great communities, remained silent when they should have spoken, and stood by and looked on when they should have stepped forward to act and to help. Once again, there came to the present generation Jeremiah's word of indictment: 'They mean to heal the hurt of my people slightly, saying: peace, peace, when there is no peace'. The sin of silence and of looking on lay upon the world.

> This disaster has come upon humanity because the moral enthusiasm and
> the moral passion were lacking. . . . Everything and all of the manifest
> forms of Jewish life has been hit by the severity of the loss and of the suf-
> fering. We must never forget what we have lost or whom we have lost.

Again, we are introduced to the sufferers, the silent witnesses who can
only speak from the grave and for whom we must say kaddish. Where
once a traditional teacher might have invoked the merit of the fathers
in a plea to God to alleviate the suffering of the children, the martyrs
are brought before us to show the inner qualities of Jewish life which
can help us surmount suffering. And the reasons for suffering are not
placed into the lives of the dead, but into the actions of the living.
Baeck's great respect and even affinity to Maimonides is here put to
the test, since his approach confronts a traditional structure where
good and evil, pain and pleasure are placed into the lives of individuals
and groups supervised and judged by an omniscient and omnipotent
God. Richard Rubenstein, in a clear presentation of the problem of
good and evil, summarizes the traditional position of Maimonides
admirably:

> Man has 'the ability to do whatever he wills or chooses among the things
> concerning which he has the ability to act' and that 'it is no way possible
> that He (God). . . should be unjust', Maimonides affirmed uncondition-
> ally that 'all the calamities. . . and all the good things that come to men, be
> it a single individual or a group, are all of them determined according to the
> deserts of man. . . in which there is no injustice whatsoever'. Mai-
> monides went so far as to insist that no feeling of pain or pleasure, no
> matter how minute, can be other than a divinely inflicted punishment or
> reward. Maimonides was so insistent upon seeing misfortune as punitive
> that he quoted with approval Rabbi Ammi's dictum that 'there is no death
> without sin, and no suffering without transgression'(*b. Shab.* 55a).[1]

The positive thinking of the 'early' Baeck had already distanced itself
from Maimonides in terms of the reasons for human suffering and in
the way of coping with the tribulations of the Jewish people. And yet,
bound to the notions of Covenant and the task of the martyr in the
world, accepting the God who 'tests' His people and permits them to
see virtue in their pain, Baeck had not broken with the traditional
approach. It was more that his emphases had shifted: one did not ask
for the reasons, but simply tried to cope with the human situation in
which suffering was a given. After the Holocaust, this was no longer a

---

1. Richard Rubenstein in his article 'Evil' in *Contemporary Jewish Thought* (ed.
A.A. Cohen and P. Mendes-Flohr; New York, 1987), pp. 204-205.

tenable position for most thinking Jews. The death of a million children in the camps could not be a punishment for sins. It could not be a testing or a purification. It was simply monstrous. As Rubinstein indicates,

> Jewish religious thinkers attempted to mitigate the harsh and uncompromising ethical rationalism of covenant theology. . . to reaffirm the abiding validity and credibility of God's relation to Israel, while rejecting the punitive interpretation of the Holocaust. Thinkers such as Arthur A. Cohen and Elieser Berkovits have limited God's role to that of a teacher of free human agents and identified the Holocaust as the work of human beings who have rejected the teachings. . . [1]

Richard Rubinstein has rejected this and various other approaches (Maybaum, Fackenheim). For him, one may accept the Covenant, or the non-punitive character of the Holocaust; but not both. As new, as yet unformulated metaphor may now have to restore the integrity of post-Holocaust Jewish theology. The quiet conviction of Baeck's affirmation of the Covenant despite the Holocaust might be respectable but unacceptable to him. Perhaps a far clearer picture must be achieved of the relationship between Baeck and the rabbis of the midrash who lived after the destruction of Jerusalem and could yet laugh with Rabbi Akiva in the face of suffering and martyrdom, and accept the teachings of Ben Zoma (read in the Haggadah by all of us on the first night of Passover):

> Rabbi Eleazar ben Azariah said: 'I am now over seventy years old; but I never understood why the story of Exodus has to be received by night until Ben Zoma expounded it thus: "the Torah states (Deut. 16.3) 'that thou mayest remember the day when thou camest out of the land of Egypt all the days of thy life'. 'The days of thy life' would imply the days only; 'all the days of thy life' includes the nights also.' "

As I have said elsewhere:

> We want to exclude the nights; we want to live in the sunlit day. But it is in the nights that the message of redemption matters most to us. VAY'HI EREV VA'Y'HI VOKER: between dusk and dawn there is the passage of the night, a middle that cannot be excluded in logic or in religion. We have to seek God in all our ways; we have to find God in all our ways. And if the God we find is not always the God we want to find, we must learn to live in that knowledge as well.[2]

1. Rubenstein, p. 209.
2. Founders Day Address, HUC 1980, Cincinnati, p. 9.

Personally, I would include both Richard Rubinstein and Leo Baeck into my reading of the Ben Zoma passage. Both bring the night of the *Sho'ah* into their understanding of God and humanity. Baeck moves from *erev* to *voker*, while Rubinstein still battles with the darkness. Both are authentic voices of Judaism. If I have taken Baeck and his teachings as structure of thought and pathway of action, demanding action from the living and seeing a continuance of a Covenant which demands the same from the individual and from the community, it does not render me unaccessible to the moral indignation and bitter challenge of an eloquent voice in our time. I would accept the charge of inconsistency against Baeck's position—but when is theology consistent? In that darkness, faith moved beyond reason.

IV

The 1946 Address to the WUPJ was a challenge to the guilty bystanders of the Holocaust. And much of Germany is included in this. There are many—my friend and colleague Lord Jakobovits, Chief Rabbi of the UK and the Commonwealth included—who to this day would not visit Germany. (The nearest he came to it was within a dialogue I helped organize for a Catholic Centre in Aachen: they crossed the border to Maastricht, in the Netherlands, where the Chief Rabbi entered into a challenging discussion with them.) But there came a time, there *had* to come a time, when Leo Baeck returned to Germany and confronted the German community. The year was 1952. It was an important year for German–Jewish confrontation. Martin Buber had come to Frankfurt to accept the Peace Prize from the Frankfurt Book Fair. And he spoke words of reconciliation. In 1978, 40 years after the *Kristallnacht*, the German Chancellor Helmuth Schmidt spoke at a commemorative occasion on the theme of 'Truth and Tolerance'. The heart of the speech was an expression of hope for a new dialogue with the Jewish community, one which would build upon the candour expressed by Martin Buber:

> Fifteen years ago, the German-Jewish philosopher Martin Buber asked in the St. Paul's church: 'Who and what am I that I could dare to express forgiveness here?'[1]

---

1. Martin Buber, 'Acceptance Speech at Frankfurt Book Fair, 1952'.

In 1939, Martin Buber had spoken of the end of the German–Jewish symbiosis, taking a position particularly espoused by Gershom Scholem in later days, although Scholem went further in his assertion that such a symbiosis had actually never existed. And it was not the intention of Buber's Frankfurt speech to renew the previous relationship. Buber saw Germany's guilt; he spoke of Auschwitz and Treblinka. But—and here he differed from many Jewish voices of that time—he did not demand that German opponents to Hitler should have chosen martyrdom. He saw them in their flaws: deaf, blind, unresponsible. And yet, unlikely as it seemed to those examining the situation from the outside, Buber did not rule out the possibility that there were those who simply did not know what was happening. Buber did recognize that there were a few non-Jewish friends who resisted, who saved lives, the *chassidei umot ha-olam* ('Righteous Gentiles'). For their sake—as Abraham pleaded at Sodom—he saw the possibility for a new beginning.

In October 1952, almost at the same time, Leo Baeck published an article in the *Merkur*, entitled 'Israel and the German People'. The opening lines of this important presentation bring together the themes of reproval and reconciliation:

> Only a profound, one almost wants to say a loving yearning for inner openness and outer clarity can permit anyone to speak about peace between Israel and the German people. Only this truthfulness in which thought and speech join together as a specific particularity, which leaves no room for ulterior thoughts or excuses, gives a justification here to confirm or to deny, to hope or to doubt. . .
>
> But now for the other pre-condition. It is, as it were, the pre-condition of a Kairos-assumption with its question which must be asked: Given, that this foundation of a matter-of-fact objectivity together with a personal dimension. . . is clearly established, should this dialogic confrontation really commence NOW? There is an old Jewish saying 'If one tries to rush the hour, it flees away'.
>
> Has the time come? Some say. . . that the Jews should make their peace with this span of time, with the goodness and monumental sadness contained in it. Centrally, with the good. But with the sadness? Sadness will come to join sadness. But was there not something else, something completely and utterly different in that time? Should peace be made with all of that otherness, with all the ways in which the image of God was destroyed at that time?

Quite simply, Baeck speaks here about honesty in human relationships, whether in a one-to-one confrontation or in the re-encountering of

Israel with Germany. The time *was* early: 1952, and Israel and Germany were moving towards a grey area of an uncomfortable relationship which has not yet been fully resolved. Baeck's call for total honesty where the intellectual and moral dimensions could join together and where sentimentality could be avoided was not heard. Over the years, large reparations were given and accepted for (partly) wrong reasons; an element of guilt was present on both sides, and awkwardness and the uncomfortable skirting around issues continues. Yet it may well be argued that Baeck's call for honesty, if not heard within the political sphere (or even in the field of religion some entrenched positions—God's punishment of German Jewry's assimilation; the sins of parents transmitted to children; etc.), has been partly realized in the area of scholarship in its secularity. Yad V'Shem (Israel's Institute of Holocaust Studies) presents the dimensions of horror in so far as one can look in the face of Medusa through a mirror. At the same time, the Avenue or Righteous Gentiles sponsored by that Institute gives recognition to those whom Baeck already recognized as standing in the shadows of the Holocaust: the rescuers who cared and refused to go along with the multitude to do evil.

The present always wants to change the past, as it wants to dominate the future. Does Hegel's owl of Minerva fly only at dusk—do we really gain understanding of that past darkness by letting our categories of understanding organize the incomprehensible horror into coherent patterns? 'The time cannot be turned around' says Baeck with Kirkegaard. But every time, every era contains new possibilities. How and when can one reach out towards these? In 1952, too close to that darkness, as Baeck knew, he still had to ask fundamental questions of both sides. The Jews? Which ones? 'Those who live today as they lived yesterday and the day before yesterday? Or those Jews who survived yesterday as through a miracle? Or those whose lives were annihilated?' Every Jew lives with those shadows—wherever he lives. Who can speak for the shadows? And from whence comes the address?

> No man can set these questions and can call forward those to whom these questions are addressed. They are asked by that which was done and was done unto them. 'It' asks, not 'he', not a person. But it is not an 'it', but a 'he', a person, which must answer. Humans, individual persons, must come to terms with a happening, with a collective happening. And it remains essential that the questions must find receptivity both here and

there. Sooner or later, there will come an answer, the true answer: that is the hope.[1]

The closing word in this powerful message by Baeck then tries to place this hope within the contemporary world in which the two sides meet:

> Two people, both of them bound into one fate, cannot permanently turn their backs towards one another and walk past each other. It can mean much to humanity if such a peace is prepared and examined honestly, that is, without forgetfulness, and, if God wills, if that peace is then established.[2]

There was, at best, a quite and sincere appreciation for these words of Leo Baeck. They did not have the impact of Martin Buber. This is not surprising. Buber was far more in the public's eye, and had earlier accepted—in 1951—the Goethe Prize of the University of Hamburg. He had not gone to Hamburg to receive it, but defended himself against the attacks from the Jewish community through letters in the public press in which Buber had stressed the need to support the decent, humane circles within Germany in their fight against the old enemies. When asked to speak in Hamburg (January 1952) Buber declined in words which link his attitude to that of Baeck:

> As much as it has been granted me in every genuine meeting with a German to accept him without reservation as a person, and to communicate with each circle made up of such persons, it has still not been possible for me up to this time to overcome the facelessness of the German public, which has persisted for me since the events of 1938 and thereafter. A public that is not made up of persons each of whom has been selected, cannot fulfil the indispensable presupposition for my speaking publicly: being able to regard every face that I turn toward as my legitimate partner. Among the burdens which the history of this age has laid on me, I experience this as one of the most difficult.[3]

Yet Buber did go to Hamburg in June, 1953, and in September he went to the Frankfurt Book Fair to accept the Peace Prize. *Pointing the Way*, his 1957 collection of essays translated by Maurice Friedman, contains the lecture in the Paulskirche, where he begins with a

1. *Der Merkur*, October 1952.
2. *Der Merkur*, October 1952.
3. M. Buber, in a letter to Bruno Snell, quoted in M. Friedman, *Buber's Life and Work*, III (New York: E.P. Dutton, 1982–83), p. 111. Here, cited from E.P. Philipson, *Buber's Jewish Self-Definition* (unpublished PhD dissertation, 1990).

statement related to the earlier Leo Baeck article—a Jewish scholar trying to come to terms with the total horror set within a humanity that was not totally depraved. And yet. . .

> About a decade ago a considerable number of Germans. . . killed millions of my people in a systematically prepared and executed procedure whose organized cruelty cannot be compared with any previous historical event. . . Those who took part in this have so radically removed themselves into a sphere of monstrous inhumanity. . . that not even hatred, much less an overcoming of hatred, was able to arise in me. And what am I that I could here presume to 'forgive'!
>
> With the German people it is otherwise. I have never. . . allowed the concrete multiplicity existing at that moment within a people—the concrete inner dialectic, rising to contradiction—to be obscured by the levelling concept of a totality constituted and acting in just such a way and no other.
>
> When I think of the German people of the days of Auschwitz and Treblinka, I behold, first of all, the great many who knew that the monstrous event was taking place and did not oppose it. . . but my heart. . . will not condemn my neighbour for not. . . becoming a martyr. Next, there emerges before me the mass of those who remained ignorant. . . and who did not try to discover what reality lay behind the rumours (representing) the anxiety. . . of the human creature before a truth which he fears he cannot face. But finally there appear before me. . . those who refused to carry out orders and suffered death. . . those opposers. . . put to death. . . those who could not stop it. . . and killed themselves. Reverence and love for these Germans now fills my heart. . . [1]

Buber continued to express his concern for what he saw happening in the Germany after Auschwitz. He had compassion for the young people, and saw the need to open dialogue with those in Germany who were involved in the battle against evil, the *homo humanus* against the *homo contrahumanus*. He felt that the Hamburg and the Frankfurt Prizes both called to him to join in the battle carried out at the present time under the darkness still covering Germany. And he heard the call addressed to him as a Jew, who cannot leave the battlefield where the struggle takes place against all that is contrahuman. Like Baeck, Buber called for candour and directness in address and answer as the precondition for genuine talk: where there is no trust, there cannot be speech. 'In a genuine dialogue each of the partners, even when he stands in opposition to the other, heeds, affirms, and confirms his opponent as an existing other' described this specific encounter for

---

1. M. Buber, *Pointing the Way*, (New York: Harper, 1957), pp. 232-33.

him as well as the human situation. In demanding truth and recognition, in building upon truth, Buber arrived at the final statement of his acceptance speech:

> The name Satan means in Hebrew the hinderer. That is the correct designation for the anti-human in individuals and in the human race. Let us not allow this Satanic element in men to hinder us from realizing man! Let us rather release speech from its ban! Let us dare, despite all, to trust![1]

It is quite clear, then, that Baeck and Buber walked the same path which travelled towards a reconciliation. In 1952 and 1953, it was a dangerous path to tread. It was more difficult for Buber, living in Israel with its open wounds and its bitter memories. Buber was pilloried there. His giving of the Peace Prize money towards Arab-Israeli reconciliation was only an extra wound for the group which had also opposed him because of his political attitude in Israel. Baeck, living in London and, at times, Cincinnati, had fewer problems, since he was surrounded by a progressive Jewish community who worshipped him (unfortunately too often from the distance) and who had less scar tissue to excise from their hearts. In some ways, Baeck moved once again into the centre of Jewish communal life: as president of the World Union for Progressive Judaism, lecturer at the Hebrew Union College, revered teacher of the Reform and Liberal movements in Israel where German refugee rabbis also formed a circle around him.

Baeck did not really write about his Holocaust experiences. He did not create a new theology of suffering or make radical changes in his teachings. The changes and new emphases had already been established in the text he finished basically in Theresienstadt: *This People Israel: the Meaning of Jewish Existence.* As has been demonstrated, it was the shift from essence to existence (his first major work was *The Essence of Judaism*). Yet the two works are one, a logical development of a clear, rational, ethical and pious approach to all of the Jewish tradition. All of Baeck's writings form a consistent, interlocking structure and are at the heart of Judaism—even when Rosenzweig tried to place him into the periphery. Buber, so often considered the great teacher of Judaism to the outside world, is far more at the edge of Jewish life— but, it must be stated firmly, totally Jewish and authentic as a Jew in every utterance he made. He moved much closer towards Germany in his attempt of dialogue and reconciliation; visited more often, pub-

---

1. M. Buber, *Pointing the Way*, p. 239.

lished, spoke, taught, and affirmed that dimension of a continuing dialogue carried on between Jews and Christians who had come out of the darkness maimed and dumb. Few Christians realized how much had been destroyed within Christianity and in themselves through the cancer of apathy and silent compliance—let alone acts of violent evil. All Jews knew that the wounds inflicted upon their family and upon themselves would not be healed within their lives; one could only learn to live with the pain. Yet remembrance and hatred are not automatic companions. There is the curious misconception among Christians that the Jewish insistence upon remembering the Holocaust rises out of implacable hatred (which many even consider to be justified). Few understand that the category '*Zachor*' is a dominant part of Judaism in which the generations are linked together, and through which God is reminded of the Covenant. But remembrance cannot live long with hatred. Baeck and Buber, in their own ways, were messengers of this to a Germany awakening out of a nightmare which had left many of them crippled in a still poisoned land.

V

In 1952, when Baeck's cautious approach to a resumption of discussions between Israel and Germany appeared, he lived in Cincinnati as a teacher of Reform rabbis, at the Hebrew Union College. I saw him most days, during the spring semester, and we spent much time together, partly to discuss my future. (I was about to be ordained). Baeck felt that it was my task to transplant something of the German Jewish heritage within the fertile soil of American Jewish life. 'Germany is finished', Baeck said to me on more than one occasion. He was certain that Jewish life would diminish and eventually disappear in that land, and that there was no need and indeed no call for me to return to my birthplace out of an obligation to German Judaism. My choice should probably be between South America and the United States. My Spanish would be of help if I were to join the German refugee rabbis Lemle or Pinkus; but Leo Baeck had come to love American Jewish life and looked forward to its growth and development. And his teaching at the Hebrew Union College meant that he could direct new disciples into a rabbinate that would have new dimensions and challenges.

Why, then, did he still look at Germany and reach out hesitatingly towards a dialogue? One must go back to the 1952 lecture then, to

Baeck's demand for truthfulness—the only pattern in which an eventual expression of repentance by Germans could eventually take place. And, as Baeck taught, there is no repentance without actions of atonement. He saw at that time that such actions had not come to the fore, and warned against rushing 'time'. A 'forgiving', a 'forgetting' would not only be a dishonest obscuring of the past, but would also deny Germany the necessary acts of atonement.

At a later time, Ernst Akiva Simon, Baeck's friend and colleague, expressed this point of view in a statement on Germany in which he still searched for acts of atonement:

> The new Germany can only 'work through' or 'overcome' its most recent past (whatever the term is) if it is ready for a genuine task of turning back (*teshuva*, return). The meaning of 'turning back is that one attempts to undo the consequences of evil deeds, to the fullest extent possible. No one who died is awakened by a return, but the return can help avoid new murders and new war. An energetic peace policy which brings Israel and its neighbours closer towards an understanding would be such an act of return. Then, Israel might be able to continue the task of rebuilding in peace and with humanity. If you (Germans) really want to return, do all in your power to let all the nations on earth find the way towards God's peace, not least Jews and Arabs in the Holy Land.
>
> We Jews were God's witnesses under the greatest oppression and deepest suffering; we hope to remain God's witnesses, in our own state, under conditions of freedom.[1]

Whether or not the time has come; indeed, whether or not Ernst Simon's hopes for Israel as well as for Germany have moved closer to fruition, continues to be a question of concern to us. But the balanced hope and doubt of Leo Baeck in this area is still applicable to our own situation. Recently, looking through my files, I came across my notes of an interview I had with Ernst Simon (on 23 December, 1965) when I was preparing my work on Leo Baeck. Most of the theological comments entered the book, but there also warm, personal statements about Baeck which again bring him to life in the re-reading. Simon did not always agree with Baeck, but defended him against Rosenzweig's criticism of being an apologete. 'Baeck, like Schleiermacher, defended religion against its despisers', said Simon. . . 'But he did not adopt any of Schleiermacher's views, despite Leon Roths's statement. . . Baeck was a great human being. . . with a hard core of

---

1. Ernst Simon, *Das Zeugnis des Judentums* (Berlin,1980).

inner integrity. . .' And Simon appreciated Baeck's traditional practices, the hour of prayer and study which opened every day of Baeck's
life. . .

In the end, Baeck inspired his colleagues as much as his students. All
of them knew: the day is short, and the work beckons. . .

And the Kairos-time may be closer than we imagine.

5

THE HUMAN BODY AND THE IMAGE OF GOD

Byron L. Sherwin

In generations to come, historians of British Jewry might very well conclude that 'Louis Jacobs' could not possibly represent the name of a single individual, but must refer to an entire school of rabbis and scholars engaged in communal service and scholarly research and writing. The scope of scholarly expertise, the breadth and depth of startling erudition, the massive corpus of published work, and the impact of rabbinic, religious, social and academic activities identified with the name 'Louis Jacobs' could hardly but convince future chroniclers that such attainments must be the product of more than one individual. Yet those of us fortunate enough to have benefited from the endearing friendship, the massive learning and the noble personality of Louis Jacobs know that he is a single and singular individual whose life and works embody the highest aspirations of Jewish learning and of British gentility.

Despite a career punctuated by controversy, his enormous intellectual and spiritual contributions have won him a permanent place of distinction in the annals of contemporary Jewish life and thought.[1] The lives of so many, including my own, have been immeasurably enriched because of Louis Jacobs. Offering my deepest gratitude and appreciation to him and extending sincere affection toward him is but a feeble attempt to reciprocate for what already has been received. For many of his American admirers, such as myself, Louis Jacobs represents the crown jewel of contemporary British Jewry. For rabbis and scholars, he is what many of us hope to become.

---

1. See Byron L. Sherwin, 'Louis Jacobs: Man of Controversy, Scholar of Distinction', *Judaism* 28.1 (Winter 1979), pp. 95-109.

The following essay, in which the imprint of Louis Jacobs's thinking upon my own may be evident, is an offering of thanksgiving, esteem and deep affection for a profound theologian, an inspired religious leader, a perspicacious scholar, and a faithful friend. In writing about the image of God, I offer a tribute to one who undoubtedly exemplifies that divine image and whose life unquestionably fulfills the purpose of the One who created him in that image.[1]

> It is proper for man to imitate his Creator, resembling Him in both likeness and image according to the secret of the Supernal Form. Because the chief Supernal image and likeness is in deeds, a human resemblance merely in bodily appearance and not in deeds debases that Form. Of the man who resembles the Form in body alone it is said, 'A handsome form whose deeds are ugly'. For what value can there be in man's resemblance to the Supernal Form in bodily limbs if his deeds have no resemblance to those of his Creator?[2]

The Ten Commandments forbid making an image of God. Yet God violated His own commandments and made an image of God. The human being is created by God in the image of God. Of all creatures, only the human creature is described as being in the image and likeness of God (Gen. 1.26).[3]

The divine image relates not only to the soul, intellect and will, but to the body as well. The body is a mirror reflecting the image of God, as well as a receptacle that embodies the divine likeness.[4]

> A parable: There were two twin brothers who lived in a certain city. One was elected king while the other became a thief. At the king's command, the thief was hanged. But all who saw the thief hanging on the gallows said, 'The king is hanged'.[5]

1. A version of this essay has been published in Polish translation by the Catholic Theological Academy of Warsaw University, 1991.

2. Moses Cordovero, *The Palm Tree of Deborah (Tomer Devorah)* (trans. Louis Jacobs; London: Vallentine, Mitchell, 1960), p. 46.

3. On the 'image of God' in rabbinic theology, see e.g. A. Heschel, *Torâ min ha-Shamayim* (London: Soncino, 1962), pp. 220-23.

4. On the identification of the 'image' (*zelem*) with intellect, see e.g. M. Maimonides, *Guide of the Perplexed*, Book I, ch. 1; J. Albo, *Séfer ha-Ikkarîm* (ed. and trans. I. Husik; Philadelphia: Jewish Publication Society, 1946), I, p. 109; D.I. Abravanel's commentary on Gen. 2.2 in his Hebrew *Commentary on Hebrew Scriptures* (Jerusalem, 1964), I, p. 89. On the identification of 'image' with moral autonomy, see e.g. J. Loew of Prague, *Tiferet Yîsraël* (New York: Judaica, 1969), p. 53.

5. *Sanhedrin* 46b.

Commenting on the verse, 'in the image of God, He created the human being', a midrash observes:

> Hillel the Elder once completed his studies with his disciples who accompanied him from the academy. His disciples asked him, 'Master, where are you going?'
> ' To perform a religious duty', he responded.
> 'Which religious duty?'
> ' To wash in the bathhouse', said Hillel.
> 'Is this a religious duty?'
> 'Yes', replied Hillel. 'If the statues of kings, which are erected in theatres and circuses, are scoured and washed by the person appointed to look after them, and who thereby obtains his maintenance through them, how much more I, who have been created in the image and likeness of God, for as it is written, "for in the image of God He made human beings?"' (Gen. 9.6)[1]

As these texts plainly observe, the human body, and not only the soul, has been created in the divine 'image and likeness'.

Whereas for Plato the business of the philosophers is to pry the soul loose and to isolate it from the body,[2] the business of the rabbis is to encourage the realization of the divine image through the exercise of moral autonomy, through the performance of sacred deeds, and through the rejection of acts of violence. (Murder, for example, is described as diminishing the divine image).[3]

The idea, so prevalent in Christianity, that God is embodied, is usually considered absent in Judaism. It was Maimonides who sought

1. *Midrash Leviticus Rabbah* 34.3; *Midrash Yalkut Shimoni*, 'Proverbs' para. 947; *Abot d'Rabbi Nathan* (ed. S. Schechter; New York: Feldheim, 1967), Recension 'B' ch. 30, p. 33b. It is important to note that in Hebrew Scriptures, no distinct term for the body exists. In rabbinic literature, body/soul dualism does not really exist. Rather, the individual human person is considered a psychophysical composite. The word '*guf*' used to designate the body in post-biblical literature only appears in Hebrew Scripture to denote a corpse, see 1 Chron. 10.12. The term '*gapo*' in Exod. 21.3 does not refer to the body, but probably to a garment, as Rashi notes in his commentary on this verse. The word '*basar*' does not denote the body, but life (e.g. Gen. 6.13) or flesh (e.g. Exod. 16.12). Nor does the term '*nefeš*' denote the soul as is often thought. Rather, '*nefeš*' usually refers to the person, i.e. to the psychophysical organism. See e.g. E. Urbach, *The Sages* (trans. I. Abrahams; Cambridge, MA: Harvard University Press, 1987), pp. 214-15.
2. Plato, *Phaedo* 67.
3. See e.g. *Tosefta-Yebamot* 8.3, *Midrash Mekhilta d'Rabbi Yishmael* (ed. Horovitz and Rabin; Jerusalem: Wahrmann, 1960), '*Yitro*'—'*ba-Hodesh*', p. 233 on Exod. 20.16.

to banish the idea of divine corporeality forever from Judaism.[1] However, the early Jewish mystics produced a treatise entitled *The Measurement of the Height (Shiur Koma)* that not only posits the existence of a divine body, but that describes in minute detail each of its limbs.[2] Subsequent Jewish mystics portrayed the *Deus Revelatus* in the form of a body, the configuration of the *Sefirot*, the Primordial Adam (*Adam Kadmon*). While admonishing against taking literally what is meant to be understood figuratively and symbolically,[3] they nevertheless insisted that the biblical description of the human being in the divine image refers to the configuration of the *sefirot* in the form of a human body. However, for the kabbalists, it must be stressed, it is the

1. See Maimonides, *Mishneh Torâh—Séfer ha-Mada,* "Laws of Repentance', 3.7 with the famous gloss of Abraham ben David to the effect that great Jewish scholars have affirmed the notion of divine corporeality. Also see Maimonides 'On Resurrection' in *Iggrot ha-Rambam* (Leipzig, 1859), p. 8a, and, of course, various sections throughout his *Guide of the Perplexed.* Note L. Jacobs, 'Kabbalistic and Hasidic Views of Maimonides', in B.L. Sherwin (ed.) *Solomon Goldman Lectures, Volume 5* (Chicago: Spertus College of Judaica Press, 1990), and L. Jacobs, *Principles of the Jewish Faith* (New York: Basic Books, 1964), pp. 120-23.

2. See the important translation and study by Martin S. Cohen, *The Shi'ur Qoma* (Lanham, MD: University Press of America, 1983), and the extensive discussion and documentation regarding all aspects of this work. Though a number of scholars, most notedly Gershom Scholem, maintain that the text describes the divine corpus in such gigantic terms so as to reject the notion of divine corporeality, there is no reason to make this assumption. The text should be taken at face-value as a description of God's body. Why else would the author take such great pains at describing each limb of God's body unless he believed that God has a body? This more literal reading was also affirmed in a conversation with Professor Moshe Idel. Furthermore, that medieval scholars who affirmed the absolute incorporeal nature of God, such as Maimonides, took such offense at this work, would lead one to conclude that many medieval readers took the work literally. Maimonides, for example, considers it a dangerous foreign import into Jewish literature. See e.g. Maimonides, *Responsa* (in Arabic and Hebrew) (ed. J. Blau; Jerusalem: *Mekitzie Nirdamîm,* 1957), I 117, pp. 200-201.

3. The insights of Moshe Idel with regard to kabbalistic views of the body are relevant here and are well-taken. Idel writes: 'the focus of the kabbalistic discussions is neither the glorification of the structure of the limbs nor even their dignity; purity or impurity, performance of the commandments or their neglect, are their major concern. The human structure is, *in potentia,* prone to perfect the divine structure or to cause its construction; thus action is the clue to understanding of human influence. Hence, limbs are no more than tools for the performance of the theurgic ritual'. See Idel, *Kabbalah: New Perspectives* (New Haven: Yale University Press, 1988), p. 185.

human being who is in the image of God, and not God who is in the human image.[1]

This notion of the human being in the image of the *sefirot* (the manifested attributes of God) reversed a trend in medieval Jewish thought of identifying the divine image exclusively with intellect or spirit. The correspondence of the human being with the sefirotic realm opened a door to taking the human body seriously as an active and necessary partner and participant in the drama of divine as well as human existence. Whereas in earlier medieval Jewish thought, self-knowledge as the conduit to knowledge of God and the universe was primarily related to the human intellect or soul, now the human body became a vehicle not only for self-knowledge, but to knowledge of God and creation as well. The Delphic maxim—'Know Thyself'—was no longer restricted to knowledge of the intellect or the soul, but now was applied to the knowledge of the body.[2]

While the Talmud and many of the medieval Jewish philosophers counselled contemplation of the body for the purpose of appreciating the *wisdom* of God, the kabbalists encouraged contemplation of the body as an entrée to the deepest truths, foremost among them being the *knowledge* of God. In this regard, compare, for example, medieval Jewish philosophical and medieval Jewish mystical interpretations of the verse from Job (19.26), 'From my flesh, I shall see God'.[3] Philosophers such as Abraham bar Hiyya interpreted the verse to mean 'from the nature of your flesh and the structure of your organs, you can comprehend the wisdom of your Creator'.[4] Jewish mystics such as

---

1. See e.g. L. Jacobs, *Seeker of Unity* (New York: Basic Books, 1966), p. 41.

2. See e.g. the now classic study by A. Altmann, 'The Delphic Maxim in Medieval Islam and Judaism' in his *Studies in Religious Philosophy and Mysticism* (Ithaca, NY: Yale University Press, 1969), pp. 1-40.

3. A comprehensive study of interpretations of this verse in Jewish sources would inevitably bring interesting results. Certainly, Altmann made some extraordinary progress in this endeavor. See e.g. Abba Mari ben Moses of Lunel who interprets it to mean that the existence of God can be inferred from contemplating the form of the human body; see his *Minhat Kenaōt* (Pressburg, 1838), ch. 7, pp. 8-9. In his work *Shivilei Emunâ* (Warsaw, 1887), Meir Aldabi notes that knowledge of the nature of the limbs of the human body leads inevitably to divine worship. He therefore offers a detailed discussion and description of each limb; see pp. 48a-55b.

4. Abraham bar Hiyya, *The Meditation of the Sad Soul (Hegyon ha-Nefeš)* (trans. G. Wigoder; London: Routledge and Kegan Paul, 1969), p. 38. Also see e.g. Bahya ibn Pakudah, *The Book of Direction to the Duties of the Heart* (trans. M. Mansoor; London: Routledge and Kegan Paul, 1973), pp. 160-61.

Judah Loew of Prague took this verse to mean, 'When one contemplates the form of the human body, one is able to arrive at a knowledge of God'.[1]

Already in early rabbinic thought, one encounters the idea of the human being as a microcosm.[2] The Jewish mystics expanded this notion to include not only the cosmos, but all worlds, especially the world of the *sefirot*. Being modelled after the *sefirot*, the human body can be a gateway to the divine. Consequently, contemplation of the human body and its actions not only grants one knowledge of all worlds—of all dimensions of existence, but also indicates how physical action can influence what happens in these worlds, including the world of the *sefirot*. In this typically kabbalistic view, each human action, each human gesture, has immense implications and influence. The physical life of the human being is related therefore not merely to the individual or social realm, but to the disposition of all that exists. From this perspective, the actions of the human body have transcendent and theurgic implications, effecting the Godhead itself. As the hasidic master, Elimelekh of Lizensk, observed:

> The main reason man was created was to rectify his Root in the upper worlds. It is written, 'For in the image of God, He made humans' (Gen. 9.6). God made humans in the form of the structure that exists on high, making each human being a precise counterpart of it. . . The main human task is to rectify the divine structure (*shiur komah*). . . Whenever a per-

---

1. J. Loew, *Derekh Hayyim* (New York: Judaica, 1969), 3.14, p. 143. Also see e.g. *Sēfer ha-Temūnâ* (Lwow, 1892), p. 25a-b.

2. See e.g. *Abôt d'Rabbi Natān*, 'A', ch. 31 (ed. Schechter), p. 46a-b. Here it is stated: 'Everything that God created, He created in man'. The term '*ōlam katān* (microcosm), does not appear in this text. Its first appearance in rabbinic literature seems to be *Midrash Tanhuma (ha-Nidpas)* (Jerusalem: Levin-Epstein, 1964), '*Pekuday*', para. 3, p. 132b, in relation to the Tabernacle which in turn is related to the creation of human beings.

The notion of man as a microcosm is common in medieval Jewish thought. See e.g. Maimonides, *Guide of the Perplexed*, I, ch. 72. The term 'microcosm' (*ha-'Ōlam ha-Katān*) is utilized by the medieval Jewish philosopher, Joseph ibn Zaddik, as the title of his major philosophical work. According to ibn Zaddik, the body is a microcosm of the physical world and the soul is a microcosm of the spiritual world (ed. S. Horovitz, Breslau, 1903, p. 4). See e.g. Bahya ben Asher on Gen. 1.27; Zohar, III, pp. 33b, 257b. See discussion and sources noted in Idel, *Kabbalah*, pp. 146-53; Altmann, pp. 19-28.

son sanctifies him/herself through a certain part of the body, that person rectifies the universes that correspond to that particular limb.[1]

While Descartes believed that the soul and the body meet in the pineal gland, for Jewish thought the rendezvous occurs in the sacred deed.[2] Without the body, the sacred deed could not be performed. Doing the sacred deed offers the body an opportunity to make manifest the divine image implicit within the self. Through the performance of the sacred deed, body and soul resolve any intrinsic tension between them by moving together toward their common goals: self-realization and divine worship. Hence, mind-body and soul-body dualism is resolved in the *miṣvâ*, the sacred act. Through observance of the commandments of God, one realizes and makes manifest the image of God.

Unlike the Zohar, which placed the 'image' below the soul but above the body, Judah Loew of Prague described the 'image' as transcendent both of the soul and the body, as higher even than the angels.[3] For Loew, the 'image' could only become manifest with the body, in the body. The 'image' requires an agent to become manifest in order to realize its essence and to accomplish its divinely ordained mission. The body is this agent. Similarly, the divine commandments (*miṣvōt*) can only be performed physically. The 248 positive commandments of the Torah relate to the 248 parts of the body, according to the Talmud. Both the body and the commandments are physical agents of the divine. Without the body, without spiritual deeds in physical form, the 'image' would remain unrealized, dormant, comatose.[4]

While care and development of the body are desired by God and are necessary to human enjoyment and life, the body is not an end in itself. Neither the destruction nor the adoration of the body is desirable.

---

1. *Noam Elimelekh 'Likkutay Shoshanâ'* (Lwow, 1887), p. 102b. This text, as is typical of kabbalistic texts, stresses the need to refrain from thinking of the upper worlds in physical or pictorial terms while proceeding to describe them in these ways.

2. René Descartes, *Meditations*, ch. 6, and *Passions of the Soul*, part. 1, Articles 31, 34.

3. On the Zohar, see Isaiah Tishbi, *Mishnat ha-Zōhar*, II (Jerusalem: Mosad Bialik, 1961), pp. 90-93.

4. For discussion and relevant sources, see Y. Jacobson's Hebrew essay, 'The Image of God as a Source of Man's Evil According to the Maharal', *Daat* 19 [Summer 1987], pp. 103-36. See also B.L. Sherwin, *Mystical Theology and Social Dissent* (London: Oxford University Press, 1982), ch. 10.

Care and development of the body provide a foundation for more elevated pursuits. The body is a vehicle, not a destination.[1]

In an 'ethical will' attributed to Maimonides, the author writes, 'Perfection of the body is an antecedent to the perfection of the soul, for health is the key that unlocks the inner chambers. When I bid you to care for your bodily and moral welfare, my purpose is to open for you the gates of heaven'.[2] But, a medieval Jewish philosopher observes, 'What profit has one in his bodily health, if one's soul is

---

1. While physical exercise is not prohibited but is encouraged, the rabbinic disapproval of sports in the Hellenistic period articulates the rabbis' objection to making the body an end in itself. In this regard, see e.g. S. Lieberman, *Greek in Jewish Palestine* (New York: Feldheim, 1965), p. 92.

In his *Treatise on Asthma* (trans. S. Muntner; Philadelphia: Lippincott, 1963), p. 6, Maimonides discusses six 'obligatory regulations' for health of the body: clean air, proper diet, sleep, regulation of emotion, moderate exercise, and proper excretion. See also his *Mishneh Torah—Sefer ha-Mada, 'Hilkhot Deot'* 4.1, 13. It is significant that Maimonides incorporates a discussion of health requirements in his *legal* code. On health of the body in Judaism, see e.g. Byron L. Sherwin, *In Partnership with God* (Syracuse, NY: Syracuse University Press, 1990), ch. 4, and sources noted there. On Maimonides view of the 'perfection of the body' and its being a foundation for moral and intellectual perfection, see e.g. B.L. Sherwin, 'Moses Maimonides on Perfection of the Body', *Listening* 9 (1974), pp. 28-37 and notes there.

One cannot deny that various trends in Jewish thought advocate weakening the body to strengthen the soul through ascetic practices. On asceticism in Judaism, see e.g. S. Fraade, 'Ascetical Aspects of Ancient Judaism', in Arthur Green (ed.), *Jewish Spirituality* (New York: Crossroads, 1986), pp. 253-88; A. Lazaroff, 'Bahya's Asceticism Against its Rabbinic and Islamic Background', *Journal of Jewish Studies* 21 (1970), pp. 11-38.

Louis Jacobs distinguishes among three religious attitudes toward physical gratification: thankful acceptance, ascetic, and puritanical. Jacobs correctly considers the first dominant in rabbinic literature, the second dominant among certain philosophers and in certain mystical trends (e.g. Hasidei Ashkenaz), and the third dominant among other philosophers (e.g. Bahya) and mystics (e.g. Hasidism). The first gratefully accepts the gift of creation and of the body. The second sets up a state of conflict between body and soul, and the third teaches that pleasure is good but should not be an end in itself. See Louis Jacobs, 'Eating as an Act of Worship in Hasidic Thought', in S. Stein and R. Loewe (eds.), *Studies in Jewish Religious and Intellectual History* (University, Alabama: University of Alabama Press, 1979), pp. 157-58. See also, L. Jacobs, 'The Uplifting of Sparks in Later Jewish Mysticism', in A. Green (ed.), *Jewish Spirituality II* (New York: Crossroads, 1987), pp. 99-126.

2. I. Abrahams (ed. and trans.), *Hebrew Ethical Wills* (Philadelphia: Jewish Publication Society, 1926), p. 105.

ill?'[1] Since the limbs of the body are the instruments of the soul, a body in ill repair leaves the soul inoperative, the self spiritually immobile. However, if the soul is diseased, health of the body becomes a premise without a conclusion, a non sequitur.

A choice is offered each individual. One's body can be all that one is; or, one's body can allow one to become more than one is. The body is a passport to transcendence, an invitation to immortality. The disposition of each human life depends upon whether one chooses to accept this invitation, to make use of this passport.

Without the soul, the body is a corpse. Without the body, the soul is a vagabond spirit. Without the soul, the body is a rudderless ship. However, without the body, there is no ship. Without the limbs of the body, the soul is mute. Or, as the Zohar directly states, 'The soul cannot operate at all without the body'.[2]

Each physical activity, no matter how mundane, can become an opportunity for realizing the divine image. This is the message of the hasidic teaching of *abōdâ ba-gašmiût*, 'worship of God through the physical'. This is true of eating, even of excretion, but especially of sexuality. Sexual relations begin with the premise that no single body is complete. Through relations with another, one can attain completion, achieve a higher level of self-consciousness than by one's self, transcend the limitations of one's own body by fusing with another, and ensure the perpetuation of one's body in the body of a child. Sexuality thereby aligns the individual with the divine image.[3]

Already in Scripture, sexual experience is described as 'knowledge'. Sexual experience, coupled with love, desire and will, penetrates not only the mystery of sexuality, but inevitably draws one to begin to decode the deeper mysteries of existence, especially the mysteries embedded in the psychophysical organism that is the self.[4] Just as the soul fills the body, so God fills the world.[5] Just as God fills the world,

1. Shem Tov ben Joseph ibn Falaquera, *The Book of the Seeker (Séfer ha-Mebakeš)* (trans. M.H. Levine; New York: Yeshivah University Press, 1976), p. 31.

2. Zohar, II, p. 244a. See Tishbi, p. 115.

3. See e.g. J. Loew, *Tiferet Yisrael*, ch. 16, pp. 53-54. I have expanded on this theme in an essay in the *Festschrift* in honor of Louis Jacobs's and my mutual friend, Seymour J. Cohen, not published at the time of this writing.

4. Gen. 4.1. See the interpretation of this verse in the anonymous medieval treatise, *Iggeret ha-Kōdeš*, ascribed to Nahmanides. See the bi-lingual (English/Hebrew) edition (ed. S.J. Cohen; New York: Ktav, 1976), pp. 40, 49.

5. *Berakhot* 10a.

He is present in each cell of the body. The universe is a disguise of God; the body is one of His masks. He awaits our unmasking Him. In encountering God beneath His garments, one also dis-covers oneself.

The body changes throughout the course of a lifetime. In a sense, one inhabits many different bodies which are the same body between birth and death. Some of the Jewish mystics discussed transmigration of souls, the view that in the course of the life of a soul, many different bodies are inhabited. They vested individual identity in an 'astral body' that transcends the individual bodies of the soul's sojourns.[1] One may extend these notions to mean that during a single lifetime, one dwells in many bodies that coalesce in the same body, in an identical self. Each of these bodies writes a chapter in the novel that is each of our lives.

The promise of the resurrection of the body—a virtual dogma of classical Jewish faith—expresses Judaism's assurance that God is concerned with each individual, that the body and not just the soul is an object of providence.[2] The resurrected body is an improved model over the one that preceded it. This notion can be extended to mean that not only after death but also during life, tragedy and trauma—a form of death during life—can become a prelude to renewed and improved life. The body that is shed can become the preface to a new resurrected self. Life after death can occur both after death or during life. Resurrection is an opportunity that mitigates the reality of mortality. By envisaging a corporeal life after life, Jewish tradition articulates its stance that embodied existence holds forth the promise of renewed life. A disembodied afterlife beyond time and space may be accepted on faith while it eludes our experience and even our imagination. An embodied afterlife reaffirms the continuing potentialities pregnant in our bodies, in ourselves.

In the theological parlance of the Jewish mystics, each individual is a limb of God (*aiber ha-šekhinâ*). The disposition of the individual human person, of the cosmic and of the divine corpus, is vested in how each limb of God articulates the image of God. Furthermore, the Jewish mystical notion that every person's soul is 'a part of God' (*helek*

1. See Tishbi, *Mishnat ha-Zôhar*, II, pp. 91-93.
2. For an erudite and thoughtful discussion of resurrection in Jewish theology, see L. Jacobs, *Principles*, ch. 14, pp. 398-454.

elōhā mi-ma'al) implies that the human essence is not merely to be in the image of God, but to become divine.[1]

Human existence is an opportunity to make manifest in the world the 'image' that we bear and that we share with God. Each human person is an envelope bearing a divine message, a divine Presence. It is our task during life to bear witness to this message by the way we live. By realizing the image of God implanted in each of us, we can bring about not only the realization of our own individual selves, but also the repair of the torn fabric of creation, and the augmentation of the Source of all creation and of all selves.[2]

---

1. Note L. Jacobs, 'The Doctrine of the Divine Spark in Man in Jewish Sources', in R. Loewe (ed.), *Studies in Rationalism, Judaism and Universalism* (London, 1966), pp. 84-144, and Jacobs's introduction to his translation of Dobh Baer of Lubavitch's *Tract on Ecstasy* (London: Vallentine, Mitchell, 1963), p. 17.

2. See e.g. Moshe Hayyim Ephraim, *Degel Mahaneh Ephraim* (Jerusalem, 1973), '*Aharei*', p. 175. Note e.g. Idel, pp. 157-67, 185-91 and sources there.

6

THE CLASSICAL TRADITION IN BYZANTIUM

Nicholas de Lange

I remember well with what apprehension (as well as excitement) we rabbinical students at Leo Baeck College received the news that Louis Jacobs was going to take over our Talmud classes. The 'Jacobs affair' had received so much press coverage and aroused so much controversy that the prospect was rather like coming face to face with Captain Dreyfus. A cultural chasm divided those of us brought up in the Reform camp from the Anglo-Orthodoxy from which he issued; to fear of the unknown was added a certain frisson at encountering a notorious heretic. In the event our fears proved groundless. We soon succumbed to the relaxed brilliance of his expositions, the apparatus of scholarship lightly worn, the good humour, the astonishing insistence of looking behind the surface of the talmudic text and its argument to the aims and methods of its editors. In time I came also to appreciate Louis Jacobs as a rabbi, and I came to learn that if I needed his advice it would always be freely given and sound. I am glad to have the chance to offer him this little tribute.

Byzantine Judaism is an unjustly neglected subject. Among the various factors which have contributed to this neglect,[1] a major one is the shortage of historical documents. The few sources we do have at our disposal afford us some intriguing glimpses of a civilization which had some curious and distinctive features. But the interpretation of the evidence poses awkward questions.

Here are two examples: The Spaniard Abraham Ibn Ezra, in his commentary on the book of Jonah, asserts in passing that the Jewish

---

1. See my historiographical study 'Qui a tué les Juifs de Byzance?', in *Politique et religion dans le judaïsme ancien et médiéval* (ed. D. Tollet; Paris: Desclée, 1989), pp. 327-33.

scholars of Byzantium identify the city of Nineveh with Troy.[1] Ibn Ezra was writing in the middle of the twelfth century. A generation later his compatriot Benjamin of Tudela mentions, also in passing, that the leaders of the small Jewish community of a place he calls Larta (probably the town of Arta) in western Greece are called Rabbi She-lahia and Rabbi Herakles.[2]

Now we may safely suppose that nowhere else but in the Byzantine empire would we find in the twelfth century a Jewish dignitary by the name of Herakles or a Jewish commentator evoking the Homeric epic in a commentary on the Bible. But these stray allusions raise the further question of how much other evidence of this kind has been lost. In other words, what part, if any, did the classical Greek heritage play in the culture of the Jews of Byzantium?

Given the nature of our evidence, any attempt to answer this question is bound to be speculative. The materials on which a conclusive answer to it might be based simply do not exist. Even the question of whether they once existed and are now lost must remain open. We have no medieval Jewish commentaries on classical Greek texts; we do not even have information about the educational syllabus followed in Byzantine Jewish schools. The surviving writings produced by Jews in Byzantium are mainly written in Hebrew and do not quote from or allude overtly to classical sources. And yet the question is worth asking, because of its bearing on the relations of Byzantine Jewish cul-

1. Commentary on Jon. 1.2. See my article 'Ibn Ezra and Byzantium', in *Abraham Ibn Ezra y sus tiempos* (ed. F. Díaz Esteban; Madrid: Asociacíon Española de Orientalistas, 1990), pp. 99-107. Ibn Ezra expresses himself as uncertain about the truth of this identification, which he mentions again on Zeph. 2.13.
2. The form 'Herakles' does not actually occur in any manuscript that I have seen, but there seems to be a consensus that Benjamin wrote 'Hercules', which would be the Latin or Spanish form corresponding to the Greek Herakles. So M.N. Adler in his translation (London, 1907), following A. Asher (London, 1840), who restored the reading *'erqules* in his text. S.B. Bowman, *The Jews of Byzantium, 1204-1453* (University of Alabama, 1985), prints 'Ercules' in his translation (p. 333), but suggests (somewhat implausibly) that this 'represents the spoken Greek form of the name Hercules' (p. 336 n. 2). (Bowman also maintains [pp. 75, 336] that the place in question is not Arta but Leukas). The Rome manuscript (Casanatensis 216) reads *'RQLYWS*, corresponding to the Greek name Heraklios. Since the most famous Heraklios was an emperor (Heraklios I, 610-41) who was remembered as a persecutor of the Jews, in fact the first ruler to decree the forcible mass-baptism of the Jews, this would seem to be an even less likely name for a Jewish leader than Herakles. I would consequently take this reading as a corruption of Herakles, the original Greek form of the name.

ture, both 'vertically' with earlier Judaeo-Greek culture, and 'horizontally', with contemporary Christian Greek culture.

The Classical Tradition in Ancient Judaism

In the Roman period, when Greek was one of the main (if not *the* main) spoken and written languages of the Jews, there was no particular difficulty about access to the classical Greek heritage. Naturally, this heritage made itself felt in many different ways among Jews, as it did among gentiles. At one end of the spectrum, it is possible for a Jew to manipulate classical Greek literary genres, in the manner of the tragic poet Ezekiel, author of a Greek drama on the subject of the Exodus, or the epic poet Philo.[1] The two Jewish writers who have left us really substantial remains, the philosopher and biblical exegete Philo and the historian and apologist Josephus, are clearly perfectly at home in the composition of literary Greek,[2] and they are both conscious of writing within a Greek tradition and of addressing cultivated Greek readers. In the case of some Greek works, despite Jewish subject-matter, it is not even agreed that they are Jewish: an example is the Greek romance on the story of Joseph and Asenath.[3]

Other evidence betrays a more tangential, but in some ways no less interesting, involvement with the Greek cultural heritage. To take an unpromising example: the Greek translation of the Song of Songs, thought to have been made in the late first century CE, is so closely attached to the Hebrew original that in places it is not really comprehensible as Greek. By the time the translation was made this cycle of erotic poems was certainly read as an allegory of the love-affair of God and the people of Israel. In the first chapter of the Song the

---

1. H. Jacobson, *The Exagoge of Ezekiel* (Cambridge: Cambridge University Press, 1983); C.R. Holladay, *Fragments from Hellenistic Jewish Authors*, II: *The Epic Poets Theodotus and Philo and Ezekiel the Tragedian* (Atlanta, GA: Scholars Press, 1989).

2. In Josephus' case it seems to have taken him some time to achieve a mastery of written Greek. In the case of Philo there is no clear evidence that he could write any other language.

3. For a succinct history of criticism see C. Burchard in *The Old Testament Pseudepigrapha* (ed. J.H. Charlesworth; London, 1985), II, p. 187. Most scholars now accept a Jewish origin: e.g. S. West, '*Joseph and Asenath*: A Neglected Greek Romance', *Classical Quarterly* 24 (1974), pp. 70-81; A.D. Momigliano, *Alien Wisdom: The Limits of Hellenism* (Cambridge: Cambridge University Press, 1975), p. 117.

woman (Israel) appeals to her beloved (God) to let her know where she can find him. Her beloved answers as follows: 'If you do not know yourself (*Ean mē gnōs seautēn*), O beautiful among women, go out yourself in the tracks of the flocks, and herd your kids near the shepherds' tents'. We need not trouble ourselves here to identify the allegorical shepherds; what is striking is the introduction of the Delphic maxim 'Know yourself ' (*gnōthi seauton*) into the sacred text.[1] For the Greek Jew, self-knowledge has become a way to God.

Let us turn now to a later example, an epitaph dated on various grounds to the first half of the third century. It is a plaque of white marble from a splendid mausoleum (now in ruins).[2] The inscription is in Greek, and in verse (however defective the prosody and the metre):

> Here I lie dead, Leonteides [i.e. the descendant of Judah, the Lion (?)], Ioustos, son of (S)aphes [or possibly 'of Sappho'], who, having plucked the fruit of all science, left the light, my poor parents still weeping, and my brothers, alas, in Besara [Beth Shearim], and departed to Hades. I, Ioustos, lie here, with many of my own, since the powerful Moira willed it. Courage, Ioustos, no one is immortal!

Here is an epitaph which is certainly Jewish from its context, and yet typically Greek in its form and language and even its theology. We note Hades, Moira, and perhaps most startling to anyone not familiar with hellenistic inscriptions, the concluding slogan, 'No one is immortal!'

Personal names can also be revealing. From around the same time as this inscription (or a little later) we have the lists of names of Jews carved on a stele at Aphrodisias in Caria.[3] The names include not merely names which are those of Greek heroes, such as Achilles, but

---

1. Cf. Origen *ad loc.*: 'the wise Solomon anticipated the well-known Greek saying'. The same interpretation is given, although without explicit reference to the Greek, in a medieval Aramaic work, the *Zohar Hadash, ad loc.* See A. Altmann, 'The Delphic Maxim in Medieval Islam and Judaism', in his *Studies in Religious Philosophy and Mysticism* (London: Routledge and Kegan Paul, 1969), p. 18. Altmann points out that in Juvenal, *Satires* 11.27, the maxim 'descended from heaven'.

2. M. Schwabe and B. Lifshitz, *Beth She'arim II: The Greek Inscriptions* (Jerusalem, 1974) 127, pp. 97-110 (in the original Hebrew edition [Jerusalem, 5727/1967], pp. 45-51).

3. Joyce Reynolds and Robert Tannenbaum, *Jews and God-Fearers at Aphrodisias: Greek Inscriptions with Commentary* (Cambridge: Cambridge Philological Society, 1987).

even Greek theophoric names such as Diogenes and Hermes (or Hermeas).

An acquaintance with the Homeric myths and even with the language of the Homeric poems is attested in various kinds of Jewish source at various periods.[1] Most interestingly, we have eight letters from the rhetor Libanius supposedly addressed to the Jewish Patriarch Gamliel VI between 388 and 393 which include Homeric allusions, and, in the words of a recent writer on the subject, 'not only show that the patriarch was on intimate terms with one of the most famous teachers of rhetoric at the time, but that they shared a similar rhetorical education and love for the Greek classics'.[2]

Greek mythology makes its appearance also in the decoration of synagogues in Palestine, from the sun-god Helios in his four-horse chariot in the centre of the splendid zodiac mosaic of the fourth-century synagogue of Hammath by Tiberias to the similar, if artistically cruder, specimen from the early sixth century at Beth Alpha, and the beautiful mosaic from Gaza in which a musician who looks like Orpheus charming the wild beasts is identified by an inscription as David, the biblical musician-king.[3]

All this is highly suggestive. Yet the contrary tendency can also be detected. In the mid-third-century apologetic work *Against Celsus*, the Christian writer Origen finds it most unconvincing that his opponent should put a quotation from Euripides in the mouth of a Jew: in his experience, Origen remarks (and we should remember that he had lived for a quarter of a century in Caesarea of Palestine), Jews are not at all well read in Greek literature.[4]

---

1. See for example M. Hengel, *Judaism and Hellenism* (trans. J. Bowden; London: SCM Press, 1974), I, p. 75; S. Lieberman, *Hellenism in Jewish Palestine* (New York: Jewish Theological Seminary, 5722/1962), pp. 112ff.
2. R.L. Wilken, *John Chrysostom and the Jews* (Berkeley/London: University of California Press, 1983), p. 58.
3. See e.g. L.I. Levine (ed.), *Ancient Synagogues Revealed* (Jerusalem: Israel Exploration Society, 1981), esp. pp. 8f., 15f., 66f., 130, 174 (David/Orpheus at Dura Europos). The same volume contains an account of the interesting series of mosaics depicting Samson, from what may be a synagogue or a church in Mopsuestia in Cilicia. Michael Avi-Yonah argues that it is a synagogue, and that Samson is chosen because he is associated with the eponymous founder of the city, Mopsos (pp. 186ff.).
4. Origen, *Contra Celsum* II.34. Cf. N.R.M. de Lange, *Origen and the Jews* (Cambridge: Cambridge University Press, 1976), p. 69. On the other hand, we should bear in mind that the context is polemical: cf. p. 6.

In another text dating probably from the third century we read the following:

> Avoid all gentile books. For what need have you of alien writings, laws and false prophets which lead the frivolous away from the faith? What do you find lacking in God's Law that you should seek those gentile fables? If you wish to read histories, you have the books of Kings; if rhetorical and poetic writings, you have the prophets, you have Job, you have the Proverbs, wherein you will find a sagacity that is greater than that of all poetry and sophistry since those are the words of our Lord who alone is wise. If you have a desire for songs, you have the Psalms, if for ancient genealogies, you have Genesis; if for legal books and precepts, you have the Lord's glorious Law. So avoid strenuously all alien and diabolical books.[1]

These words were written in all probability by a Jew converted to Christianity. But there is nothing Christian in them, not even a mention, which we might have expected, of the books of the New Testament. There is no reason to doubt that they represent a certain Jewish attitude of the time. Yet its polemical tone confirms a contrary tendency for Jews to read the pagan authors. Indeed, we have hints of Jewish participation in traditional Hellenic education at the highest level much later than this time: we hear of 'Jews instructed in liberal studies' who acted as advocates;[2] and in the late fifth and early sixth centuries we know of a number of learned Jews, such as the philosopher Zeno of Alexandria, the mathematician Domninos, and the doctors Jacob of Alexandria, Domnos, and Agapios. We can also detect traces of Jewish influence in the neoplatonic writers of the period.[3]

The Decline of Classical Studies

The closing of the Academy of Athens by Justinian in the year 529 must have had a disastrous effect on classical studies generally, even if a certain amount of scholarship survived. A law of the same year for-

---

1. *Apostolic Constitutions* 1.6, as translated in Cyril Mango, *Byzantium, the Empire of New Rome* (London: Weidenfeld and Nicolson, 1980), p. 131.

2. *Cod. Th.* 16.8.24; see Wilken, *John Chrysostom and the Jews*, p. 60.

3. See Alfredo M. Rabello, *Giustiniano. Ebrei e Samaritani alla luce delle fonti storico-letterarie, ecclesiastiche e giuridiche*, I (Milan: Giuffre, 1987), pp. 445f. Some doubts are in order about the Jewish origins or continuing Jewish allegiance of some of those mentioned: see M. Stern (ed.), *Greek and Latin Authors on Jews and Judaism*, II (Jerusalem, 1980), pp. 671-78.

bids any heretic to teach, permitting only those of orthodox (Christian) faith. Does the prohibition cover Jews? Samaritans, as it happens, are mentioned expressly, but Jews are not. As Alfredo Rabello has recently argued,[1] even if Jews are not automatically included, it might always be open to a judge to include them if he deemed it opportune. In any case, the climate thenceforth was scarcely conducive to classical studies among the Jews in Byzantium. It is conceivable (even if it cannot be proved) that Greek scholarship was stronger among Jews in Palestine and Syria in the early period of Arab rule than in Byzantium itself.[2]

How late did Jews continue to read the classics of Judaeo-Greek literature, and to compose works in the same vein? This is a question that cannot be firmly settled in the present state of our knowledge, in fact the evidence is so slight as to be virtually non-existent. Books 12 to 14 of the *Sibylline Oracles* appear to have been composed (in the traditional Greek hexameters) in Alexandria in the third to fifth centuries, and perhaps even later: it has been argued that Book 14 contains a reference to the Arab conquest of Egypt.[3] 'Presumably they represent an ongoing tradition which was repeatedly updated'.[4]

To summarize our findings so far: there is plentiful evidence for an attachment to the classical tradition among (some) Jews, even if from the third century we have found some signs of hostility to it. (This could be reinforced by reference to Talmudic texts, which are however notoriously difficult to date or localise). The continuity of a learned tradition depends on education. After the crisis of the sixth century, which undermines both the existence of the pagan schools of classical learning and the status of the Jews in the Christian empire, the survival of a continuous classical tradition among Jews becomes highly problematical. But is it possible that such a tradition, once lost, could be revived? This question cannot be approached in isolation from the Byzantine Christian context.

---

1. Rabello, II (1988), pp. 726f.
2. It has been suggested that such may have been the situation among Christians; see Mango, *Byzantium, the Empire of New Rome*, p. 137.
3. E.g. A.D. Momigliano, 'Sibylline Oracles', in his *Ottavo Contributo alla storia degli studi classici e del mondo antico* (Rome, 1987), pp. 349-53. [This article originally appeared in *The Encyclopedia of Religion*, XIII (New York, 1987)].
4. J.J. Collins in *Jewish Writings of the Second Temple Period* (ed. M.E. Stone; Assen/Philadelphia, 1984), pp. 379f.

The Christian Experience

Although it is quite proper to attribute to Christian Byzantium the credit for having kept the ancient Greek learning alive during the long centuries when it was more or less forgotten in the West, it would be a mistake to imagine that the classical culture of Christians in Byzantium was uniform down the ages or even uniformly rich at any particular time. The closure of the Athens Academy and related measures of the Christian Empire had more or less destroyed the structure of higher education, at least outside the main centres. Even in Constantinople there is no firm evidence of a formal, state-supported institution of higher learning between the early seventh and the mid-eleventh century. It is no accident that this period coincides with the decline and revival of the cities.[1] Some signs of a revival of learning begin to appear from the early ninth century, however, and by the tenth century there is a good deal of interest in the classical heritage. This is the period of the great Byzantine dictionaries, encyclopaedias and anthologies. It is also the period when ancient copies of the classical texts were collected and recopied in the minuscule script. It is thus a period which is crucial in the history of classical studies, and one which laid the foundations for the expansion of classical learning in the eleventh and twelfth centuries.

During the eleventh century there were both qualitative and quantitative improvements in education; yet inevitably there were still great inequalities in the educational level of the populace. A small minority could read the classics with pleasure and insight (an even smaller minority could actually write classical Greek correctly and with elegance); but many more were apparently able to recognise certain classical allusions, and the Greek myths enjoyed a wider currency still. These differences have to be borne in mind when we try to envisage the level of Greek culture practised by the Jews. What is at issue is, on the one hand, an education, which was based on the Greek language and the Greek classics. To be able to drop a classical allusion, or

---

1. See on this particularly Mango, *Byzantium, The Empire of New Rome*; also 'Discontinuity with the Classical Past in Byzantium', in *Byzantium and the Classical Tradition* (ed. M. Mullett and R. Scott; Birmingham, 1981), pp. 48-57; A.P. Kazhdan and Ann Wharton Epstein, *Change in Byzantine Culture in the Eleventh and Twelfth Centuries* (Berkeley, Los Angeles and London: University of California Press, 1985). On Byzantine scholarship more generally see N.G. Wilson, *Scholars of Byzantium* (London: Duckworth, 1983), and P. Lemerle, *Le Premier humanisme byzantin* (Paris: Presses Universitaires de France, 1971).

recognise one, was the hallmark of an educated man. But implicit in all this there was also a question of identity. To be a Greek was to be the heir of heroes of old. Anna Comnena compared her father, the emperor Alexios I, to Herakles and also to Alexander the Great. Byzantine Christians recognized the biblical roots of their faith, but they tended to attempt some form of reconciliation between the two elements of their double heritage, for example by weaving together biblical and Graeco-Roman history into a single story (following in the footsteps of Josephus and other ancient Jewish historians).

Jewish Knowledge of the Greek Heritage

We may reasonably ask ourselves which elements of this picture can be transposed from the better attested Christian milieu to the less well-documented Jewish one. The first thing to be said is that the interruption in education between the sixth and tenth centuries must have weighed even more heavily upon the Jews than upon the Christians. Indeed it would seem, although we cannot trace the details clearly, that during this period Jewish education in the Byzantine empire was totally transformed. When the darkness lifts in the eleventh century the education is based not on the study of Greek grammar and the Greek classics but of Hebrew grammar and the Hebrew Bible. The discoveries of the Cairo Genizah shed some light on this, and the documents in question, though only rarely dated, belong most probably to the eleventh and twelfth centuries. We have letters in which Greek-speaking Jews correspond even with members of their own families in Hebrew, albeit a rather rudimentary Hebrew influenced by Greek and making occasional use of Greek words; and we have glossaries in which Hebrew words from the Bible or the Mishnah are listed with their Greek equivalents.[1] It is significant that when Greek words are written in these manuscripts they are almost always given in Hebrew letters: Jews were apparently more at home with the Hebrew than the Greek alphabet at this time, an indication that the goal of primary edu-

---

1. For examples see N.R.M. de Lange, 'Some New Fragments of Aquila on Malachi and Job?', *Vetus Testamentum* 30 (1980), pp. 291-94; N.R.M. de Lange, ' Two Genizah Fragments in Hebrew and Greek', in *Interpreting the Bible: Essays in Honour of E.I.J. Rosenthal* (ed. J.A. Emerton and S.C. Reif; Cambridge: Cambridge University Press, 1982), pp. 61-83 [together with a fragment of Ecclesiastes in Greek]; J. Starr, 'A Fragment of a Greek Mishnaic Glossary', *PAAJR* 6 (1953), pp. 353-67.

cation was to be able to read the Hebrew Bible, not the Greek classics. It is also significant that the Greek of these texts is generally the vernacular language rather than the classicizing literary Greek, another indication of an educational rift between Jews and Christians.[1]

The Cairo Genizah documents also reveal the presence in the Byzantine towns of numbers of Arabic-speaking immigrants, from Egypt and elsewhere, apparently well integrated in the Jewish communities. It seems that the revival of the Byzantine cities attracted immigration, as did the loss of certain eastern, Arabic-speaking territories. Even though in time the immigrants seem to have abandoned Arabic in favour of Greek, this movement of population must have had an impact both on the education and on the self-identification of Greek-speaking Jews. Henceforth they were part of an international Hebrew-based culture.

From the tenth century[2] on we have works composed by Byzantine Jews in Hebrew, and despite the presence of Greek words and phrases they seem to have been intended for an international Jewish readership. At any rate, we know that some of them were read and copied in other countries.[3] The question of whether there was a separate, parallel activity of Jews writing in Greek characters is very difficult to answer; to the best of my knowledge it has never been seriously tackled. The earliest Greek manuscript written in a minuscule hand (the form of writing that came into favour among Christians from the ninth century) for which a Jewish origin has been posited dates from

---

1. 'To write ideal attic was possible in Byzantium only if one read the ancient authors (through rhetorical education in the schools) and used an atticising lexicon for writing' (H. Hunger, in *Byzantium and the Classical Tradition*, p. 43). The only continuous text we have in attic for which a Jewish authorship has been claimed (it even uses the doric dialect to render the Aramaic portions of the Bible) is the so-called *Graecus Venetus* (see below).

2. Possibly even a little earlier, particularly in Byzantine south Italy. The south Italian hymnographers Amittai of Oria and Zebadiah may be dated to the late ninth century: see H. Schirmann, *New Poems from the Genizah* [Hebrew] (Jerusalem, 5727/1967), p. 422. Kalon of Rome (Schirmann, *New Poems*, p. 424) may also be a Byzantine poet of the same period. The conventional dating of the Iosephon, a Hebrew reworking of the Latin Josephus, in the mid-tenth century has been challenged recently in favour of a ninth-century date. The *Book of Medicines* of Asaf may also have been written in the ninth century (see below).

3. See e.g. S. Buber's introduction to his edition of the *Leqah Tob* of Tobias ben Eliezer of Kastoria (Vilna, 1880), fol. 23ff.; J.E. Rembaum, 'The Influence of *Sefer Nestor Hakomer* on Medieval Jewish Polemics', *PAAJR* 45 (1978), pp. 155-85.

no earlier than the fourteenth century.[1] From occasional specimens of Greek writing which are found preserved in Hebrew manuscripts, often in the form of readers notes or odd jottings, it would appear that Jews clung even at this late date to a form of the uncial script, and did not make the transition to the minuscule hand—a reminder of the barriers that separated Christians from Jews in everyday cultural life.

Some of the Byzantine works written in Hebrew make use of sources in Greek. This is most apparent in medical or philosophical writings, but can be observed also elsewhere, for example when biblical commentaries quote from Greek Bible translations. A few illustrations will give some idea of the range and character of the sources used. It should be emphasized that relatively little work has been done so far on identifying the Greek sources of Hebrew writings; it is likely that further research would reveal a wider range of source materials.

Leaving aside the *Iosephon*, a work which, though compiled by someone with a knowledge of Greek, is based on the ancient Greek writer Josephus only at second hand, via a Latin translation, the earliest Byzantine prose works to interest us are medical writings. The *Book of Medicines* attributed to Asaf, according to the latest study[2] 'may well be a product of Byzantine Italy in the ninth or tenth century'.[3] It is an encyclopaedic work, essentially not unlike the Byzantine encyclopaedias. As the study in question makes plain, the work, although based in part on earlier Jewish writings such as *Jubilees*, also contains 'paraphrased abridgments of. . . Greek works such as the Hippocratic *Aphorisms* and the *Materia medica* of Dioscorides'.[4] The influence of Hippocrates, Dioscorides and Galen can also be discerned in the *Book of Mixtures* of Shabbetai Donnolo[5] (born in Oria in Apu-

---

1. This is a translation of the Pentateuch and other biblical books known as the *Graecus Venetus*. It is by no means certain that the scribe was a Jew: see G. Mercati, *Se la versione dall' Ebraico del codice veneto VII sia di Simone Atumano* (Rome, 1916). Cf. A. Turyn, *Dated Greek Manuscripts of the Thirteenth and Fourteenth Centuries in the Libraries of Italy*, pp. 212f.

2. Elinor Lieber, 'Asaf's *Book of Medicines*: A Hebrew encyclopedia of Greek and Jewish medicine, possibly compiled in Byzantium on an Indian model', *Dumbarton Oaks Papers* 38 (1984), pp. 233-49.

3. Lieber, 'Asaf's *Book of Medicines*', p. 237.

4. Lieber, 'Asaf's *Book of Medicines*', p. 238, cf. pp. 244ff., and for references to Galen, pp. 243, 245.

5. See A. Sharf, *The Universe of Shabbetai Donnolo* (Warminster: Aris and Phillips, 1976), pp. 94f. Cf. pp. 98ff. for an account of the Greek medical tradition on which Donnolo may have relied.

lia in 913, d. after 982). A third medical work, the *Practica*, of uncertain authorship,[1] also makes use of Greek medical sources.

A little later, in Constantinople and perhaps in some other large centres, we find a considerable output of works in Hebrew, by both Karaite and Rabbanite authors, which are spattered with words and phrases in Greek. Sometimes the Greek word serves simply to explain an obscure Hebrew one, or to supply an expression which is lacking in Hebrew. These words and phrases are of great interest, and would repay study by Hellenists. Writing of the Greek words in Jacob ben Reuben's *Sēfer Ha'ōšer*, Zvi Ankori observes: 'The words range from "bread" to various kinds of fish; from simple work-tools to specialized terms in building techniques, textile industry, etc.; from parts of the human body to medical names for diseases and physical defects; from different articles, of wear and even armour, to official designations, such as titles of Byzantine officials, measures and coinage; from courtesy phrases to theological expressions'.[2] Sometimes the words appear to go back to earlier Greek sources, but since indications of source are not given it is hard to be certain about the origin.[3]

All this evidence is at best only mildly encouraging. It shows us the Greek-speaking Jews as being at home in their environment, perfectly familiar with the colloquial Greek language and, beyond that, with Greek institutions, technical terminology, even possibly some contemporary Greek texts. But there is no convincing indication of a familiarity with the classical tradition.

It is interesting in this connection to consider one item which might on the face of it seem to point the other way. George Gemistos Plethon (c. 1360–1452), one of the outstanding Greek intellectuals of his day, is said to have studied Aristotle with a Jew, Elissaios (Elisha). But our sole source for this claim is a later Greek writer, George Scholarios,

1. Sharf thinks it may be by Donnolo; Lieber (p. 237) thinks it may originally have been part of the *Book of Medicines*.

2. Z. Ankori, *Karaites in Byzantium. The Formative Years, 970–1100* (New York and Jerusalem, 1959), p. 198.

3. On Greek philosophical terminology in Judah Hadassi's *Eshkol ha-Kofer* see P.F. Frankl, *MGWJ* 33 (1884), pp. 448-57, 513-19; J. Perles, *BZ* 2 (1893), p. 576. This probably indicates an acquaintance with contemporary Greek literature rather than the classical sources, just as his familiarity with Christian theological vocabulary (see W. Bacher, *JQR* 8 [1906], pp. 431-44) probably does not indicate an acquaintance with classical patristic sources so much as with current Christian usage. It is possible that we possess some tracts written in Greek by Jewish converts to Christianity; so far none has been certainly identified or published.

and he makes it quite plain that Elissaios's acquaintance with Aristotle was mediated through Hebrew translations of Averroes and other Islamic commentators. Moreover, although Scholarios describes Elissaios as a 'Hellenist' (as opposed to a believing Jew), it is not at all clear that he was a Greek Jew. In another text Scholarios says that Gemistos went abroad to study under him, 'at a time when he enjoyed great influence at the court of the barbarians'—presumably the Ottoman Turks.[1] Consequently even this initially promising lead does not really advance us in our quest.

What then of the evidence from which this quest began, the commentary on Jonah by Abraham Ibn Ezra and the travelogue of Benjamin of Tudela? How much weight can we give to such stray items now that we have explored the wider background?

To begin with Ibn Ezra's identification of Nineveh with Troy. The reference to Troy is in itself mildly interesting: it not only betrays a knowledge of the Homeric legend (which at this basic level is no great surprise), but points to a society in which Jewish biblical commentators and their readers (including presumably Ibn Ezra himself, a Spaniard who had spent some time in Rome) could share the point of such an allusion. But what is more interesting is the use to which the reference is put:[2] it appears to be an attempt to reconcile a history based on the Bible with that based on the Homeric epic. Now this is an enterprise which is attested also in the Christian chronographers of Byzantium at the same time. By way of example, Constantine Manasses, following the earlier chronographers Malalas and Kedrenos, locates the Trojan War during the reign of David, who was one of the allies rallied by Priam after the death of Hektor. According to this view, Homer was a contemporary of Solomon; but John Tzetzes maintains that he must be dated later, since he refers to the *Solymoi*, the people of Jerusalem, who were named after Solomon.[3] The attempt

---

1. For a discussion of the whole question of Elissaios see C.M. Woodhouse, *George Gemistos Plethon, the Last of the Hellenes* (Oxford: Oxford University Press, 1986), esp. pp. 23-28; E. Wust, *Pe'amim* 41 (1989), pp. 49-57.

2. 'What is interesting is not so much who could quote Homer, or even who read him, but the purpose for which Homer was read, the place of knowledge of Homer in the life of Byzantine society, and the extent to which study of Homer led to results, direct or indirect, which go beyond the pleasure of the immediate reader' (R. Browning, 'Homer in Byzantium', *Viator* 6 [1975], p. 15).

3. See the references in A. Vasilikopoulou-Ioannidou, *Hē anagennēsis tōn grammatōn kata ton IB' aiōna eis to Byzantion kai ho Homēros* (Athens, 1971),

to align the book of Jonah to the Iliad, mentioned by Ibn Ezra, fits well against this background. On the other hand, it must be admitted that it is a small snippet, and I have not yet found any more material of the same type in the actual remains of Byzantine Bible commentary of this period.

The question of Benjamin of Tudela's 'Rabbi Herakles' needs to be studied with all the resources of Byzantine Jewish onomastics. A word of caution is in order from the outset. Although most of the names of Byzantine Jews known to us are Hebrew, it is likely that the preponderance of Hebrew names is due at least partly to the nature of our sources. Even in Hebrew documents some Hebrew names are accompanied by their Greek equivalents. A good example is the 14th-century scholar commonly known as Yehuda Ibn Moskoni, who signs himself with great care *'ani yehûdâ hamekhûnē leon ben harav moshē hamekhûnē mosqoni*.[1] In other words (as Steven Bowman was the first to point out), he had two names, which could be used for different purposes: his Hebrew name was Judah son of Moses, while his Greek name was Leo son of Moskhon or Moskhoni. Again, a scribe who on one manuscript[2] signs himself as Menahem ben Joseph Vivante elsewhere gives his name as Menahem Parigori ben Joseph Vivant.[3] A contemporary signs himself Menahem Parigori b. Shabbetai Pangalo.[4] *Parigoris*, 'the consoler', is the Greek equivalent of the Hebrew *Menahem*, and it is plausible to suppose that many more Jews had Greek names as well as Hebrew ones. Apparently they still kept their Greek names; but since most of the documents that survive are in Hebrew, these names have been lost. (Women mentioned in the documents almost invariably have Greek, not Hebrew names. This does not mean that Byzantine Jewish parents gave their daughters Greek names and their sons Hebrew ones, but rather that they gave their sons both Greek and Hebrew names and their daughters Greek names alone.)

The medieval records concerning Greek-speaking Jews are mainly in Hebrew (and the rest are mostly rather later than the time of Benjamin of Tudela, dating from the thirteenth to fifteenth centuries, after the Latin conquest); consequently we find very few Greek men's

---

pp. 116, 120. It is surprising that this very detailed monograph on the uses of Homer in 12th-century Byzantium makes no mention of the reference in Ibn Ezra.

1. See S. Bowman, *The Jews of Byzantium, 1204–1453*, p. 133 n. 11.
2. Paris BN héb. 308, dated 1467.
3. Bodley Opp. Add. 40 24, dated 1446.
4. Cambridge UL Add. 485, note of sale dated 1469.

names in them. I have only found sixteen in all, and Herakles stands out in the list in being a name from classical antiquity. The rest are for the most part either traditional Greek Jewish names (Anastasios, Marinos, Moskhon, Paregoris, perhaps Protos) or names that might be borne by contemporary Christians (such as Angelos or Niketas). Most of the names which had been common on the earlier Jewish inscriptions have seemingly fallen out of use, including such 'classical' names as Alexander or Iason. The only other name which may possibly contain a classical allusion is Disos, which is attested once in the fifteenth century and may perhaps be a shortened form of Odysseus. But the identification is too uncertain and the date too late for any serious analogy to be drawn with the Herakles mentioned by Benjamin of Tudela

The name of Rabbi Herakles would appear, then, to be an oddity, due possibly to a local tradition, or a desire to imitate or pay a compliment to a non-Jew (although the name is not common among Christians either).

Conclusions

This has been, as I remarked at the outset, a speculative investigation, and the few conclusions that may be drawn are for the most part negative ones. There is really very little evidence of familiarity with the classical heritage after the 'dark ages' of the seventh to the tenth centuries. What can be seen instead, I believe, in the slim dossier I have brought together, is a certain contact with the majority Greek culture, particularly among Jewish scholars who had a particular reason to consult Greek texts or Greek scholars. Insofar as there is a classical 'tradition', then, it belongs to the Christians, even if not all Christians share it. From a Hellenic point of view, this signifies an impoverishment of Jewish culture by comparison with earlier times. The principal reasons for this development are two. In the first place, a deliberate and conscious rupture—legal, social and cultural—between Christians and Jews, maintained and enforced by the government and the church. And secondly, the arrival of a strong outside influence, which filled the vacuum created by this schism, namely Rabbinic Jewish culture, with its emphasis on the Hebrew language and the biblical heritage. The study of this fundamental development lies outside our present scope, although it may properly be observed here that analogous tensions, between the classical and the biblical heritage, can be discerned on the Christian side as well.[1] Later we find a revival of interest in the scientific portion of the Greek heritage among some Byzantine Jews, but this question, too, lies outside the confines of the present study; it must be explored on another occasion.

1. 'The true culture of Byzantium. . . was dominated, not by classical antiquity as we understand it, but by a construct of the Christian and Jewish apologists built up in the first five or six centuries AD. This body of doctrine was very consistently worked out and its ingredients were mostly biblical with an admixture from other sources, both classical and oriental, but always subordinated to the teaching of the Bible' (C. Mango, in *Byzantium and the Classical Tradition*, p. 57).

7

AKKADIAN MEDICINE IN THE BABYLONIAN TALMUD[1]

M.J. Geller

For the past several years, Rabbi Louis Jacobs has offered an important Talmud seminar at University College London for staff and students, although it is not a typical Talmud *shiur*. This seminar offered an opportunity to analyse the text critically, with an attempt to reconstruct the editorial work of the compilers, while grappling with the ruthless logic of the argumentation. Rabbi Jacobs's mastery of the

---

1. The bulk of this article has been redrafted from the author's review of Pablo Herrero, *La thérapeutique mésopotamienne* (Paris, 1984), which appeared in *Bibliotheca Orientalis* 43 (1986), pp. 738-46; permission to reprint much of the review article was kindly granted by the editor, Professor Marten Stol. Corrections from Professor Franz Köcher are also gratefully acknowledged and incorporated into this version. Additional data was collected by the author for lectures given at the Seminar für Assyriologie, Heidelberg, and the Institut für Assyriologie und Hethitologie, München.

BAM	=	Franz Köcher, *Die Babylonisch-assyrische Medizin in Texten und Untersuchungen* (Berlin, 1963–), I–IV
AMT	=	R.C. Thompson, *Assyrian Medical Texts* (Oxford, 1923)
AS	=	*Assyriological Studies* (University of Chicago)
CAD	=	*Chicago Assyrian Dictionary*
CT	=	*Cuneiform Texts in the British Museum*
JNES	=	*Journal of Near Eastern Studies*
KAR	=	E. Ebeling, *Keilschrifttexte aus Assur religiösen Inhalts*
MSL	=	*Materials for the Sumerian Lexicon* (edited by B. Landsberger, M. Civil, *et al.*)
PRSM	=	*Proceedings of the Royal Society of Medicine*
RA	=	*Revue d'Assyriologie*
SAHG	=	D. Goltz, *Studien zur altorientalischen und griechischen Heilkunde* (Wiesbaden, 1974)
TDP	=	R. Labat, *Traité akkadien de diagnostics et pronostics médicaux* (Paris and Leiden, 1951)

subject was not only enlightening, but in no small part it inspired the interest in the Talmud of the present contribution, offered with gratitude to his Festschrift.

The Babylonian Talmud is a great repository of information about Babylonia in the first five centuries CE, and its contents often reflect the learning and practices of contemporary and earlier Babylonia. The Aramaic passages of the Talmud which originated in Babylonia (and not Palestine) can occasionally be compared to Akkadian texts with spectacular results, since many of the ideas of the Babylonian Jewish community can be traced back to local traditions, in such diverse fields as law, magic, and medicine. No systematic studies have yet been attempted to collect similar passages from Akkadian and Babylonian Jewish Aramaic texts. The following sample of magico-medical texts is offered as a foray into a difficult but fruitful area of research.

B. Ab. Zar. 28b

פיקעא תתאה מאי? לייתי תרבא דצפירתא דלא אפתח וליפשר
ולישדי ביה. ואי לא לייתי תלת תרפא קרא דמייבשי בטולא
וליקלי וליבדר עילויה.[1] ואי לא לייתי משקדי חלזוני.[2] ואי לא
מייתי משח קירא ולינקום בשחקי דכיתנא בקייטא ודעמר גופנא
בסיתווא.

> For a split in the lower part of the anus, what to do? Let him (the healer) take the fat of a virgin goat and melt it, and pour it upon (the patient). If (that does) not (work), let him take three leaves of a *gourd*, which are dried in the shade, and let it be roasted and sprinkled upon (the patient) (var. let it be roasted, ground up, and wrapped upon him). If (that does) not (work), let him take *snail shells* (var. let him take *snail shells* and let it be roasted and *left* upon him). If (that does) not (work), let him take oil and wax and wrap (the patient) in a worn linen in summer and in cotton in winter.

A number of Babylonian medical texts deal with proctology (cf. Herrero, p. 36, Labat, *TDP* XIV, pp. 32ff., and *inter alia BAM* 89, 102, 105, 258). The recipes prescribed here are similar to those found in Akkadian medical texts, namely a salve (cf. Akk. *napšaltu*; Goltz, *SAHG*, p. 70; Herrero, pp. 98-99), a powder (Akk. *qēmu*; cf. Ritter, *AS* 16, pp. 308f.), or a 'poultice' (Goltz, *SAHG*, p. 71). The medical

1. תלתא תרפי דקרי דיבשי בטולא וליקלי ולישחק וליכרך עליה.
2. ליתי משקדי חלזוני וליקלי ושביק עליה.

texts themselves refer to '30 drugs (used) in bandages for a rectal ailment' (*BAM* 159, iii, 53), or '(the patient) will drink the seven drugs in a potion, (dissolved) in wine, for a rectal ailment' (*BAM* 164, rev. 25; see Ritter, *AS* 16, pp. 313-14). Moreover, the format of the recipe is set out in a similar fashion to its Akkadian counterpart, which uses KI.MIN 'ditto' to mean 'another remedy', i.e. if the previous one does not work. The following terms have either cognates or close parallels in Babylonian medical texts:

trb': abdominal fat, corresponding to Akkadian *lipû* (ì.udu) 'tallow' (Herrero, p. 53) and *himṣu* (^{uzu}me.hé) 'fatty tissue around the intestines' (*CAD* H 192) found in rituals. See also *BAM* 1, iii, 6 ^úgi-ir-gi-ru-u: *šammu*(ú) KI.MIN (= DÚR.GIG) *itti*(ki) *lipî* (ì.udu) *tuballal*(hi.hi) 'mix fat with a *girgirû*-plant for a sore anus'.

ṣ'yrt' dl' 'pth: a virgin goat = Akkadian *unīqu la petītu* (cf. Ritter, *AS* 16, p. 309a); Aramaic *l' 'pth* appears to be a borrowing from Akkadian.

wlšdy: Jastrow (*Dictionary*, p. 1524b) suggests an etymology from the root *ndy*, which fits well with Akkadian *nadû* (Herrero, p. 65; Goltz, *SAGH*, p. 45), although Akkadian *nadû* is never attested in the III-stem in medical texts.

dmyybšy btwl': dried in the shade = Akkadian *ina ṣilli tubbal* 'you will dry it in the shade' (*AMT* 6,1.10, and Goltz, *SAHG*, p. 29).

qly: roasted = Akk. *qalû* (Herrero, pp. 69-70).

bdr: sprinkled, corresponding to Akkadian *zarû* 'sprinkle' (Herrero, p. 113; Goltz, *SAHG*, p. 74). Cf. *ta-qal-lu teṭên^{en}*(àr) *tazarru*(mar) 'you roast, grind, and sprinkle' (*BAM* iii, 2), and for an ailing rectum, [*ina*] *šuburri*(dúr)-*šú tazarru*(mar.meš)-*ma* 'you sprinkle (materia medica) on his anus' (*BAM* 494, 152, rev., iii, 9).

lyšhq wlykrk (variant): For the Akkadian equivalents *tasâk. . . talammi* 'you pound. . . wrap', see *CAD* S 83.

mšh oil, corresponding to Akkadian *šamnu* (ì.giš) (see Herrero, pp. 53, 55).

qyr': wax, corresponding to Akkadian *iškuru* (gaba.làl), (see Herrero, p. 52); oil and wax frequently appear together in Akkadian medical texts, as in the Talmud passage; see *BAM* 3, ii, 51, *ina šamni iškura*(gaba.làl) *tuballal ina maški*(kuš) *teṭerri^{ri}*(sur) *taṣammid*(lá)-*ma* 'you mix (the materia medica) in oil and wax, smear it on a leather (poultice) and make a bandage'.

kytn': linen garment = Akkadian *kitinnu/kitû*. See *BAM* 543, 3 *kitâ*(túg.gada) *šamna tasallah*(sù) 'you sprinkle linen with oil'; see also *CAD* K 475a.

bqyyṭ' . . . bsytww': summer. . . winter; cf. *RA* 53, 4.13 *šum₄-ma kuṣṣu*(en.te.na) *ina šur-šum šikari*(kaš) *šum₄-ma um-ma-a-tú ina mê*(a) *kasî*(gazi^{sar}) *tu-ba-har taṣammid*(lá) 'if it is winter, you heat (the

materia medica) in beer, if it is summer (you heat it) in beet-juice, and
you make a bandage' (see *CAD* B 307a; see also *BAM* 522 7').

B. *Ab. Zar.* 28b

נפק מר שמואל ודרש עין שמרדה מותר לכוחלה בשבת. מאי
טעמא? דשורייני דעינא באובנתא דליבא תלו. כגון מאי? אמר
רב יהודה כגון רירא דיצא דמא דימעתא וקידחא וחחלת אוכלא
ולאפוקי סוף אוכלא ופצוחי עינא דלא.

Mar Samuel went and taught: It is permitted to treat a runny eye with antimony (*koḥl*) on the Sabbath. What is (the reason)? Because the sinews of
the eye are attached to the projections (lit. fingers) of the 'heart' (internal
anatomy). What (is it)? Rab Judah said, for example: a discharge, a
squeezing, blood, tears, and heat. At the beginning of the pain, and
excluding the end of the sickness and the brightening of the eye (i.e.
increased sightedness), (it is) not (permitted to treat on the Sabbath).

This is the only Talmudic passage of this group which can be dated,
since Mar Samuel, of the Nehardea academy, died in 254 CE (Strack,
Introduction to the Talmud and Midrash, p. 121), while Rab Judah,
who taught in Pumbeditha, died in 299 CE (Strack, p. 123).

kwḥlh: Antimony was widely used for eye treatment in Egypt and Greece, as well
    as in Akkadian medicine as *guḥlu* (see *CAD* G 125).
šwryyny d'yn' b'wbnt' dlyb': Veins of the eye in 'fingers' of the 'heart'. These are
    Akkadian terms, as in Labat, *TDP*, p. 50 iv 9 (*CT* 37 50):
    šumma(diš) *šer'ān*(sa) *īnē-šú kīma*(gim) *ubāni*(šu.si) *ku-bu-*[*ur*] 'if
    the veins of the eyes are thick like a finger'. In the Aramaic passage,
    the term '*wbnt*' corresponds to the Akkadian (plural) of *ubānu* which
    can refer to 'projections' of the lung (*ubān haši*, see *CAD* H 144b).
dm': Jastrow translates the term here as congestion, but without supporting evi-
    dence. The basic meaning of 'blood' is supported by Akkadian evi-
    dence: *T D P* V ii 6-9: *s'umma īnā-šú dama*(úš)
    malā(diri)/*imtanallā*(diri.meš) 'if his eyes are filled with blood'. See
    also *BAM* 522 5', *šumma amīlu*(na) *īnā-šú damu iṭ-ri-ma izzi*[z]*iz*(gub)
    'if a man, in whose eyes blood coagulates and stays. . .'; *BAM* 510 i
    35' *šumma amīlu īnā-šú dama šu-un-nu-'a* 'if a man's eyes are sticky
    (with blood). . .'
dym'h: tears, cf. BM 54641+54826 (unpub.) *šumma amīlu inā-šú dimātu*(ér) im-
    mal-la-a 'if a man's eyes are filled with tears. . .'
qydḥ': heat (or inflammation), as in *BAM* 510 i 9 (+*AMT* 20,2 7') *šumma amīlu*
    īnā-šú marṣā(gig)*-ma u ḥa-an-ṭa* 'if a man's eyes are diseased and
    hot'.

'wkl': hurting, a calque adapted from Akkadian *akālu* 'to be in pain'; cf. *TDP* V 1
    šumma marṣu īn imittīšu ikkalšu 'if a patient, whose right eye causes
    him pain. . .'

The Aramaic passage can be compared with the following passage
from an eye disease text (*BAM* 514 ii 27', dupl. 510 ii 16'), in which
similar symptoms are described:

šumma   amī lu   īnā-šú   marṣā(gig)-*ma dama*(úš) *m a l ā*(diri)
baluhhā(ᶴⁱᵐbuluh.hi.a) *dama ul-ta-ta-ni-'a damu dīmtū*(ér) *ina libbi* (šà)
inē-šú ittaṣâᵃ(è) *ṣillu*(gissu) *lamassat*(ᵈlamma) *inē-šú ú-na-kap a-ši-tu ana
ṣilli itūr(gur).

If a man's eyes are diseased and filled with blood, they were constantly
bloodshot with blood and *mucus* (resin), tears came out from the middle of
his eyes, and a film has *encircled* the pupil of his eye, and blurring has
turned to shadow. . .

B. Git. 69a

לשברירי דליליא ניתי שודרא ברקא וניסר חדא כרעא מיניה
וחדא כרעא מכלבא וניטרפו ינוקי חספא אבתריה ולימרו ליה
"אסא כלבא אכסא תרנגולא". ולינבי שב אומצי משבעא בתי
וליתבינהו ניהליה בציגורא דדשא וניכלינהו בקלקולי דמתא. בתר
הכי לפשוט שודרא ברקא ונימרו הכי "שברירי דפלוני בר
פלוניתא שבקינהו לפלוני בר פלוניתא" וליחרו לכלבא בבביתא
דעיניה. לשברירי דיממא ליתי שבעה סומקי מגווא דחיותא
וניטוינהו אחספא דאומנא וליתיב מגואי ואיניש אחרינא
מאבראי ונימא ליה "עירא הב לי דאיכול". ונימא ליה "האיך
פתיחא סב איכול". ובתר דאכיל ליתבריה לחספא דאי לא הדרי
עילויה.

For night blurriness let (the healer) take a rope of white strands and bind
together one of (the patient's) legs and a leg of a dog, while children toss
potsherds behind him and say to him (the incantation): '*heal* the dog, *hide*
the cock'. Let (the healer) collect seven pieces of meat from seven houses,
and position them for himself on the door-pivot, and let them (the dogs?)
eat (the meat) on the town's refuse-heap. After this, undoing the white
rope, let (the healer) say 'O blurriness of So-and-so, depart from So-and-
so', and let them stab (or blow at) the dog in the pupil of the eye.

For daytime blurriness, let (the healer) take seven red (pieces) from the
belly of animals, and let him roast them in a craftsman's vessel. Let (the
healer) place himself inside, with the other man outside, and let (the healer)
say to (the patient), 'Blind one, give that I may eat'. Let (the patient) say to

him, 'Open-eyed one there, take and eat'. After it is eaten, let him break the vessel, that (blurriness) not return to him.

The ailment to be treated in this passage is *šbryry*, which is a loan from Akkadian *barāru* 'to be filmy (referring to the eyes)' (*CAD* B 106), the *šafel*-form of the Aramaic word being characteristic of Akkadian loanwords into Aramaic.

The passage should be compared with the following eye disease recipe (*BAM* 516 ii 30ff.; see R.C. Thompson, *PRSM* 1926 41):

šumma amīlu ūma(u$_4$) *kalama*(dù.a.bi) *lā*(nu) *immar* (igi.du$_8$)
mūša(ge$_6$) *kalama*(dù.a.bi) *immar*(igi.d[u$_8$]) ^{d}*sin-lu-ur-ma-a*
šumma amīlu ūma(u$_4$) *kalama*(dù.a.bi) *immar*(igi.du$_8$)
mūša(ge$_6$) *kalama*(dù.a.bi) *lā*(nu) *immar*(igi.du$_8$) ^{d}*sin-lu-ur-ma-a*
šumma amīlu īnā-šú si-lu-ur-ma-a ma-ku-ut ga-bi-di
ša imēri(anše) *šīr*(uzu) *la-ba-ni-šú*
ina pitilti(šu.sar) *ta-šak-kak ina kišādi*(gú)-*šú*
tašakkan^{an}(gar) *egubbâ*^{a}(a.gúb.ba) *tukân*^{an}(gub)
ina še-rim šahhâ(^{túg}sà.ha)
ana pān(igi) ^{d}*šamaš*(^{d}utu) *tarakkas*^{as}(lá) *niknakka*(níg.na)
burāši(^{šim}li) *tašakkan*^{an}(gar) *amīlu*(lú) *šú-a-tú*
ina ku-tal šahhî(^{túg}sà.ha) *ana pān* ^{d}*šamaš*
tuš-z[a-a]s-su mašmāšu(maš.maš) 7 *akali*(ninda)
inašši^{si}(íl) *šá īnā-šú marṣú marṣa*-(gig) 7 *akali*(ninda)
inašši^{š}(íl)-*ma*
[*mašmāšu a*]*na marṣi*(lú.tu.ra) *mu-uh-ra nam-ra i-ni i-qab-bi*^{r}
[lú.tu.r]*a ana mašmāši mu-uh-[ra] bal-ṣa i-ni i-qab-bi*[
[....................*m*]*a-ku-ut ga-bi-di ta-har-ra-aṣ*
[....................*m a š*]*māšu ṣehrūti*(lú.tur.meš) *tu-pa-har-ma*
ki-a-am i-qab-bu-u
[....................] ^{r}*i*^{1}-*qab-bu-u himēta*(ì.nun) *u šamna rešta*(sag)
išteniš^{niš}(diš) *tuballal*(hi.hi) *īnā-šú teteneqqi*(mar.meš)
[ak.ak.bi] *šu-a-tu* šu.bi.gin$_7$.nam
[ka.inim.ma *mu*]-*úh-ra* ^{d}*é-a liš-ma-a* ^{d}*é-a lim-hu-ra*
[*a-m*]*ur nam-ra i-ni a-mur bal-ṣa i-ni* tu$_6$.én.

If a man cannot see everything by day and can see everything at night, (it is) *sinlurma*-disease. If a man can see everything in the daytime, but cannot see at nighttime, (it is) *sinlurma*-disease. If both of a man's eyes (suffer from) *sinlurma*-disease, you shall thread the 'pole' of a donkey's belly and its neck sinews on a cord and place it on (the patient's) neck. You set up the ritual-water vessel, and in the morning spread a linen cloth in the sun, and prepare a censer with juniper. You make that man (the patient) stand behind the linen cloth, in the daylight. The incantation priest will raise up seven loaves and the one with the sick eyes will raise seven loaves, and [the priest] will say to the sick man, 'Receive, O bright of eye'. The sick man will say to the incantation priest, 'Receive, one with staring eye'. [. . .] you will chop up the 'pole' of the belly [. . .] you (with the ?) incantation priest will assemble children, who say thus. . . they will say. . . You mix the ghee and best quality oil and repeatedly daub his eyes. [Its ritual]: It is the same. [Incantation]: 'May Ea hear the prayer, may Ea receive (it). See O clear eyed, see O staring-eyed.'

There are many common features between the Aramaic and Akkadian passages which make them worthy of comparison, particularly the similar dialogues between healer and patient, the positioning of the patient and healer 'inside' and 'outside', the references to seven pieces of meat or bread, and the recitation of the children. The incidences of similarity are too numerous to be entirely coincidental.

Occasionally, the Talmudic recipes appear to be closely related to Akkadian rituals which occur in incantation contexts. *Shab.* 110b, for example, includes the instruction to take a speckled swine (*ḥwṭrn'*), tear it open and apply to the patient's 'heart'. The following ritual occurs in a Sumerian-Akkadian bilingual incantation (CT 17 6 10):

šah-tur-ra ki-bí-in-gar-ra-bi-šè u-me-ni-sum
    MIN-*a a-na pu-hi-šú i-din-ma*
uzu-uzu-bi-šè mud-mud-bi-šè u-me-ni-sum šu ha-ba-ab-ti-gá
    še-ra ki-ma še-ri-šú da-me kīma da-me-šú i-din-ma lil-qu-ú
lipiš sag-šà-ga-na-ke₄ u-me-ni-gar šà-ga-gin₇ u-me-ni-sum
    šu ha-ba-ab-ti-gá
    lìb-ba šá ina rēš lìb-bi-šú taš-ku-na ki-ma lìb-bi-šú
    i-din-ma lil-qu-ú

Give over a small pig as (the patient's) substitute,
give its flesh as his flesh and its blood as his blood, so that it takes (the evil) away,
position its 'heart' which is at its epigrastrium and position it like his 'heart', so that it takes (the evil) away.

In both cases, the pig acts as a substitute for the patient's organs, and receives the illness from the patient through direct contact between the pig and the patient's body.

In addition to these lengthier passages, there are a number of isolated phrases in the Babylonian Talmud which appear to be technical *calques* borrowed from Akkadian medical recipes. *B. Git.* 70a, for instance, gives instructions for medicines to be taken on an empty stomach, which is directly analogous to the Akkadian *balu patān: balu patān išattīma iballuṭ*, 'he shall drink (the medicine) on an empty stomach and he will get better' (*CT* 23 46 iv 6), or *balu patān ikkalma u mê išattīma ina'eš*, 'he will consume (it) on an empty stomach but he can drink water, and he will improve' (*BAM* 77 32', see *CAD* B 72). Other terms can actually be identified as Akkadian loanwords, such as the symptom *ṣimra'*, defined by Jastrow, *Dictionary*, p. 1277, as 'fever', but probably derived from Akkadian *ṣimru* 'distended', referring to the bloating of the intestines (*CAD* Ṣ 127, 200). Similarly, Aramaic *ṣmyrt'* (Jastrow, *Dictionary*, p. 1288, 'inflammatory fever') derives from Akkadian *ṣemertu* (*CAD* Ṣ 126).

Moreover, one of the main features of Mesopotamian medicine is the large number of plants in recipes, which were collected by ancient scribes into long lists, including descriptions of the physical properties of the plants themselves. It seems to have escaped notice that most of the plant names mentioned in Talmudic medical contexts either have Akkadian cognates, or even derive directly from Akkadian plant names. The following list has been culled from a few pages from one tractate, *Gittin*, and by no means represents a systematic collection of Talmudic plant names. Nevertheless, the parallels with Akkadian terminology are striking:

TALMUD			AKKADIAN
Git. 67b	*sykwry*	=	*sikkūrat eqli*
Git. 68a	*'s'*	=	*asu* 'myrtle'
Git. 68a	*byn'*	=	*bīnu* 'tamarisk'
Git. 68a	*šwrbyn'*	=	*šurmēnu* cypress'
Git. 69a	*'spst'*	=	*aspastu* 'lucerne' (Pers. *asp-ast*)
Git. 69a	*thly*	=	*sahlû* 'cress'
Git. 69a	*ptylt'*	=	*pitiltu* 'Palmblast strick'
Git. 69a	*pryd'*	=	*pirindu* 'Fruchtschnitze'
Git. 69b	*sysyn*	=	*sissin libbi*
Git. 69b	*glgyl'*	=	*galgaltu*
Git. 69b	*nynyy'*	=	*nīnû*

Although not a plant name, we would also include *mwnyny* (*Git.* 69b) as a corruption of *mê nūni* 'fish brine', as coincidentally defined by Jastrow, *Dictionary,* p. 744. There is only one plant name in this passage which derives from Greek terminology, namely *pylwn* (*Git.* 69b), which is Greek *phyllon*, 'leaf', although the meaning of the Greek indicates that it was a general term, misunderstood in Babylonia as a plant name.

A Traditional Quest

Incantations

The subject of medicine is never far removed from magic and incantations, which offered closely associated therapeutic procedures. The following two passages reveal the relative uses of Babylonian and Greek magic in the Talmud:

B. Ket. 61b

ההוא רומאה דאמר לה לההיא איתתא מינסבת לי. אמרה ליה
לא. אזיל אייתי רימני פלי ואכל קמה. כל מיא דצערי לה
בלעתיה ולא הב לה. עד דוג לה לסוף אמר לה אי מסינא לך
מינסבת לי. אמרה ליה אין. אזיל אייתי רימני פלי ואכל קמה.
אמר לה כל מיא דצערי לך חוף שדאי חוף שדאי עד דנפקא
מינה כי הוצא ירקא ואתסיאת.

There was a Roman who said to a certain woman, 'Favour me (sexually)'. She refused. He went and brought pomegranates, cut and ate (them) in front of her. (Since) all liquids caused her pain when she swallowed, he did not give (the pomegranate juice) to her. When she was in agony, he finally said to her, 'If I heal you, favour me (sexually)'. She agreed. He went and brought pomegranates, cut and ate (them) in front of her. He said to her, 'As for all liquids which cause you pain, *twp šd'y, twp šd'y*', until (the ailment) departed from her. When the *sputum* was brought out, she was healed.

Although the story refers to a Roman trying to seduce a woman, the rituals involved are well attested in Babylonian incantations, which specifically suggest that a woman be given apple or pomegranate to ingest in order to interest her in intercourse. Note, for example, the following rituals from Babylonian 'potency' (šà-zi-ga) incantations (Biggs, *TCS* II 70):

dù.dù.bi *lu* <ana> *hašhūri*(^{giš}hašhur) *lu ana nurmî* (^{giš}nu.úr.ma)
šipta(én) 3-*šú tanaddi*(šub) *ana sinništi*(mí) *ta-dan*
   mê(a.meš)-*šu-nu tu-šam-zaq-ši*
sinništu šuāti(bi) *illak*(du)-*ku tarâm*(ág)-*ši*

Its ritual. Either to an *apple* or to a pomegranate, you should
recite the incantation three times. You shall give (them) to a
   woman and have her suck their juices.
That woman will come to you; you can make love to her (*KAR* 61 8-10).

The same ritual prescribes aphrodisiac rituals *ana sinništi šudbubi* 'to make a woman have intercourse' (Biggs, *TCS* II 22).

In the Talmudic passage, the woman cannot imbibe the pomegranate juice because of a throat ailment, which prevents her from swallowing any liquids. The intended paramour offers to heal her by pronouncing an incantation, which will allow her to swallow the pomegranate juice, and hence become interested in intercourse, to which she presumably submits. Although the paramour is called a Roman, the story probably originated in Babylonia and has little to do with Hellenistic magic.[1]

B. Pes. 112a

> (A Beraita): A man should not drink water on Wednesday or Saturday night, and if he does, he is responsible for fatal consequences (lit. his blood is on his head), because of the danger. What is the danger?—an evil spirit. But if he is thirsty, what is the remedy? Let him recite (Ps. 29.3-5, 7-9). If (that does) not (work), let him say thus:
>
> lwl špn 'nygrwn 'nyrdpyn (var. 'ndryp')
>
> If (that does) not (work), if there is a man sleeping near him, let him awaken him and say to him, 'So-and-so, son of So-and-so, I am thirsty for water', and he returns and drinks.

The passage is in Hebrew, dating from the Tannaitic period (pre-220 CE), and includes an incantation which can only be deciphered if understood as Greek:

לול שפן אניגרון אנדריפא (אנירדפין)

lwl špn 'nygrwn 'ndryp' ('nyrdpyn)

λαλει σαφα ἀνεγείρειν ἀνδρα ὕπνου

Speak *clearly* to rouse a man (from) sleep.

The obvious point is that the Beraita incorporates an incantation which turns out to be an instruction in Greek which is repeated in Hebrew, namely to wake up a sleeping man (in order to disturb an evil spirit lurking near the water jug). The Hebrew Beraita was composed in Palestine during a period when Greek was still current, but by the time the story was transmitted to Babylonia and was edited for the Babylonian Talmud, knowledge of Greek was remote, and the Greek instruction became a meaningless incantation. The passage serves as an instructive warning against the indiscriminate comparisons between Greek and Babylonian-Talmudic medicine, since the likelihood is that

---

1. For a similar case of Akkadian terminology being quoted in a Talmudic passage, cf. *BiOr* 45 (1988), pp. 631-32, comparing the expression *lmšql 'pr' mtwty kr'yh* (*b. Sanh.* 67b) to Akkadian *eper šēpē šabāšu* 'gather the dust from under the feet' in magical contexts.

Greek and Babylonian-Talmudic medicine, since the likelihood is that the Babylonian Jewish scholars of the third and later centuries had little or no first-hand knowledge of Hellenistic literature, language, or science.[1]

1. The question of Greek influence in Babylonian Jewish Aramaic, particularly in magical and medical contexts, must take into account the important group of two magic bowls and one amulet published by Joseph Naveh and Shaul Shaked, *Amulets and Magic Bowls* (Jerusalem, 1985), pp. 104-22, 188-97, and now also a duplicate magic bowl from Jena published by Joachim Oelsner, *OLZ* 84 (1989), pp. 39-41. Although the provenance of the amulet is unknown, Naveh and Shaked judge it to be Palestinian, and both the contents and language of the amulet and magic bowls are close enough to assume derivation from the same text tradition. The remarkable feature of the incantation is the presence of Greek words, such as the name of the demon Sideros (= Greek 'iron'), and the expression *plgws ym' rbh* (Naveh and Shaked, pp. 110, 190-91), which includes the Greek word *pelagos* 'sea', with an Aramaic gloss *ym' rbh* 'great sea'. The story incorporated within the incantation became widely quoted in Medieval magic in many languages (Naveh and Shaked, pp. 111f.). Nevertheless, the evidence for Greek influence per se cannot be established for this incantation, since the Greek word *pelagos* was translated into Aramaic, probably because it was no longer understood. Even if the incantation stemmed from a Greek original, it cannot be assumed that a demon name, Sideros, would have been known in Babylonia with the meaning of 'iron'. The likelihood is that Greek terms brought from Palestine to Babylonia (like those in the Mishnah) are not sufficient proof that Greek was read or used by Babylonian Amoraim.

8

PSYCHOANALYTIC APPROACHES TO BIBLICAL NARRATIVE
(GENESIS 1–4)

Adrian Cunningham

The three years Louis Jacobs spent as visiting professor at Lancaster University were as entertaining as they were profoundly informative for those who attended his classes and staff seminars. One might hesitate at the appropriateness of an essay on psychoanalysis and the Bible in honour of someone who has so sharply criticized 'infantile religion' in psychoanalytic writings (*Faith, A Jewish Appraisal*, 1988). As will be seen, I do not dissent from the broad lines of that criticism but do suggest there are further points worth considering in psychoanalytic studies, taken at least as variants upon the application of biblical narratives, figures and motifs to present and personal times.

Among Louis Jacobs's teachers was Rabbi E.E. Dessler, one of the founders of the Gateshead Kolel. As Paul Morris has pointed out to me, it is indeed striking that one of the few secular references in his *Mikhtav Me-Elijahu* of 1955 is a discussion of Freud's drive theory in connection with the *Yetzarim* or 'inclinations' of rabbinic anthropology, which can be related to Gen. 2.16. The discussion stands so awkwardly in the general context that one wonders if the idea had been put to Dessler by one of his students. . .

The Claims of Psychoanalysis

Any account of origins is necessarily a failure or, at best, a restatement of a paradox, for origin is itself a presupposition of an account about anything. If to this resistance of origin stories to any settled explication are added our own resistances to psychoanalytic accounts of why we resist recognizing certain truths about ourselves, and our origins in particular, then reflection on psychoanalytic views of the biblical origin story requires quite substantial introduction.

Unlike almost any other line of approach even the initial plausibility of this one cannot be assumed. Anthropological, existentialist, feminist, structuralist, and currently de-constructionist readings of scripture have become part and parcel of interpretation. Certain broad themes, at least, of psychoanalytic understanding are as much part of our tacit experience, yet they rarely feature in academic work in religion, exegesis, or theology. There are some egregious examples of how not to read the Bible, arising from the general difficulties in too simply relating procedures rooted in extensive analysis of contemporary individuals to mythic or traditional stories. Nonetheless, as compared with attempts at the application of psychoanalytic insights and methods in, say, literature, history, anthropology or politics, their absence in the professional religious and theological fields is striking.

In the broadest terms, the claims of psychoanalysis (for convenience here I use this term equally for Freudian and Jungian thought) which I take to merit serious consideration involve the following four items:

1. A practice concerned with the understanding and possible illumination of disturbances of the emotional life.
2. A theory, or set of theories, about this practice which emphasize the substantial, even determining, role of fantasy in our desires and the location of the deepest fantasies in our infant formation.
3. A claim that, with all our unique experience and experiences of ourselves as unique, there are certain significant regularities in the intellectual and emotional lives of all human beings.
4. A general account of human development which can illuminate, even explain, basic features of cultural, historical and social institutions.

It should be stressed that, contrary to the practice of many psychoanalysts and their critics, there is no necessary link between these four elements—any one might be true or false independently of the other three. Particularly awkward problems arise, especially for the present purpose, with the third and fourth points. Very few even of the ardent believers nowadays make much use of Freud's 'primal horde' account of human origins, but the appeal to contemporary individual dreams and fantasies to get at the 'real meaning' of ancient narratives is still very common.

Psychoanalysis is the only comprehensive attempt at a non-religious account of how selves come to be. It is based upon the inescapability of human conflict and the ambiguity of our responses to it, especially those of which we can only with the greatest difficulty become consciously aware. With Freud the locus of conflict lies in the universality of the Oedipal situation through which we are expelled from the simple gratification of instinctual, especially 'sexual' desires into a social, and thus specifically human, existence. With Jung our expulsion from paradise arises as much from internal drive as external compulsion. For him there is a 'conflict at the heart of sexuality itself', a 'force compelling [us] towards culture', and ultimately beyond culture to an achievement of individual integration indistinguishable from the appropriation of what he calls the 'image of God'. For both Freud and Jung the never-wholly-forgotten experience of violent separation from our point of origin is the unavoidable mark of our existence as individual conscious beings. Whether described as sacrifice, mutilation, expulsion, or merely socialization, we come to hesitant consciousness in the second act of our own drama, of which the first and decisive act will always be beyond the reach of either our nostalgia or our fear. An angel with flaming sword forever bars the way back.

Psychoanalysis is an attempt to defy the angel and think in general terms about what is autobiographically unthinkable. It essays a reconstruction, with necessarily devious and multiple manoeuvres, of what those primal desires and fears may have been and still are. It should thus be especially well-equipped to investigate the myths which deal with the paradoxes of origin. What is required to start following this through is that we at least entertain the claim that there is only a limited repertoire of moves in any infantile situation and that any individual development of a sense of identity shaped out of this situation will continue to encounter both attraction and repulsion with regard to inescapable experience of the body, close kin, the significant dead, sexuality—to name some of the most obvious. This is a large claim but not necessarily a foolish one. But the patchy plusibility of many psychoanalytic interpretations of origins stories, and the Garden of Eden in particular, owes much, I think, to rushing ahead of this general, but defensible, ground of a common infancy, which might help clarify tantalizing apparent similarities between various collective myths, rooted in particular cultural settings, and the experience of specific individuals, rooted in diverse times and places. Overall, I shall suggest that the deficiencies in psychoanalytic views of origin stories, and myths generally, lie in an historically understandable but in principle unnecessary pitching of the case at an inappropriate level. Psychoanalysts often disregard the difference between the ways in which a common childhood might leave its mark in the life of groups (and thus their myths) and the life of individuals in such groups.

There is the additional complication of whether the myths the psychoanalyst wishes to investigate are living ones among (at least part of) the audience addressed. We may read and be persuaded by Freud's use of the Oedipus motif to understand a basic human situation. Or we may, as in currently fashionable and often fascinating Jungian studies, consider myths like those of Osiris or of Aphrodite for their psychological significance. There is, however, an inescapable change of gear when we consider the stories of living rather than dead traditions. In the former case the episodes and figures are, in one way or another, part of publicly shared beliefs and practices. Such stories live in interaction with members of a tradition, they are part of complex structures of organization and ritual celebration. This means that there are constraints to be taken account of which may not apply to a rather more free-wheeling private appropriation of classical stories.

Questions about the appropriate pitch or angle of approach in psychoanalytic views of myth can be taken under three headings: subscription to the 'archaic illusion'; a tendency to literalize the symbolic; a confusion between mythic exegesis and mythic application.

By the archaic illusion (Lévi-Strauss's term) I mean that fatefully muddled and still extant commonplace that what is (1) deep in contemporary individual experience, (2) what lies far away in our individual childhood, (3) what we might imagine is deep in the whole human past, and (4) what is 'far away' in contemporary so called 'primitive' societies, are somehow all the same thing. Under the spell of this illusion it is obvious, indeed scientific, to use evidence from any one of these areas to illuminate any or all of the remaining ones. Psychoanalysis was sharing in a very widespread set of assumptions here but they proved extraordinarily damaging for it. In the case of the first two, a link between the depths of one's own present experience and one's lost childhood is part of the psychoanalytic framework most of us can entertain, but note that a link is, of course, not an identity. What the archaic illusion assumes is that there is an identity between metaphorical usages of the term 'childhood' such that comparisons might be made between 'the dawn of humanity' or 'childhood of the human race' and our own childhood and/or either of these and far-away people whose culture is seen as still in its 'childhood'. This is nonsense, but powerful nonsense. It should be clear that this is a distortion of, or failure to tackle at the right level, the idea of a possibly common childhood. It we entertain this latter then we might consider what evidence there is for such a claim and, if plausible, how groups and individuals within groups build diverse identities in the light of it. The archaic illusion, on the contrary, collapses any growth and diversity into a ludicrous picture, if spelled out, of there being but barely distinguishable differences between the infant and the adult in the deep past and the far away. The archaic illusion, with its unmistakable convenience for western and colonially minded cultures, is, ironically, a fantasy close to the heart of many psychoanalytic efforts to dissolve fantasies of origins.

The second heading under which misgivings about the pitch of psychoanalytic views of myth can be organized, one of major importance for some earlier Freudian work, concerns a naive view of the relation between the symbolic and the 'actual'. This view is often linked with the short-circuiting of what, if any, connection there may be between, for example, Adam's 'rib' and a motif in a present-day dream. Relying upon a misleading use of a medical model of the human person, there can be a tendency to think of fantasies about the body as if they were of a similar order as overtly organic disturbances. The bodies in question are ultimately, if mysteriously related, of course, but they are not the same. The terms 'phallus' and 'penis', for instance are related but also belong to different kinds of discourse and reality. The former may be a characterization of certain kinds of masculine power of use in the description of contemporary family situations or even whole ages, the latter is not. Similarly, women have vaginas but the motif of the 'vagina dentata' is of a different, symbolic, order. What I am stressing is what can easily go wrong in the use of physical *metaphors* (which can indeed have specific bodily reference in the symptoms of individuals) for states which are not primarily or exclusively physical. The supposed remark of Jung's that the penis is only a phallic symbol has a certain cogency. I think that the Jungians are generally in the right in giving a greater relative autonomy to the symbolic, especially so in attempting to link clinical findings and traditional narratives.

The third general area in which some initial clarification is required concerns the difference between exegesis of myths and applications of

myth. By the latter I mean, say, the use of the Oedipus story to identify a psychological complex or, especially widespread in contemporary Jungian work, the use of classical stories like those of Aphrodite
or Narcissus to clarify individual psychological states of affairs. The
archaic illusion is often at work here but the use of such stories to
amplify the fragmentary evidence of dreams and images for the individual, creating a wealth of possibilities for association, is not essentially tied to this. One might consider such uses of stories as akin to,
even an extension of, homiletic treatment or application to personal
situations familiar in religious contexts. What does need careful
scrutiny is the tendency to assume that the relationship between dreams
and myths can attain symmetry or provide for equal two-way traffic
between them, as if at root we are dealing with the same thing.
Psychoanalytic findings about, for instance, the process of mourning
may indeed illuminate the behaviour of a figure like Gilgamesh or
Proserpina, and it may just be possible that a single case-history could
prompt a new insight into the Garden story but great caution is needed
if free-flow two-way traffic is not to get out of hand.

The elaborated, multiple, versions of classical stories, the figures
that can be traced in these diverse accounts, can provide at least a
sounding boards for our experiences, if not perhaps, as some could
claim, an originating focus. Many biblical characters are, by contrast
pretty sparse in their biographical detail and number of canonical
stories. Interesting psychoanalytic studies have been done of some
biblical figures who offer at least the basis for a 'biography' (Kluger,
Lacoque and Lacoque, Wiener, Zelligs, for instance). The Eden story,
as an origin story, works on a different scale. If anything, we are
dealing with factors of a pre-biographical kind. This drama precedes
an imaginable human life and the Reformed Christian traditions in
particular have jealously safeguarded against any attempt to explain or
justify the primordial failures of the human relation to the divine. We
are looking at roles (stereotypes and deep prejudices too) and situations rather than individuals with characters and biographies. 'In the
beginning' also means in principle or in essence this is how things are,
these are the ground rules upon which the historical and traceable
development of groups and individuals arise. The ur-factor in origin
stories means that analysis based on the detail of particular biographies, the essence of psychoanalysis, should always observe a discipline
of tentative and vague, suggestive rather than definitive or over-par-
ticular, applications. The professional drive of psychoanalysis to get

behind or below the appearance to what is 'really' the case is necessarily going to be frustrated, whether the reality sought is that of a history—of a primal crime or of a prior matriarchy, say—or the penetration of a primal human fantasy.

Questions of appropriate psychoanalytic approach to narratives with possible biographical or possible pre-biographical reference can be further illustrated by comparison with some of the parallels found in the Jewish derashic level of interpretation or Christian typology and the register in which they are appropriately pitched. In such traditional exegesis certain *intra-textual* motifs (for instance, Benjamin in the well and Jonah in the whale) can be claimed, not as allegories, but as part of the basis of belief. The thematic scheme can be continued into liturgical practice. To take a Christian example, the derivation of Eve from the side of the sleeping Adam can be seen as the model for the symbolic derivation of the community of believers from the spear-pierced side of the dead Jesus. These two images in turn can be related to the immaculate womb of the divine font from which neophytes emerge as believers, frequently mentioned by Jung regarding Paul's gloss on Gen. 2.24 (Eph. 5). In these three cases there are images of penetration and fecundation—the opening of bodies, the parting of waters (in the Easter liturgy by the generative plunging of the paschal candle). All three are clearly 'odd' images of birth or rebirth and the cross-references heighten the oddity vis à vis ordinary birth in such a sophisticated and deliberate way that psychoanalytic explanations in terms of suppression or repression of material are unlikely to have much purchase. When the typological register shifts to numerological examination of the measurements of Noah's ark, something else is happening and we are on the slope towards such questions as whether Adam and Eve had navels, Adam was born with a beard, or Celtic was the language in which the animals spoke with him.

Comparable care with regard to the register of reference needs to be exercised in questions of alleged 'parallels', the abuse of which is certainly not confined to psychoanalysis but is certainly characteristic of it. Thus, to look at the Oedipus or Prometheus stories as Greek 'versions' of the Eden myth might yield insights into the variety of concerns with senses of trespass and a seeming necessity of conflict and disobedience for the human realm to be established both in terms of and over against the divine realm. There is a change of scale, however, when particular items of these different narratives are examined as parallels. A different order of comparison is involved in taking the textually questionable view that 'rib' is what Eve is formed from and comparing this with Aphrodite's formation from the blood of her castrated father's penis, or further afield citing the Rig Veda (X, 85.23) where the Manu generates womankind through his daughter called 'rib' (*parsu*). Such connections are not necessarily foolish ones but without substantial further argument they cannot be taken as offering any kind of evidence about the significance of any particular item in its context.

Motifs of the Eden Story

Psychoanalysis has been called, by Paul Ricoeur, a hermeneutics of suspicion, and psychoanalytic writers apply to our text skills developed in the unravelling of individual self-deceptions—the teasing out of the projections, inversions, condensations, substitutions and displacements by means of which disavowed memories and desires are accommodated. Indeed, Eve's birth from Adam, *contra naturam*, seems to demand such an interpretative strategy. Otto Rank was the first to apply the method of reversal to the Adam and Eve relationship so that the 'real' text would be one in which Adam, being born of Eve, is related to her as son to mother. Thus the inducing of Adam to eat of the fruit of the forbidden tree shifts to Eve the blame for Adam's seduction of her. In this primordial example of son-mother incest longing, the serpent too is taken as having undergone a reversal, being in fact the guardian of the father's exclusive access to the mother. As Freud commented on Rank's theory in a letter to Jung (18.12.1911) following a lecture by Sabina Spielrein:

> Equally strange is the motif of the woman giving the man an agent of fruitfulness (pomegranate) to eat. But if the story is reversed, we again have something familiar. . .

As in the case of Proserpina a man giving a woman a fruit to eat is an old marriage rite. Freud expresses considerable contempt for the story as we have it:

> in all likelihood the myth of Genesis is a wretched, tendentious distortion devised by an apprentice priest who, as we know, stupidly wove two independent sources into a single narrative (as in a dream). It is not impossible that there are two sacred trees because he found *one* tree in each of the two sources. . .

Freud's interest in the Hebrew bible focused throughout his adult life upon the figure of Moses, the founder of Judaism in Exodus rather than upon the prehistory of humanity in the early chapters of Genesis.

There is, of course, a famous or notorious reference in Ch. 4, Sec. 6 of *Totem and Taboo* (1912) picked up in *Moses and Monotheism* a quarter of a century later. What is striking is the indirectness of the reference, for Freud makes no attempt to show how his theories of original totemism and taboo behaviour are applicable to the origin story of Adam. In trying to establish a collective event or series of events, analogous to the Oedipal crisis of individual development, in which 'the beginning of religion, morals, society and art converge', he simply argues back from Christ to Adam in terms of a deeply rooted law of talion. Argument is, perhaps, too strong a word for a dubious line of thought. There is no doubt, says Freud, that in the Christian myth the original sin was one against God the Father. If redemption from the burden of original sin came with Christ's sacrifice of his own life 'then we are driven to conclude that the sin was a murder'. 'And if this sacrifice of a life brought about atonement with God the Father, the crime to be expiated can only have been the murder of the father'. The guilty primeval deed is acknowledged in Christian doctrine 'in the most undisguised manner' for the Christian communion is essentially 'a fresh elimination of the father, a repetition of the guilty deed'.

> The very deed in which the son offered the greatest possible atonement to the father brought him at the same time to the attainment of his wishes against the father. He himself became God, beside, or, more correctly, in place of, the father. A son-religion displaced the father-religion. . .

Stirring stuff indeed but its particular application to the Adam story is entirely unclear and it is noteworthy that with the sole exception, I think, of Theodor Reik none of the later Freudian interpreters attempt to make such a detailed application.

Psychoanalytic interpretations of motifs like the trees, the serpent, the rib, are not necessarily consistent, but early on Herbert Silberer had warned that differences of interpretation should not be exaggerated for:

> Genesis itself is welded together from heterogeneous parts and different elaborations [of the primal pair motif]. Displacements, inversions, and therefore apparent contradictions must naturally lie in such material. . .

In 1917 Levy identified a variety of sexual symbols in the story and saw them as representing a set of general ambivalences about the mystery of sexuality. He cites parallels for the fruit, as apple relating to the female breast and as fig to the penis as also, more obviously, does the serpent; for eating and ploughing as analogues of sexual intercourse; for the linking of death and what is in French *la petite mort* or orgasm.

Levy is particularly interesting on the two trees which had so irritated Freud. Following Midrash Agada, he takes them as one. Thus, the tree of knowing, with the sexual connotation of carnal knowledge and the tree of life are to be identified and the forbidden fruit seen as coitus. This may not be evident from a plain reading of the text as we have it but the assumption that sex, a serpent, forbidden fruit, and a fall are related as a key to the story is evident in contemporary popular belief and imagery, which is one reason for taking Freudian views of the story with some initial seriousness.

Both Freudian and Jungian interpreters can see an ambisexual character in the tree or trees of paradise. Roheim, for instance, views the Tree of Life as primarily a sign of paternal phallic authority (see de Monchy on the flaming sword at the exclusion from paradise) but, citing the psalm on the wife as 'fruitful vine', also takes account of the tree's fruit-bearing aspect. Jung, taking the Tree of Life as general psychic energy, libido, sees it as having a bisexual or hermaphrodite character, like the primal Adam.

The possibilities of the serpent in terms of sexual symbolism are fairly obvious. Roheim, following Levy, sees the serpent's condemnation to crawling upon (mother) earth as symbolic of coitus. At least one Jewish traditional story has the serpent as the form in which Satan had intercourse with Eve with menstruation as the result. The curse on the serpent is not only a harbinger of enmity between humanity and the serpent but, more specifically, with the serpent as a phallic representative, of enmity between female and male sexuality.

Given the claimed principle of reversal, of course, the enmity between Eve and the serpent can also be seen as a hidden identity, and there are numerous, medieval at latest, iconographical examples of a female serpent which can indicate a subtle mixture of sexuality as itself a female area into which man is snared and of a direct liaison as in the Jewish tradition about a woman and phallic serpent which can both exclude and threaten as well as fascinate the male. The pornographic possibilities of trespass, as both threat and male-controlled spectacle, here are captured in some of the late-nineteenth century Austrian painter Franz Stuck's paintings, one of which Jung uses as an illustration in *Symbols of Transformation*. The shocking power of such representations makes the seemingly bizarre psychoanalytic discussion of 'the phallic woman' (Fodor) less unreal than it might at first appear.

The last particular item of psychoanalytic significance in the story which I wish to consider is that of the generation of Eve from a rib of Adam. The word 'rib' is obviously questionable but of some antiquity and can be taken for granted in the sources I am using. The creation of Eve from a rib of Adam means that while he gains a companion he loses a rib, which *qua* rib is, of course, of little consequence. The symbolic loss, and an important one, however, can be construed in a variety of ways. There can be, for instance, two contrasted views of woman vis à vis the rib taken as penis—as castrated or castrating. In the former case, the 'borrowed' or derived nature of the rib operation emphasizes the idea of the woman in terms of lack of the male member. In the latter case, the woman 'taking' and making the erect penis disappear in intercourse leads into the motif of the castrating woman or devouring mother.

In this connection and on a larger scale it is important to note Theodor Reik's work on the Genesis story, for of all the psychoanalysts he wrote most on biblical themes and Jewish ritual practices. He outlined his ideas on the story in conversations with Freud and Otto Rank in 1912 and 1913, but it was more than forty years before he published his worked-out conclusions. Written towards the end of his life *The Creation of Woman* is an odd mixture of astute attention to wide-ranging material and conversational thinking aloud. In *Myth and Guilt* he had tried to establish that the episode of the eating of the forbidden fruit was a disguised account of the Semitic version of a primal cannibalism—a valiant effort but no more finally convincing than the concluding section of Freud's *Totem and Taboo*. In the new book he follows other authors in seeing the birth of a woman from a man as a rejection of cults of a mother goddess and an assertion of patriarchy, what he calls the 'Stone Age hoax'. He is surely right in arguing that whilst daughters may be born of fathers, like Pallas Athene from the head of Zeus, there seems to be no other myth in which a wife is born of her future husband and that any adequate account of the Genesis story must focus upon this motif. What is new is Reik's linking of the rejection of the primacy of the mother to a feature that he had always found questionable in Rank's reversal argument, namely that it did not fully explain the extraordinary anomaly of the birth of Eve from Adam and the sleep of Adam and the rib operation in particular. It is his contention that this most puzzling motif does make sense in the context of widespread male initiation rites of which he had published a psychoanalytic interpretation in 1915 in Freud's journal, *Imago*. In these rites the pubescent boy is reborn, or really born, into a society of males—the birth from the mother often being symbolically downgraded. The mutilating removal of the rib would thus be an equivalent of circumcision and fit the pattern in which the initiand undergoes an ecstatic sleep, is given a new name, and subsequently entitled to take a wife.

Reik's argument is, of course, based upon the assumption that modern ethnographic findings about circumcision can be taken as evidence for a reconstruction of the remote past. Of the various psychoanalytic arguments touched upon so far, however, this is certainly one that deserves further investigation.

Having looked at some applications to particular motifs in the story, we can now turn to the wider themes under which I suggest, psychoanalytic contributions can be grouped: incest, separation and disobedience, and growth of human consciousness.

Themes of the Eden Story

Incest

In general, the psychoanalytic interpretations, to my mind, tend to stay too close to occurrences of actual incest or fantasies about it arising from clinical experience. In their discussions of the taboo on incest and putative primal crimes this clinical dimension leads too easily into the old assumption that the forbidding of something indicates a powerful desire to do it. This may be so but it is not a necessary assumption and tends to miss what one could call the conceptual, philosophical, or even metaphysical issues of incest. Emphasizing that the forbidding of certain relationships simultaneously prescribes others, Lévi-Strauss has argued that by compelling social reproductive relations outside the biological unit the taboo is coterminous with society as such (the rational core, if any, to Freud's primal myth). If avoidance of incest and the origins of human society, and thus of humanity as recognizably such, are linked as Lévi-Strauss suggests, then one can see a possible root for the horror which incest evokes, for in it the whole social world, the world of distinctions and conceptual classification, is thrown back into chaos.

It is not only a problem of monogenetic theory, like the biblical one, running into an insuperable conflict between divine commands to procreate and to avoid incest which raise problems about the nature and justice of God. We are dealing as much with the inherent paradoxes of attempts to describe the origins of kinship and all other classifications of the world, social and natural. How can one offer a picture, by definition classificatory, of a world prior to classification? Can we even speak of such a 'world'? What terms, then, can be given to the first man and first woman before kinship and categories like husband, wife, father, mother, daughter and son exist? There is a conceptual profundity to puzzles of Eve born of Adam but Eve as mother of *all* the living, of whether the pair are mother and son, father and daughter, as well as husband and wife, that many accounts rarely raise. Eden may be a paradise of the unawakened and the undifferentiated but it also represents the necessity of division and the horror of chaos. Symbolically, then, the incest taboo and any conceivable human order, a social and lingusitic rather than simply biological state of affairs, are inextricably linked. To break the taboo is not just to go against a prohibition or give way to a powerful fantasy of sexual identification between parents and children, it is to step outside and thus threaten the very possibility of a human world. That is why, I think, that the motif of incest (as in Oedipus at Colonnus, or the ritual/symbolic royal incest of ancient Egypt) can on occasion be a sign of the sacred and of transcendence. Oedipus is not only an accursed outcast from human society, he finally transcends the human world and is assimilated to a non-human, divine world.

Short of this dimension of metaphysical speculation, psychoanalytic contributions to the incest issue in our story are, nonetheless, striking and inventive. Roheim, for instance, noted that Adam's designation of his wife as 'mother of all the living' comes immediately after God's declaration of punishments. Since the name cannot itself be one of them, the juxtaposition unconsciously gives the reason for the punishments—incest between mother and son. This is confirmed by the preceding condemnation to re-entry into the (maternal) earth.

> Anxiety, shame, an invisible divine voice and punishment then appear in the world; that is, the Oedipus complex is repressed and gives rise to the Super-Ego. . . (p. 26).

In this view, sexual desire is disobedience to the father and the main themes of the story are oedipal ones of aggression, conflict, and the sense of sexual maturity as a misfortune, robbing us of infantile security.

The cross-culturally common analogy between ploughing and sexual intercourse can also be developed in this connection, for Adam is to till the ground from which he was taken. Erich Fromm saw this as the root of the prohibition of work on the Sabbath:

> That which was to be primarily averted on the Sabbath was the incestuous appropriation of Mother Earth. . . The Sabbath was originally a reminiscence [!] of winning the mother. . . (1927, p. 234).

In similar vein Reik stresses that Cain, who in one Jewish legend was Abel's rival for the affections of an older sister, was an agriculturalist and that his crime was of an incestuous kind. His punishment, as a divinely protected rebel, to be a wanderer, excluded like his father Adam, links in Reik's view with Israel's obedience to the father's command: repression of incestuous feelings for the mother and the seeking of a promised land as a substitute for her.

> All wanderings of nations are a search for an original home, just as all sex desire in the individual is a search for the mother, the never abandoned object of one's first love. . . (1923, p. 54).

This idea of a promised land, of paradise lost and sought in a new Jerusalem, a messianic age or ultimate redemption, as nostalgia for an intra-uterine bliss free from the curse upon work and sexual reproduction, is widespread in psychoanalytic writings. Mario Jacoby's study, from a Jungian standpoint, is a particularly careful and compelling one (see also Landy).

Disobedience and Separation

One of the topics upon which the diverse psychoanalytic views of Genesis tend to agree is the necessity of the (to use the Christian term) 'fall', like the 'necessity' of incest discussed above; it is certainly, *O felix culpa*. Indeed, in one Freudian opinion (de Monchy) the necessity of disobeying the father's rule is of far more importance than the sexual elements undoubtedly present. Parallels with Prometheus as a necessary sinner who benefits mankind are not uncommon (Edinger, de Monchy, Neumann, for instance). As Jung says:

> The fall legend shows a dim presentiment that the emancipation of ego
> consciousness was a Luciferian deed. . . (*Collected Works*, 9.1,
> p. 230).

Roheim stresses the usurpation of Yahweh by Adam. Using 'parallels'
with the Babylonian Adapa story and the Epic of Gilgamesh, he highlights the motif of a struggle over trees of life:

> the apple torn from the tree was a challenge to the old king, or divine
> being, by a younger being. . . (p. 131).

and he cites Frazer's priest of Nemi. Similarly Neumann makes use of
the 'Gnostic' picture of Yahweh as the vengeful old god while Adam,
in league with Eve and the serpent, is the hero, bringing new knowledge to mankind.

The idea that the primordial parents, or heaven and earth, cling to
each other, thus preventing creation from fully emerging until they
are forced apart (and possibly slain) occurs in a wide variety of creation myths. A number of writers have seen the separation of the primal parents as the core of the Eden myth, though who or what is
involved in the separation varies. Before psychoanalytic attention to
the story, Edward Stucken had focused upon linked motifs of castration and separation. He saw a parallel between the sleeping Noah and
the sleeping Adam, both symbolically emasculated father figures
(Noah by his son, Adam by the removal of his rib) and cast Yahweh as
the separating son-god breaking the Adam–Eve unity (cited in Silberer, p. 75). On the other hand, assuming that the gift of the fruit is
a reversal (i.e. symbolizes Adam's impregnation of Eve) then for Otto
Rank, Adam is the separator of the Eve-Yahweh pair. (In the Lurian
Cabala, Adam Kadmon divided the primal King and Queen, sundered
Shekinah from her spouse). Rank later saw the actual experience of
birth as the primal trauma underlying all later anxieties and desires
revolving around separation from the mother. In this context, the fruit
of the paradise story is seen as a child and its being torn from the tree
expresses the trauma of birth. In the prohibition of eating of the tree
can be seen the father's hostility to the child being born—the sometimes neglected parental side of the oedipal situation. The woman's
true offence is breaking off the fruit, giving birth.

The Growth of Consciousness

My last class of materials is at once the broadest and the one most likely to be of an appropriate register, as discussed above.

Extra-biblically, the Eden story can be put in a world-wide context of creation stories taken as symbolic correlates of the awakening of human consciousness. Motifs such as emergence from water, separating of the elements, dismemberment of a primordial being can be taken simply as different versions of the origins of consciousness, or, more ambitiously, as images of different phases of a single development.

Intra-biblically, the growth of human consciousness may be traced in the 'psychodynamics of its leading personalities', the development of a collective super-ego, growing out of oedipal conflict, portrayed as a group drama (Zelligs). It may be claimed that unlike the hero of other mythologies, gratifying instinctual wishes of *overcoming* the father, the story of the biblical hero is one of *identifying* with the father and his commandments for instance, the submissiveness of Isaac to Abraham (Dreifuss, Wellisch). It is a story of renunciation and sublimation, a working through of the inevitable generational conflicts. The biblical hero offers an ego-ideal upon which development can be modelled and provides an image of the struggles against the people's (and/or the self's) resistance to change. In a Jungian perspective, the biblical theme can be seen as one of the growth of inner identity. For Jung, at his most radically unorthodox, this culmination is in sight from the time of Job: 'Because his creature has surpassed him, he must regenerate himself. . .' (*Collected Works*, XI, p. 405). Yahweh's decision to become man is a symbol of the development that had to supervene when man became conscious of the sort of God image he is confronted with. In the Bible, then, from this position we have for the first time a single transcendent creator and this unity of God makes possible the psychological unity of man. There is a single common source for both inner and outer experience (Westman).

The theme of separation of the world-parents and separation from them is also of great significance in the Jungian view. I shall take Erich Neumann's as the most systematic and ambitious of attempts at a mutual illumination of creation stories and psychoanalytic hypotheses regarding the development of consciousness. His work received the highest of commendations from Jung for 'consciousness and insights which are amongst the most important ever to be reached in this field'.

It is not possible here to give more than a sketch, let alone a critique, of Neumann's handling of this topic in a book of some five hundred pages. Basically, he follows Jung's position in the 1912 battle fought out in the rival publications *Totem and Taboo* and *Symbols of Transformation*—works that only make sense in the light of one another. That is, Neumann sees the primary task of the hero as liberation from the *mother*. In terms of both historical and personal evolution (which he always dovetails), it is only on the ground of a necessarily always incomplete separation from the mother that the struggle with the father can be undertaken. Neumann claims that the archetype of the castrating or castrated father and dismembering of the monster and the archetype of the devouring, sucking back and also castrating mother belong together and, in one way or another, can be found in all creation myths. He sees the alchemical image of the uroborus, the serpent biting its tail, as representative of the primal condition of the self from which the emergence of ego-consciousness is a desperate struggle against the inertia of the unconscious, represented in its profoundest aspect by the image of the engulfing Great Mother. The primal deed of separation is 'theologized' in the great religions and it is necessarily accompanied by sin, apostasy, disobedience and rebellion. The 'fundamental liberating act of man which releases him from the yoke of the unconscious' entails, like every liberation, sacrifice and suffering. The experience of separation involves not only a passive suffering and loss, it is an actively destructive deed, 'symbolically identical with killing, dismemberment and castration'. For 'Mutilation. . . is the condition for all creation'. Like Jung, Neumann incorporates the Eden text in a study of other creation stories and uses gnostic, alchemical and cabalistic material to illustrate the archetypal motifs, including the androgyny of the primal Adam.

A slightly more accessible Jungian perspective, one less dependent upon controversial theoretical innovation, is provided by Edinger. The four-fold garden is taken as a mandalic representation of the primitive stage of the self, suggesting the ego's original oneness with nature and with deity. There is as yet no conflict for the ego is contained in the womb of the self. The passive, narcissistically inflated sense of the earliest infantile fantasies becomes, with the claim 'you shall be as gods' an active inflation. And with the offer of fruit comes consciousness, the knowledge of opposites, the necessary initial polarization of energies that psychic development requires. What God forbids is any attempt to combine the unthinking, dreaming, immortality of instinctual life and consciousness. In God's condemnation there is both a primal curse and a primal blessing: a curse upon psyche's primordial inertia, a blessing on the painful move from infantile, even intra-uterine, blissful dependence towards independent action. If there is a fall, it is a fall upwards! It is only on the other side of trespass that names are given and Adam confronts Eve as a truly *other* person. Adam and Eve's eyes open and the realization of wholeness in individuality becomes possible, as it was not for the world-parents in their defensive-exclusive embrace.

In general I favour these Jungian accounts because they cannot only make psychological sense, as do many of the Freudian ones, but they also tend to be pitched at an appropriate level of generality and are thus better able to account for the continuing appeal of the myth. They are less likely to confuse speculative reconstruction of possible original meanings and functions with later, long-established (say theological) readings of the material that can no longer be identified or equated with such an origin except by a severe and dubious reduction; or, in the case of the primal crime by recourse to discredited views of a phylogenetic transmission of pre-historic events. True, Neumann's work is premised upon an ontogenetic/phylogenetic parallelism but it can, I think, be presented without this assumption. Individuals may indeed find echoes of childhood guesses at and confusions about sexuality in the ambiguities of the material, and the puberty rite parallels may be fascinating and fruitful. It is, however, a mistake to take such individual echoes or parallels as somehow directly indicating the imaginative function of the story in contemporary collective belief and ritual.

I suggest that these major themes of incest, separation and growth of consciousness provide an over-arching frame of reference that may both give weight to psychoanalytic claims about an 'original' meaning (I prefer to say depth appeal) and provide insights into the continuing uses of the story far removed from an putative cultural origins.

All the psychoanalytic claims examined here, perhaps even the most bizarre, can prompt us to pursue new lines of thought, to explore new facets of the material. We remain, however, with a story that is about the origins of human life; about relationships between the human and the non-human, animal and divine; about an unnatural birth; about sexuality, trespass, work, and death.

Origin myths are myths because they point to what cannot otherwise be spoken of, what happened in the beginning when the categories of intelligibility which come after do not yet exist. To this extent they must necessarily be resistant to even the most ingenious attempts to get behind them.

BIBLIOGRAPHY

Cronbach, Abraham, 'The Psychoanalytic Study of Judaism', *Hebrew Union College Annual* 8-9 (1931–32), pp. 605-740.

de Monchy, S.J.R., 'Adam–Cain–Oedipus', *American Imago* 19 (1962), pp. 3-17.

Dreifuss, Gustav, 'Issac, the Sacrificial Lamb, a Study of some Jewish Legends' *Journal of Analytical Psychology*, 16 (1971), pp. 69-78.

—' The Binding of Isaac (Genesis 22—The Akedah)', *Journal of Analytical Psychology* 20 (1975), pp. 50-56.

Edinger, Edward F., *Ego and Archetype: Individuation and the Religious Function of the Psyche* (New York: Putnam's Sons, 1972).

— *The Bible and the Psyche: Individuation Symbolism in the Old Testament* (Toronto: Inner City Books, 1986).

Fodor, A., 'The Fall of Man in the Book of Genesis', *American Imago* 11 (1954), pp. 201-31.

Freud, Sigmund, *Totem and Taboo* (1912).

— *Moses and Monotheism* (1939).

— *Standard Edition of the Complete Psychological Works*.

Fromm, Erich, 'Der Sabbath', *Imago* 12 (1927), pp. 223-34.

— *You Shall Be As Gods: A Radical Interpretation of the Old Testament and its Tradition* (New York: Holt, Rinehart & Winston, 19) .

Jacoby, Mario A., *Longing for Paradise: Psychological Perspectives on an Archetype* (German original, 1980; Boston: Sigo Press, 1985).

Jung, C.G., *Aion* (1959).

— *Psychology and Religion, West and East* (1958).

— *Symbols of Transformation* (1956).

— *Collected Works* (London: Routledge and Kegan Paul).

Kluger, Rivkah Scharf, *Psyche and Bible, Three Old Testament Themes* (Zurich: Spring Publication, 1974).

Landy, Francis, 'Two Versions of Paradise; the Metaphor of the Garden in the Song of Songs and the Garden of Eden', *Harvest* 28 (1982), pp. 112-29.

Lacoque, André and Lacoque, Pierre-Emmanuel, *Jonah, a Psycho-Religious Approach to the Prophet* (Columbia, SC: University of South Carolina Press, 1990).

Lévi-Strauss, Claude, *The Elementary Structures of Kinship* (French original, 1949; London: Eyre and Spottiswoode, 1969).

Levy, Ludwig, 'Sexual-symbolik in der Paradiesgeschichte', *Imago* 5 (1917–19), pp. 16-30.

McGuire, William (ed.), *The Freud/Jung Letters* (London: Hogarth Press and Routledge and Kegan Paul, 1974).

Neumann, Erich, *The Origins and History of Consciousness* (German original, 1949; Princeton, NJ: Princeton University Press, 1954).

Rank, Otto, *The Myth of the Birth of the Hero* (German original 1909; Nervous and Mental Disease Monographs; New York, 1910).

— *The Trauma of Birth* (German original, 1924; London: Routledge and Kegan Paul, 1929).

Reik, Theodor, 'Psychoanalytische Studien zur Bibelexegese', *Imago* 5 (1917–1919), pp. 325-63.

— *Der Eigene und der Fremde Gott* (Leipzig, 1923) (cited by Cronbach).

— *The Creation of Woman* (New York: Braziller, 1960).

— *Myth and Guilt* (New York: Braziller, 1957).

Roheim, Geza, 'The Garden of Eden', *Psychoanalytic Review* 27 (1940), pp. 1-26, 177-99.

Silberer, Herbert, *Hidden Symbolism of Alchemy and the Occult Arts* (German original 1914) (New York: Dover, 1970).

Theodoropoulos, Jane, 'Adam's Rib', *Psychoanalytic Review* 54 (1967), pp. 150-52.

Wellisch, E. *Isaac and Oedipus* (London: Routledge and Kegan Paul, 1954).

Westman, Heinz, *The Springs of Creativity: The Bible and the Creative Process of the Psyche* (New York: Atheneum, 1961).

— *The Structure of Biblical Myths: The Ontogenesis of the Psyche* (Dallas: Spring Publications, 1983).

Wiener, Aharon, *The Prophet Elijah in the Development of Judaism: A Depth Psychological Study* (London: Routledge and Kegan Paul, 1978).

Zeligs, Dorothy F., *Psychoanalysis and the Bible: A Study in Depth of Seven Leaders* (New York: Bloch, 1974).

9

SAUL LEVI MORTEIRA'S EULOGY FOR
MENASSEH BEN ISRAEL*

Marc Saperstein

Menasseh ben Israel was a rabbi, not a prophet; he died convinced that his mission to London had failed, unaware that he had already set into motion the forces that would make possible the emergence in England of a great community of Jews who, in Morteira's words, 'would call upon the name of God in that country'. It is not unreasonable, however, to surmise that he would have taken pride in distinguished rabbis who would lead that community, and especially the rabbi honored by this volume, who shares with Menasseh more than what some may detect as a physical resemblance (compare Rembrandt's famous etching [*EJ*, XI, p. 855] with the photograph [*EJ*, IX, p. 1237]). The common elements include: a career combining synagogue responsibilites and outstanding scholarship, prolific writings in many areas of Jewish thought, an eminent reputation among both Jewish and Christian scholars (I was privileged to get to know Louis Jacobs as a faculty colleague during his year as visiting professor at Harvard Divinity School), the courage of conviction despite controversy with a rabbinic establishment, an enduring legacy of words both spoken and written. *Yibbadel le-ḥayyim arukim!*

In September of 1655, Menasseh ben Israel, prayerful yet exuberant, set out from Holland for London on a widely publicized mission to reverse the Expulsion of 1290. In October of 1657, he

*   I discovered the eulogy for Menasseh while I was a fellow at the Institute for Advanced Studies of the Hebrew University in the Spring of 1989; my gratitude to the Institute is deep and enduring. I am also grateful to Yosef Kaplan for first drawing my attention to the manuscript of Morteira's sermons, and to Rabbi Jozsef Schweizer, Director of the Rabbinical Seminary in Budapest, for allowing me access to the original and for granting permission to publish the text.

England devastated by a series of setbacks and personal tragedies. Though Oliver Cromwell appeared sympathetic to his appeal, adverse public opinion impelled the Lord Protector to refrain from a formal announcement that the Jews would be readmitted. Despite his best efforts, Menasseh's mission seemed to have ended in dismal failure. What is more, he had run out of funds; requests to Cromwell for a stipend received a favorable response, but no money was forthcoming from the Treasury. The illness of his only surviving son, Samuel Soeiro, further drained his financial and emotional resources. On his death bed, Samuel implored his father to have him buried not in London but in Holland.[1]

Menasseh thus returned to Holland with little cause for elation, except perhaps the relief at having put London and its politics behind him. His first task was to arrange for Samuel's burial. Though only 53 years old, his own health was precarious. Whether because he was too weak to travel or because he no longer felt comfortable in the city where he had spent most of his life, he decided not to return to Amsterdam, and settled instead in Middleburg. He died in mid-November 1657, some ten weeks after his son, less then two months after his return from England. His body was brought to Amsterdam and buried in the cemetery of the Portuguese community at Ouderkerk.[2]

Among the final tributes was a eulogy delivered by his senior colleague, the leading rabbi of the Portuguese community in Amsterdam, Saul Levi Morteira. The text of this eulogy has recently been discov-

---

1. Cecil Roth, *Menasseh ben Israel* (Philadelphia, 1934; henceforth 'Roth'), pp. 268-72. Menasseh's older son, Joseph, died suddenly on a business venture to Poland in the late 1640s (Roth, p. 68). His emotional state is undoubtedly reflected in the following passage from *Nishmat Ḥyyim*, published in 1651: 'It is as we see at the deaths of beloved children. The parents are overcome by trembling in the cemetery; they cannot bear to leave their children, to turn away from them. With unceasing lament and distress, they go to the graves even during the seven day period of mourning; they want nothing more than to be there in the company of their children. Afterward, the powerful love and affection abate gradually with time' (Leipzig, 1862, Book 2, Chap. 18, p. 41a).

2. Roth, pp. 272-73; on the actual date of Menasseh's death, see below, p. 163 n. 1. I do not know the basis for the assertion by Aaron Katchen in *Christian Hebraists and Dutch Rabbis* (Cambridge, MA, 1984), pp. 127 and 313 n. 70, that Menasseh was first buried in Middleburg and later reinterred in Ouderkerk; the present eulogy makes it clear that his remains were immediately brought to Amsterdam.

ered among the voluminous manuscripts of Morteira's sermons.[1] The eulogy tells us nothing about Menasseh's biography that was not previously known, but it is important evidence for his contemporary reputation following the greatest failure of his career, and yet another impressive example of Morteira's homiletical art.

Detailed information about the relations between these two rabbis is not abundant in published sources. Morteira was probably one of Menasseh's teachers, and he may well have ordained the brilliant young scholar.[2] Menasseh mentions his older colleague only once in his voluminous works, in the introduction to his *Thesouro dos Dinim* (he had consulted with 'o dotissimo e clarissimo Senhor Hacham Saul Levi Mortera');[3] Morteira wrote an approbation for that book, but I have not found any reference to Menasseh in Morteira's own writings, with the exception of this eulogy.[4] With the merger of the three Portuguese synagogues in 1639, Menasseh became third in the rabbinical hierarchy; his perennial rival, Isaac Aboab da Fonseca, was Morteira's senior assistant. Menasseh was to preach once a month while Morteira would preach three times, and his salary was considerably lower than that of either colleague. Feelings of hurt and slight undoubtedly rankled.[5]

1. The manuscript, number 12 in the collection of the Rabbinical Seminary in Budapest, includes five large volumes of sermons, each written by Morteira himself in Hebrew before the delivery (which was undoubtedly in Portuguese). The Menasseh ben Israel eulogy is in volume 3; the pages are not numbered, but if they were numbered consecutively, the original sermon would be on folios 169r-v and 172r, the addition for the eulogy is 171r-v (it is placed backward in the volume); 170r-v is blank.

2. Roth, p. 33

3. H.P. Salomon, introduction to Saul Levi Morteira, *Tratado da Verdade da Lei de Moisés* (Coimbra, 1988; henceforth 'Salomon'), p. lxxx. Menasseh's *Nishmat Hayyim* appeared six years after Morteira's *Giv'at Sha'ul*, which contains an extensive discussion of the judgment of the soul in the sermon on *Va-Yelekh*, but Menasseh does not refer to it, nor have I found reference to Morteira in Menasseh's work of biblical exegesis, *the Conciliator*: see 'Bibliographical Notices' in the English translation (London, 1842), pp. xvii-xxxii.

4. Morteira appears to use a youthful unpublished work by Menasseh on grammar, without citing the author's name, in one of his eulogies for David Farar delivered in 1624; I am publishing these texts elsewhere.

5. Roth, pp. 49-51; Salomon, p. lxv; A. Wiznitzer, 'The Merger Agreement and Regulations of Congregation Talmud Tora of Amsterdam 1638–39', *Historia Judaica* 20 (1958), pp. 117-18.

On the other hand, Menasseh was chosen to deliver the welcoming oration at the visit to the synagogue on May 22, 1642 by Queen Henrietta Maria of England and the Prince of Orange.[1] Morteira, not the easiest man to get along with, may have been jealous at Menasseh's growing reputation in the Christian world. Tension between the two rabbis impelled the lay leaders of the Ma'amad to intervene in June of 1642—less than two weeks after Menasseh's triumphant oration[2]—and again, more vigorously, a decade later. Four documents recently published by H.P. Salomon reveal a conflict that became something of a public scandal.

The first, dated the 19th of Adar I, 5413 [February 16, 1653] refers to a dispute of unspecified cause, resulting in the temporary suspension of both rabbis from preaching or teaching Jewish law. The second, from the following month, calls for a reconciliation between the two rabbis and warns them not to offend or contradict each other in their sermons. A year later, on March 21, 1654, a new problem has arisen: both rabbis are suspended without pay for a period of two months, and Menasseh is fined twenty florins, to be given to charity, for 'having raised his voice in the synagogue and violated the agreement'. The document ends with a threat that any further such incident will lead to their 'exclusion from the service of this congregation'. The final document, dated some three weeks later, attempts to establish a mechanism for the resolution of disputes over the teaching and preaching of the law.[3] David Franco Mendes, writing in 1788, concluded that 'the wardens of the community made peace between them, but from that

---

1. David Franco Mendes, *Mémorias do Estabelecimento e Progresso dos Judeos Portuguezes e Espanhoes nesta Famosa Citade de Amsterdam* (Amsterdam, 1975), pp. 51-52; Roth, pp. 66-67; Henri Méchoulan, 'À propos de la visite de Frédéric-Henri, Prince d'Orange, à la synagogue d'Amsterdam', *Lias* 5 (1978), pp. 81-86, including a French translation of the oration, which is not in the form of a sermon. The text was immediately published in Portuguese, Dutch and Latin (Roth, pp. 67, 300-301); David Franco Mendes wrote in *Ha-Me'assef* 4 (1788): 168 that Menasseh delivered the oration *be-lashon Sefaradi*.

2. Salomon, p. lxxiv.

3. Salomon, p. xcii; documents published pp. cxli-cxlii; the date at the beginning of the first document should be corrected to 16 February. Menasseh's raising of his voice in the synagogue violated the regulations of the Talmud Torah Congregation; see Wiznitzer, p. 125. For an analogous case in Mantua, 1671, where the community stopped paying the salaries of both quarreling rabbis until they made peace with each other, see Shlomo Simonsohn, *History of the Jews in the Duchy of Mantua* (Jerusalem, 1977), p. 579.

day on, Menasseh decided to leave Amsterdam'.[1] Not long after that he departed for London; Morteira never again saw Menasseh alive.

Morteira was thus faced with rhetorical challenges that transcended the poignance of eulogizing a former student and younger colleague. He had to express well-deserved respect for the deceased despite the known tensions between them. And he had to give due praise to the successes of a spectacular career despite the notorious failure of Menasseh's final endeavors.[2] In addition, he decided to use the occasion of Menasseh's burial in Ouderkerk to reiterate his position on an issue that apparently aroused strong feelings within the community: the practice of some of the wealthier members to erect lavishly ornate tombstones for their families. The plain simple tombstones of both Menasseh and Morteira indicate that opposition to ostentatious and elaborate monuments was a point on which the two rabbis agreed.[3]

For his eulogy, Morteira took an older sermon that he had delivered many years before and adapted it to the purpose at hand. It was not at all unusual for Morteira to reuse sermons after sufficient time had elapsed, and he routinely recorded these subsequent occasions, either beneath the final line of the text or on the back of the sheet (sometimes in a different color ink): 'I preached it a second time in the year. . . ;' 'I preached it a third time in the year. . . , and I added. . .' That is what we have here. The original sermon was on the lesson *Ḥayyei Sarah*; the theme-verse (*nose*) was Gen. 23.17. On the back of the second page, we find, 'I preached it a second time in the year 5401 (1640)'. Then a new page bears the heading, 'And I preached it again in the year 5418 (1657) at the conclusion of seven days from the burial of the Hakham Rabbi Menasseh ben Israel, may the memory of the righteous be for a blessing. He passed away in Middleburg, on his way from London. This was on the second day of the week, the 20th

1. David Franco Mendes, in *Ha-Me'assef* 4 (1788), p. 168.
2. On Menasseh's sense of disillusion and failure upon his return from England, see Jonathan Israel, 'Menasseh ben Israel and the Dutch Sephardic Colonization Movement of the Mid-Seventeenth Century (1645–1657)', in *Menasseh ben Israel and His World* (ed. Yosef Kaplan, Henri Méchoulan, and Richard Popkin; Leiden, 1989), pp. 152-53.
3. On ornate sculptured gravestones, with figures of humans and angels, see David Henriques de Castro, *Keur van Grafsteenen op de Nederl. Port. Israel. Begraffplaats te Ouderkerk a/d Amstel* (Leiden, 1883), plates 9-12; Alvares Vega, *Het Beth Haim van Ouderkerk* (Amsterdam, 1975), p. 22. Contrast the plain stones of Menasseh ben Israel and Morteira, shown in Vega, p. 19. Cf. Yirmiyahu Yovel, *Spinoza and other Heretics* (2 vols.; Princeton, 1989), I, pp. 54-57.

of the month of Kislev (Monday, November 26).[1] And I added what follows.' The text on this single page, front and back, contains just the 'additions' to the original sermon; in some cases, these passages replaced sections of the original.

Although it is not possible to reconstruct with absolute certainty precisely how the new material fitted together with the old, there is little question about the structure and content of what was said. Neither the theme-verse from *Hayyei Sarah* nor the *ma'amar, Genesis R.* 58.8, which plays on the name 'Machpelah' in that verse, had played an integral role in the original sermon, and they could be readily replaced. The new theme-verse, Gen. 38.30, was from the current Torah lesson, *Va-Yeshev: Afterward his brother exited, by his hand the crimson thread; he was named Zerah.*[2] The new *ma'amar, Genesis R.* 82.10, which had been discussed in the body of the original sermon, deals with the burial not of Sarah but of Rachel.

Like most contemporary eulogies, a large portion is of a general homiletical nature, without direct reference to the deceased. The

1. This raises anew the question of the date of Menasseh's death. Morteira's statement is, unfortunately, ambiguous, as the word 'this', associated with the date, could syntactically refer to Menasseh's death, his burial, or to the delivery of the eulogy. According to the Portuguese inscription on Menasseh's tombstone, he died (*faleceo*) on 14 Kislev (Tuesday, November 20). If he had been buried in Amsterdam the same day, then Morteira's date of 20 Kislev (Monday, November, 26) would fit perfectly for the seventh day, on which the eulogy was delivered. However, since it would have taken several days for Menasseh's remains to be brought from Middleburg to Amsterdam, his burial could not possibly have been on the day of his death. If then Morteira's date refers to the burial, then the eulogy would have been delivered on 26 Kislev (Sunday, December 2). But the eulogy uses the *parashah Va-Yeshev*, read on Saturday, December 1, and Morteira is not likely to have used the previous week's *parashah*. It may therefore be necessary to look again at the date for Menasseh's death recorded by hand in a copy of the 1652 edition of *Nishmat Hayyim*: November 15, 1657; see Yosef Kaplan, 'Le-Berur Ta'arikhei Petiratem shel Benei Mishpahat Nunes Henriques u-Sheloshah mi-Gedolei Rabbaneha shel Amsterdam', *Kiryat Sefer* 54 (1979), pp. 611-13. Kaplan concluded that this date was simply wrong, but it is consistent with Morteira's date if the burial was on November 20 and the eulogy delivered on November 26. This, of course, requires a conclusion that the tombstone erroneously gives the date of burial as the date of death (it might have been taken from the community register of burials by the engraver, who assumed that, as was usually the case in Amsterdam, the date of death was the same). None of these solutions is completely satisfying.

2. I have translated *yaşa'* as 'exited' and *al yado* as 'by his hand' in order to preserve the ambiguity used by the preacher in the homiletical application of the verse to Menasseh at the end of the sermon: see below.

introductory section of the original sermon was apparently re-used without change; it is worth citing at length.

> What is the meaning of the verse, '*Bless the Lord, O my soul, and all that is within me bless His holy name*' (Ps. 103.1)? He replied, Come and observe how the capacity of human beings falls short of the capacity of the Holy One blessed be He. It is in the capacity of a human being to draw a figure on the wall, but he cannot invest it with breath and spirit, entrails and viscera. But the Holy One blessed be He is not so; He shapes one form in the midst of another, and invests it with breath and spirit, entrails and viscera. That is what Hannah said: '*There is no one holy like the Lord, for there is none beside You, there is no* ṣur [rock] *like our God*' (1 Sam. 2.2). What is the meaning of '*There is no* ṣur *like our God*?' There is no artist [ṣayyar] like our God (*Ber.* 10a).

> From this we see that the difference between the forms made by human beings and the forms made by the Creator is that the former have only external, superficial significance, while the latter have inner content and substance. This same difference applies within the category of forms that God has made. The 'drawing made upon the wall' may indeed be beautiful to behold, pleasing in its colors, adorned with fine clothing and ornaments, a great delight to the eyes, yet it has no breath or spirit; a person who reaches out to touch it grasps nothing at all.[1] Even so there are some forms not 'drawn upon the wall', but rather made from the mold of the first human being, yet all their aspirations are for external ornaments. These people may be quite beautiful to behold—fashionable, bedecked in jewels, lacking none of the accoutrements of glory and prestige. But there are no 'breath and spirit, entrails and viscera' within them, for they have no real substance. Inside they are nothing but intrigue and deceit, and every vile blemish.[2]

> Indeed, such people are worse than those pictures, for the pictures have no inner content at all, while the people are filled with violence and corruption. . . Thus man must make it his goal to achieve perfection in those inner qualities that truly make him human, and not aspire to gain perfection in external things, which he shares in common with a painted portrait. And if this is so while he is alive, how much more is it so at the time of his death, after which he will be rendering account for all.

---

1. Cf. the argument used by Savonarola, that 'there is a certain living quality in natural things which art cannot express'; no matter how beautiful painted grapes may appear, birds will never fly to them: Robert J. Clements, *Michelangelo's Theory of Art* (New York, 1961), pp. 148-49.

2. Savonarola made a similar point: without the beauty of the soul, the body must necessarily lose its beauty: Clements, p. 6.

The aggadic passage, expressing the well-known topos of God as artist (*Deus pictor*),[1] had an obvious appeal for Jews living in an environment where portrait painting was highly valued. Leon Modena used it at the beginning of the opening sermon in his *Midbar Yehudah*—the first sermon he delivered in the Great Synagogue of Venice—and this was a book Morteira must certainly have owned.[2] Even more than his older Venetian colleague, Morteira reveals an aesthetic appreciation of the achievements of contemporary painters, and we may assume that most of those in his audience could envision some of the crowning examples of Dutch portraiture as he spoke.[3] Yet it is clear that the aesthetic dimension of human artifice is not a supreme value and will have to be transcended in favor of some religious ideal. Painting serves here not primarily to highlight the glories of God's handiwork, but to introduce the sermon's central motif: the contrast between external appearance and inner qualities not readily observable to the eye.

This contrast undergirds the preacher's criticism of those whose lives were excessively oriented toward the trappings of wealth and prestige, such as ostentatious clothing and jewelry. This was not the first time Morteira had forcefully addressed the problem, which was an important theme in the sermons of contemporary Dutch Calvinist preachers as well.[4] For the purpose of the eulogy, however, the emphasis would eventually have to be not on rebuke but on praise. Everyone knew that Menasseh ben Israel could not be included in the category of those concerned only with externals. For most of his life he was beset by financial problems, lacking the resources for ostentatious comportment. The introduction to the eulogy therefore establishes the basis for emphasizing the inner qualities of Menasseh—his

1. Cf. E.R. Curtius, *European Literature and the Latin Middle Ages* (Princeton, 1953), p. 562; Clements, pp. 81, 145. Note that the God as painter topos is ordinarily used to exalt paintings as a kind of *imitatio dei*, while the aggadah uses the topos to denigrate painting.

2. Leon Modena, *Midbar Yehudah* (Venice, 1602), p. 5a; cf. my *Jewish Preaching 1200-1800* (New Haven 1989), p. 409 (the citation of the aggadah is omitted).

3. Possibly in their homes. According to Salomon (p. lxi, n. 19), there is a Portuguese responsum by Morteira in manuscript in which he permits Jews to have paintings and sculptures in their homes. The codex is identified as Biblioteca Nacional de Madrid 18282, fols. 132-35.

4. Cf Morteira's sermon in *Jewish Preaching*, pp. 272-85. For contemporary Dutch preaching denouncing the display of costly ornaments, see Simon Schama, *The Embarrassment of Riches* (Berkeley and Los Angeles, 1988), p. 331.

intellectual prowess and his spiritual fortitude—and for the climactic pronouncement that the apparent failure of his mission in external terms was not ultimately decisive.

The introductory section in all of Morteira's sermons ends with a succinct statement of the central subject of the sermon and an invocation of God's help in the delivery. The body of the sermon often begins on a somewhat different tack, but in this case the fundamental dichotomy is immediately reinforced by a quote from the great oration in Isa. 58.5-6 denouncing the outward forms of religious observance devoid of genuine concern for the underprivileged. It might seem that the prophet himself substitutes another set of actions—to unlock the fetters of wickedness, to untie the cords of the yoke—but Morteira seizes on precisely the terms that underline his emphasis on inwardness: *if you remove* from within you *the yoke... and extend* your soul *to the hungry* (Isa. 58.9, 10).[1] 'These are things that the painter cannot paint, for they are components of the divine form in which inward perfections may be found'.

The same point, he continues, is made by the ethical instruction of the sages: 'It is not the position that honors the man, but it is the man who honors the position', one of the two most important rabbinic statements in the eulogy.[2] For the present purpose, Morteira rewrites the discussion in the original sermon, sharpening its focus. 'We should not understand this assertion simplistically to mean that the position bestows absolutely no honor upon the man. Several biblical verses indicate otherwise... [Prov. 4.8; 22.29; 25.7] Rather, the meaning is that a truly distinguished man does not need to be honored by his position; his own distinction brings honor to the position even if it has no distinction of its own. But if the position is one of honor, it adds to the honor of the one who holds it'.

This reformulation of the original statement is illustrated through an analysis of the examples given in the Talmud. Mt. Sinai and the vari-

1. This interpretation of the phrases as speaking of inwardness may have been influenced by Abravanel's commentary on Isa. 58.9 and 10; Abravanel points to the rabbinic interpretation of Isa. 58.10 in *B.B.* 9b as a source.

2. *Ta'an* 21b. In rendering the Hebrew word *maqom*, the word 'office' would probably best reflect what the preacher is discussing. I have used the word 'position' to convey some of the ambiguous connotation of both geographical place and occupational status. I assume that the preacher translated the rabbinic text by the Portuguese word *cargo*, used for the Rabbi's position in the documents of the community (see Salomon, p. cxlii: 'ese tal sera excluido de seu cargo').

ous locations in the wilderness where the Tent of Meeting stood had absolutely no distinction of their own. They were sanctified only by the presence of God; as soon as the Divine Presence departed, the places remained devoid of any special holiness. By contrast, the Temple Mount, and Jerusalem as a whole, retain their sanctity even after the destruction of the Temple because they had special distinction prior to the Temple. The holiness of Jerusalem was not merely the result of God's presence during the time the Temple stood. Unlike the wilderness of Sinai, even pre-Israelite Jerusalem was a source of honor to God, and God responded by honoring it even more. Thus it exemplifies the conclusion that while 'a man honors his position, if his position itself is distinguished, each brings honor to the other'.

As will become apparent, Morteira's rewriting, which moves away from the original statement by emphasizing the capacity for mutual honor between person and position (a point made only incidentally at the end of the section in the original) is by no means accidental. As soon as he cited the rabbinic statement, it was obvious to the attentive listener that he would eventually apply to Menasseh. Yet he did not want to imply that Menasseh's position—as rabbi in Amsterdam—was like the wilderness of Sinai, with no intrinsic distinction of its own, honored only because Menasseh filled it. That would be demeaning to the incumbents of the position, and to the listeners themselves. It is Jerusalem rather than Sinai that would serve as the model for the Amsterdam rabbinate.

We recall that at the end of the sermon's introductory section, Morteira concluded that the aspiration to attain perfection in inner qualities rather than externals applies both to a person's life and to his death. Having discussed the problem in the context of the lifetime by means of the first rabbinic statement, about the honor of a position, Morteira turns to the subject of externals in the context of death, citing another statement that is crucial for the eulogy:

> The same idea is taught by the statement in the Yerushalmi, Tractate Shekalim, chapter 2: 'With what is left from the funeral expenses one builds a monument over the grave. Rabban Simeon ben Gamaliel said, We do not build a monument for the righteous; their words are their memorial'. Maimonides incorporated this as a halakha in the fourth chapter of *'The Laws of the Mourner'*. The reason for this is that people want to honor the deceased through 'the honor of position' (a monument that will distinguish the place of burial), and this implies that the deceased have no other source of honor. But the righteous do not need this [external honor], for their

words are their memorial. However, this principle seems to be contradicted by Jacob's erecting of a tombstone for Rachel, as the Bible tells us: *'Rachel died. She was buried on the road to Ephrath, now Bethlehem. Over her grave Jacob set up a pillar; it is the pillar at Rachel's grave to this day'* (Gen. 35.19-20). If this is improper, how did Jacob do it? And the same with other righteous people as well. This truly needs to be answered.

I would say that the general purpose in building a tombstone and a monument over the grave is so that the name of the deceased will not be forgotten by his relatives and neighbors. When people pass by the grave and see his name, they will remember him as if he were alive.[1] This has led some individuals to extremes, making such monuments exceedingly prominent so as to attract the attention of passersby, in order that the deceased will thereby be remembered more. The Psalmist referred to this explicitly in Psalm 49.11-12: *'One sees that the wise die, the fool and the ignorant both perish, leaving their wealth to others. They think to themselves that their houses will endure forever, their dwelling-places to all generations, proclaiming their names far and wide'*. This refers to those whose sole ambition is to have built for themselves a magnificent grave and a costly sarcophagus, so that these edifices in which they will dwell forever will cause their name to be remembered throughout the land.[2] Yet they have forgotten that the essential thing is to clear the space and prepare what is necessary to enter into the splendor of the King, for without this, all the glory of their graves is futile.

Beginning with a conceptual problem—the Talmudic statement codified as halakha by Maimonides which does not fit the reality either of biblical times (Rachel's monument) or of the present (monuments that are indeed used for Jews considered righteous)[3]—Morteira returns to the preaching of rebuke. The matter of overly ornate, ostentatiously elaborate tombstones is not raised by the literary sources he is discussing. It arises rather from the practice of his own

1. On the link between the tombstone and memory, see Solomon Ganzfried, *Kiṣur Shulhan Arukh*, 199.17; cf. Philippe Ariès, *The Hour of our Death* (New York, 1982), pp. 202-203, 229-30.

2. The interpretation of Ps. 49.12 as a reference to tombstones is based on a long tradition, reflected in the Targum, which reads *qirbam* as an inversion of *qibram*; cf. Ibn Ezra and David Kimhi ad loc. Morteira develops the criticism of elaborate tombstones implicit in Ibn Ezra, as Hatam Sofer would later do; see *Oṣar Tehillot Yisrael* (Tel Aviv, 1958), VI, pp. 322-25.

3. For a discussion of the contrast between the Talmudic statement codified by Maimonides (though not by later codifiers) and the contemporary practice of building elaborate memorials even for *ṣaddiqim*, see Aaron ben Moses of Modena, *Ma'avar Yaboq* (Jerusalem, 1989), 5.40, p. 224a; Solomon Kluger, *'Ein Dim'ah* (Zolkiew, 1834), p. 2a.

community, as can be seen to this day in the monuments built for
wealthy members of the Portuguese congregation dating from the
mid-17th century in the Ouderkerk cemetery.[1] Knowing that Menasseh
would have a plain stone bearing only his epitaph, he used the
opportunity to work his criticism of the new practice into the general
theme of externals versus inner qualities, applying it to death as well
as to life, and thereby coming closer to the actual occasion of the
address.

He is not yet finished, however, with the conceptual problem; he still
needs to explain Jacob's erection of a monument at Rachel's grave.
After his discussion of the general purpose of tombstones, cited above,
he continues, 'However, the monuments and tombstones placed at the
graves of the righteous, such as Rachel, serve a different purpose'. For
this he turns to the rabbinic statement read at the beginning as the
ma'amar immediately following the theme-verse. It is a midrash
(*Genesis R.* 82.10) on Gen. 35.20 which gives two explanations for
Jacob's behavior: to teach us that 'Israel is known by Rebecca's name',
and because Jacob foresaw that his descendants would pass into exile
by that site and wanted Rachel to be in position to pray on their behalf.
This midrash is discussed extensively in the original sermon, and it is
unclear how much of this discussion, if any, was incorporated into the
eulogy. In the additional material, Morteira writes simply that both
explanations show that 'the honor of the place publicized the honor of
the *ṣaddiq*'.

At this point, with all the main themes of the sermon introduced, it
is time for the preacher to apply them to the deceased. The first
explicit mention of Menasseh brings together two central rabbinic
statements already discussed, both of which related to the contrast
between externals and inner qualities in the context of life and of
death. As in this case of Rachel,

> this *ṣaddiq* does not need an imposing monument or sarcophagus to honor
> him for the sake of his position. 'His words are his memorial': the words
> in the books he wrote will preserve his memory. Indeed, the truth is that he
> did have an honored position; his position honored him and he it. His
> position honored him, for he was a teacher and a mentor from his youth in
> this distinguished place, in the greatest congregations of the region. And he
> honored his position through his distinguished achievements, which

---

1. See above p. 162 n. 4.

earned him constant praise and glory and honor. Thus his position was fitting for him, and he for it.

Having emphasized Menasseh's tenure in Amsterdam, Morteira begins to address the final mission that would take him away from Amsterdam for the remainder of his life. He introduces the subject through an analogy with a midrash on Joseph, appropriate to the lesson for the week when the eulogy was delivered.

> He recognized the glory of his place, for the same thing that happened to the righteous Joseph happened to him. The sages gave a parable of thieves who entered a cellar and stole a barrel of wine. The owner said to them, 'You have drunk the wine, now return the barrel to its place'.[1] Even so the Bible tells us, '*The bones of Joseph, which the children of Israel brought up from Egypt, were buried at Shechem*' (Josh. 24.32). So it was with this *ṣaddiq*: his lofty ideas stole him from his place (for thoughts are called 'friends' and 'brothers', as in the verse '*How precious to me are Your friends, O God*' [Ps. 139.17]), and brought him to England in his desire to establish there a community that would call upon the name of God in that country.[2]

The analogy between Menasseh and Joseph works on several levels: a man removed from his home by a kind of *force majeure*—in Menasseh's case a compelling idea—never to return alive; by implication, a man playing a role in a providential plan which may not be clear to superficial observers.

Here Morteira confronts directly the painful subject of the apparently total failure of Menasseh's mission. 'His effort is well known; and even if he did not succeed in completing all that he intended, nevertheless the reward is his, and his recompense precedes him'. This assertion is buttressed by a Talmudic statement (B. *Ber.* 6a), analyzed in the classic homiletical style:

1. *Genesis R.* 85.3. Morteira must have assumed his listeners would not remember the statement at the beginning of this midrash, which would have been highly inappropriate in the present context: 'Whoever begins with a *miṣvah* and does not finish it buries his wife and his sons'.

2. The original Portuguese may have echoed the conclusion of Menasseh's Portuguese broadside, sent to various Jewish communities on September 2, 1655 to explain his mission to England as he set out upon it. He asks his fellow Jews to pray that Cromwell 'may give us liberty in his land, where we may similarly pray to the most high God for his prosperity' (para que nos dem em suas terras liberdade, donde possamos também orar ao Altissimo Senhor por sua prosperidade) (Roth, p. 227; Portuguese text in Salomon, p. cxliii).

'*It shall be written in a book of remembrance before Him concerning those who revered the Lord and think of His name*' (Mal. 3.16). What is the significance of "who think of His name"? Rab Ashi said, Whoever thinks of doing a *miṣvah*, and, for reasons beyond his control, is unable to do it, is considered in this verse as if he had indeed performed it'.

Now it may well be asked, how is this interpretation related to the beginning of the verse, about which the rabbis said, 'How do we know that when two sit together and study Torah, the Divine presence is with them? From the verse, "*Then those who revere the Lord converse with each other; God listens, and notes, and it shall be written*" (Mal. 3.16)'.

A close analysis reveals that the two points are beautifully interconnected. For when two sit and study Torah in depth, one may conclude that something is forbidden while the other concludes that it is permitted. Now certainly one of them is not saying what is true. But since his intention was to clarify the truth, it is considered as if he had actually hit upon the truth.[1] So those who revere the Lord, who tremble at His word in fear of sin, do not actually perform any act. All these qualities pertain to intention and thought. That is why they are written in the book in a separate category, inscribed together with those who think of His name. Hence, 'Whoever thinks of doing a *miṣvah* and, for reasons beyond his control, is unable to do it, is considered in this verse as if he had performed it', and it is written in the book. So it is with this *ṣaddiq*. *His reward is his, and his recompense precedes him*' (Isa. 40.10).

This kind of passage raises the danger that the preacher will become so entangled in the exegetical problem and the solution given that the listener will be distracted from the main point. Morteira deftly avoids this pitfall. The digression is brief and succinct; the fundamental assertion—that Menasseh will be rewarded by God as if he had succeeded in his mission—is linked with the underlying thesis of the sermon, that inner qualities are more important than externals, in life and in death, and firmly rooted in traditional texts.

Having disposed of the unsuccessful mission, Morteira returns to the present. Some may have been puzzled that Menasseh lingered in Middleburg rather than returning to Amsterdam; the preacher defuses this by emphasizing the significance of Menasseh's return to Holland, and the half-consolation that his grave would not be on foreign soil, in a

---

1. It is not unlikely that in this passage, Morteira is alluding to the apparently bitter disputes between himself and Menasseh that marred their last years together in Amsterdam, as recounted above. Certainly some of the listeners may have made this association. It is, however, difficult to determine whether the message would have been, 'It makes no difference which one of us was right when we disagreed', or 'It makes no difference that Menasseh was wrong when we disagreed'.

country without Jews. 'God has granted him the reward about which the righteous of old felt so strongly, for which they made such great exertion: to be buried in the graves of their ancestors. Both Jacob and Joseph acted accordingly, exacting a stringent oath, for they considered the matter extremely serious, of utmost consequence.[1] They therefore called it a matter of *'true kindness'* (Gen. 47.29). Miraculously, he has arrived here, for *'God will not deprive the soul of the righteous'* (Prov. 10.3). He has come to his place, which he loved so much, thereby revealing his own merit, and giving us the merit that comes from burying him and from mourning him in a manner appropriate to our master and teacher'. Part of the reward promised for the intention of the unsuccessful mission is already manifest in Menasseh's burial near the graves of his father and his teacher.

The conclusion of the eulogy links Menasseh's death with the recent loss of another rabbinic colleague, through an ingenious application of the theme-verse:

> This new pain of our sorrow is especially great, for only eight months ago the pious scholar Rabbi David Pardo departed from us (may the memory of the sacred pious be for blessing).[2] And *afterward, his brother* [i.e. Menasseh] *exited*, as we said at the beginning in our theme-verse, *by his hand the crimson thread* (Gen. 38.30). To understand this, recall that crimson is a metaphor for splendor of speech and eloquence, as in the verse, *'Your lips are like a crimson thread, your speech is lovely'* (Song 4.3). And his beautiful eloquence, his delightful words, were not in his mouth alone, but also *by his hand*, in his books which he wrote in such an elegant style. *'Therefore he was named Zerah'* (Gen. 38.30), shining, for his radiance has shone throughout the world.

This peroration leaves the listeners with the thought not of the failure that embittered Menasseh's final months, but of his widespread reputation and his vaunted mastery of language. The motif of eloquence, unexpectedly read into the theme-verse, gives special substance to the rabbinic assertion, 'their words are their memorial'. The eulogy ends

---

1. Cf. *Genesis R.* 96.5. The midrashic passage assumes that the desire of Jacob and Joseph was to be buried in the Land of Israel; Morteira applies this to burial in the cemetery of the Jewish community of Amsterdam. For Menasseh's view on the importance of being buried next to compatible people, see *Nishmat Ḥayyim,* 2, 26, p. 38d.

2. David Pardo, son of Joseph Pardo, the first rabbi of the Beth Jacob congregation, and father of Josiah Pardo, Morteira's son-in-law, died on March 19, 1657. Cf. Kaplan, 'Le-Berur', p. 612.

in Morteira's accustomed manner; returning to Isaiah 58, he contrasts the reward of the deceased with the painful obligations of the living: ' *"May God shine upon him, and fill his soul with splendor"* (Isa. 58.11). But our duty is to affirm the decree, and to say, "Blessed is the Judge of Truth".'

The following Hebrew text intersperses the additions for the eulogy with the original sermon, entitled *Massevat Qevurat Rahel*; to represent my best reconstruction from the manuscript pages of what Morteira said on the occasion. Annotation has been kept to a minimum.

(הוספות להספד, 171ב)

ודרשתי אותו עוד בשנת התי״ח בתשלום שבעה ימים לקבורת החכם כמהר״ר מנשה בן ישראל זצ״ל נפטר במידילבורג בבואו מלונדריס והיה זה ביום ב׳ כ׳ לחדש כסליו והוספתי הנמשך.

א. ואחר יצא אחיו אשר על ידו השני ויקרא שמו זרח.[1]

(מצבת קבורת רחל, 169א)

בברכות פרק ראשון [י.]: א״ל מאי דכתיב ברכי נפשי את ה׳ וכל קרבי את שם קדשו.[2] א״ל בו וראה שלא כמידת הקב״ה מדת ב״ו. מדת ב״ו צר צורה על גבי הכותל ואין יכול להטיל בה רוח ונשמה קרבים ובני מעים והקב״ה אינו כן צר צורה בתוך צורה ומטיל בה רוח ונשמה קרבים ובני מעים, והיינו דאמרה הנה אין קדוש כה׳ כי אין בלתך אין צור כאלהינו,[3] מאי אין צור כאלהינו? אין צייר כאלהינו ע״כ. מזה ראינו כי הפרש צורות הנעשות ע״י אדם לנעשות ע״י הבורא ית׳ הוא כי אלו אין בהם אלא החיצוניות וההוראה השטחיית ואלו יש בהם תוך וממש. ההפרש הזה עצמו נ״ל שיש בין הצורות עצמם הנעשות על ידו ית׳, כי כמו שהצורה הנעשית ע״ג הכותל הנה היא יפה מראה ונאה בצביעה מקושטת בבגדיה ובתכשיטיה ותאוה היא מאד לעינים[4] אולם רוח וממשות אין בה ואם ישלח איש את ידו יאסוף רוח בחפניו,[5] כן יש כמה מן הצורות בלתי נעשות על גבי הכותל והם נעשות בחותמו של אדם הראשון[6] אולם שימו מגמת שלמותם בתכשיטים החיצונים והנם יפים למראה מתוקנים ומקושטים

1. בר׳ לת,ל: פסוק הנושא של ההספד.
2. זה׳ קג,א.
3. ש״א ב,ב.
4. ע״פ בר׳ ג,ו.
5. ע״פ מש׳ ל,ד.
6. ע״פ משנה סנה׳ ד,ה.

עד מאד ולא יבצרו מהם כל[1] עניני הכבוד וההדר, אולם אין בהם רוח
ונשמה קרבים ובני מעים כי אין בהם ממש וכל חוכם מלא תוך
ומרמה[2] וכל מדה רעה. הלא אלה הם פחותים מן הצורות האלה כי
הצורות אין להם תוך ואלו מלא חמם מלא חמם ועול... ולכן צריך שישים האדם
את כל מגמתו למלא חדריו הפנימים[3] במה שהוא בהם איש ולא ישים
תקותו להשתלם בחצונותיו באשר הוא בהם צורה מצויירת. ואם בחייו
כך הנה במיתתו אשר אחריה הוא עתיד ליתן דין וחשבון[4] עאכ"ו...

ענין מיוחד אל הנשא אשר אנו עליו הוא מה שאמר הנביא ישעיהו
סי' נ"ח בענין הצום. אמר, הכזה יהיה צום אבחרהו יום ענות אדם
נפשו הלכוף כאגמן ראשו ושק ואפר יציע הלזה תקרא צום ויום רצון
לה'[5] ר"ל הלא כל אלה יוכל מצייר לצייר נשלם שבפנים כצורה
ע"ג הכותל מעולה מאד מאד ממה שהם עושים כי כל אלה ענינים
חצוניים הם. הלא זה צום אבחרהו פתח חרצובות רשע התר אגודות
מוטה ושלח רצוצים חפשים וכל מוטה תנתקו[6] וכו' אם תסיר מתוכך
מוטה[7] וכו' ותפק לרעב נפשך,[8] כי כל אלה לא יוכל המצייר
לצייר כי המה תנאי ופרטי הצורה האלקית אשר בהם השלמיות
הפנימים רוח ונשמה קרבים ובני מעים ובהם יבדלו בתכלית ההבדל
רצוני להיותם אנשים חיים או צורות מדומות כהבדל ממש אשר בין
היש ובין האין. על הכונה הזאת עצמה יסוב המוסר אשר למדונו ז"ל
בפ"ג דהתענית [כא:] תניא ר' יוסי אומר לא מקומו של אדם מכבדו אלא
אדם מכבד את מקומו, שכן מצינו בהר סיני שכל זמן שהשכינה עליו
אמרה תורה גם הצאן והבקר אל ירעו אל מול ההר ההוא,[9] נסתלקה
השכינה ממנה אמר תורה במשוך היובל המה יעלו בהר.[10] וכן מצינו
באהל מועד שבמדבר שכל זמן שהוא נטוי אמרה התורה וישלחו מן
המחנה כל צרוע,[11] הוגללו הפרוכות[12] הותרו זבין ומצורעין ליכנס
שם.

(הוספות להספד, 171ב)
ואין להבין הכלל הזה כפשוטו שאין המקום מכבד את האדם מכל וכל

1. ע"פ בר' יא,ו.
2. ע"פ חה' נח,יב.
3. ע"פ דה"א כת,א (כאן במשמעות מטפורית).
4. ע"פ אבות ג,א.
5. יש' נח,ה.
6. יש' נח,ו.
7. יש נח,מ.
8. יש' נח,י.
9. שמ' לד,ג.
10. שמ' יס,יג.
11. במ' ה,ב.
12. בשעת נסיעתם של בני ישראל (רש"י).

שהרי כמה כתובים מורים ההפך כגון סלסלה ותרוממך[1] וכן חזית
איש מהיר במלאכתו לפני מלכים יתיצב,[2] כי טוב אמר לך עלה
הנה[3] וכו'. אלא הכוונה היא שאין צורך לאדם נכבד יכבדהו מקומו
אלא די כבודו לכבד את מקומו אעפ"י שמאליו המקום אינו נכבד אבל
אם המקום נכבד יוסיף כבוד לכבודו. והביא ראיה מהי"ח מהר סיני כי
לא היה נכבד מאליו כי הוא שפל שבהרים כי לכך בחרו ה'[4] והיה
כבודו בעוד השכינה עליו ולא אחרי כן להורות כי כל כבודו תלוי
בשכינה. וכן המדבר לא היה נכבד מאליו בהיותו ארץ אשר לא עבר
בה איש[5] ובעוד אהל מעד נטוי היה בו הכבוד.

לא כן הר ציון כי היה המקום נכבד והשכינה מכבדו ולכן אחרי
הסתלקות השכינה נשאר בו הכבוד שנ' והשימותי את
מקדשיכם[6] אפי' אחר חרבן הם בקדושתם[7] וכמו כן ירושלים כי
קדושה ראשונה קדשה לשעתה וקדשה לעתיד לבא.[8] וכל כך למה
כי היו המקומות האלו נכבדים מאליהם כמו שאמר המשורר ויבן כמו
רמים מקדשו הארץ יסדה לעולם.[9] ויבן כמו רמים שאז"ל בית
המקדש של מטה מכוון כנגד בית המקדש של מעלה.[10] הארץ יסדה
לעולם זו ירושלים כי מתחילה נקראו מלכיה מלכי צדק[11] ובמקומות
האלו כבדו את ה' וה' כבדם על דרך את ה' האמרת[12] וה'
האמירך[13] והם ממש כנגד סיני ואהל מועד מקום התורה והנבואה. כמו
כן כי מציון תצא תורה ודבר ה' מירושלים[14] כי על כן נקראת
ירושלים גיא חזיון שכל נביא שלא מכר שם עירו הוא מירושלים כמו
שאז"ל.[15] הרי כי הכוונה היא אין צורך לאדם שיכבדהו מקומו אלא
הוא מכבד את מקומו אולם אם מקומו הוא נכבד זה מכבד לזה וזה
מכבד לזה.

ג. הכוונה הזאת ילמדנה מה שאמרו הירושלמי דשקלים פ"ב [מז.] על
הא דתנן מותר המת המת בונין לו נפש על קברו תני רבן רבן שמעון בן גמליאל
הצדיקים אין בונין להם נפש וכו' דבריהם הם זכרוניהם, וכן פסק

1. מש' ד,ח.
2. מש' כב,כט.
3. מש' כה,ז.
4. הש' במדבר רבה יג,ג.
5. יר' ב,ו.
6. ויק' כו,לא.
7. ב' מגילה כח.
8. הל' בית הבחירה ו,סז.
9. תח' עת,סט.
10. מדרש תהלים ל,א.
11. עי' פרושו של הרמב"ן לבר' יד,יח.
12. דב' טו,יז.
13. דב' טו,יח.
14. יש' ב,ג.
15. איכה רבתי פתיחה כד.

הרמב״ם ז״ל להלכה בפ״ד מה׳ אבל,[1] מפני שרוצין לכבד הנקבר
בכבודו של מקום ונר׳ שאין להם כבוד אחר והצדיקים אין להם צורך
בזה כי דבריהם הם זכרוניהם. אולם ק׳ נגד זה מה שעשה יעקב
במצבת רחל כמו שכתוב

(מצבת קבורת רחל, 169ב)

ותמת רחל ותקבר בדרך אפרתה היא בית לחם ויצב יעקב מצבה על
קבורתה היא מצבה קבורת רחל עד היום.[2] ואם הדבר אינו הגון איך
עשאו יעקב אע״ה? וכמו כן בצדיקים אחרים? באמת הדבר צריך
תשובה. והנה נר׳ לומר כי התכלית הכללי בבנין הציון והנפש על
הקבר הוא כדי שלא ימחה שם המת מאת אחיו ומשער מקומו[3] וכי
יעברו על הקבר ויראו את שמו זכרונהו ויעלה על לב[4] בתוך החיים.
ומזה ימשך שכמה מן האנשים יפלינו ציונים אלה להיותם מעולים מאד
לבעבור יהיו יותר יותר ממשיכים להם הראות וההבטה ומתוך כך יזכר יותר
האיש הנקבר שם. וזה הבל ואינו ראוי לצדיקים כי אינם צריכים לזה
כי מעשיהם ודבריהם הם זכרונם. וכבר דבר המשורר הזה על זה
בבירור בס׳ מט׳ אמר, כי יראה חכמים ימותו יחד כסיל ובער יאבדו
ועזבו לאחרים חילם קרבם בתימו לעולם משכנותם לדור ודור קראו
בשמותם עלי אדמות,[5] ר״ל שמו כל מגמתם לבנות להם קברות
מפוארים ובנינים יקרים להיות הבתים אשר בקרבם ישכבו לעולם סיבה
להזכיר שמם עלי אדמות ולא זכרו מן העיקר להשתדל לפנות להם
מקום ולהכין להם צידה ליכנס ביקר המלך, ומבלעדי זה כל כבוד
קבריהם הבל.

(הוספות להספד, 171ב)

ד. אולם נר׳ כי מאמרנו הקודם[6] בא לתרץ הענין הזה הכל כבדרוש
בכל א׳ משני הפירושים כי באו להורות כי כבוד המקום היה מפרסם
כבוד הצדיק, אם שבמצבה היה נראה שישראל נקראו על שם רחל
ואם כדי שתתפלל בעדם.
(171א) כמו כן הצדיק הזה אין צורך לנפש ובנין גדול לכבדו בשביל
מקומו כי דבריו הם זכרונו בספריו אשר חבר הם זכרנהו.
אולם האמת הוא כי היה לו מקום נכבד ומקומו כבדו והוא כבד את
מקומו. מקומו כבדו בהיותו מורה הוראה ומלמד מנעוריו במקום נכבד
כזה בקהילות הגדולות אשר בארץ. והוא כבד את מקומו בפעולותיו
הנכבדות ובהיותו תמיד מהודר ומסולסל ונכבד באופן כי מקומו היה נאה

1. הל׳ אבל ד,ד.
2. בר׳ לה,יט-כ.
3. ע״פ רוח ד,י.
4. ע״פ יר׳ ג,טז.
5. תה׳ מט,יא-יב.
6. בר׳ רבה פב,י (מצוטטת אחרי דנושא בתחילת ההספד. מורטירא מפרש אותו
   באריכות בדרשה המקורית ואפשר שהכניס כאן חומר נוסף).

לו והוא נאה אל מקומו.

והוא ז"ל הכיר כ"כ יקר מקומו כי קרה לו כאשר קרה ליוסף הצדיק
כאשר אז"ל מלה"ד ללסטים שנכנסו למרתף וגנבו חבית של יין א"ל
בעל הבית שתיתם היין החזירו החבית למקומו. זהו שנ' ואת עצמות
יוסף אשר העלו בני ישראל ממצרים קברו בשכם,[1] בשכם מכרוהו
לשכם החזירוהו.[2] כך הצדיק הזה עשתונתיו ודרמות גנבוהו ממקומו
(כי המחשבות נקראו רעים ואחים כמו מה יקרו רעיך אל[3])
יוליכוהו לאינגלטירא בתשוקתו ליסד שם קהל לקרוא בשם ה' שמה
והשתדל כידוע ואם לא יכול לגמר את כל אשר זמם הנה שכרו אתו
ופעולתו לפניו[4] כאמור במאמרנו בברכות פ"א [ו.] ויכתב בספר זכרון
לפני ליראי ה' ולחושבי שמו.[5] מאי ולחושבי שמו? אמר רב אשי
חשב מצוה ונאנס ולא עשתה מעליו עליו הכתוב כאילו עשאו ע"כ.
וצריך לשאול איך יקשר הפירוש הזה עם ראש בפסוק כי שם אמרו
מנין לשנים שיושבים ועוסקים בתורה ששכינה עמהם שנ' אז נדברו
יראי ה' איש אל רעהו ויקשב ה' וישמע ויכתב.[6] אולם בטוב
ההתבוננות הנה הוא יעלה יפה יפה כי שנים שיושבים ומתבוננים
בתורה זה אומר אסור וזה אומר מותר ודאי א' אינו אומר אמת ובהיות
כונתו לברר האמת הנה יחשב לו כאילו קלע אל האמת. וכן [?] ה'
החרדים על דברו[7] ויראים מן החטא הנה לא יפעלו שום פעולה הנה
כל אלה זכותם בכונה ומחשבה, ולכן נכתבים בספר בפני עצמם
ונכתבים ביחד עם חושבי שמו, וזהו חשב מצוה ונאנס ולא עשאו
מעליו עליו הכתוב כאילו עשאו ונכתב בספר. ככה היה הצדיק הזה
ולכן שכרו אתו ופעולתו לפניו.

ונתן לו ה' השכר אשר עליו נתרגשו הצדיקים ונתחבטו בו מאד:
להקבר בקברות אבותיהם. ככה עשה יעקב ככה עשה יוסף בשבועה
חמורה כי הדבר חמור מאד והיה נוגע לנפשם והיו קורי' אותה חסד
ואמת.[8] ולכן בדרך נס הגיע הנה כי לא ירעיב ה' נפש צדיק[9] ובא
אל מקומו אשר חבב כל כך זכה חיכה אותנו בקבלתנו אותו לספוד
אותו כחובתנו למורנו ורבינו ובפרט בהתחדש היגון בצערנו כי זה כח'
חדשים יצא ממנו כמהר"ר דוד פארדו זצוק"ל, ואחר יצא אחיו, כאשר
התחלנו בפסוק נושאנו,[8] אשר על ידו השני, הרצון כי השני הוא
כינוי אל תפארת הדבור וההלצה כמו שכתוב כחטם השני שפתותיך

1. יה' כד,לב.
2. הש' שמ' רבה סוף פרק ב.
3. תה' קלט,יז ע"פ פרוש של ראב"ע.
4. יש' מ,י.
5. מל' ג,טז.
6. שם.
7. הש' יש' סו,ה.
8. בר' מז,כט.
9. מש' י,ג.
8. בר' לח,ל.

ומדברך נאוה,[1] ולא בפיו לבד היה בהלצתו היפה ודבריו הנעימים
אלא על ידו, בספריו אשר כתב ביופי הלשון, כי בזה נקרא שמו זרח
אשר זרח אורו בכל עולם. כן זרח עליו ה׳ וישביע בצחצחות
נפשו.[2] ועלינו להצדיק את הדין ולומר ברוך דיין האמת.

1. שיר ד,ג.
2. יש׳ נח,יא.

10

OWNERSHIP AND AUTONOMY:
ELEMENTS OF COMPOSITION IN THE 'BOOK OF THE COVENANT'

Jonathan Magonet

It is a great privilege to be invited to contribute a chapter in honour of Rabbi Dr Louis Jacobs. It was my good fortune to be able to study Talmud and Zohar with him at Leo Baeck College and subsequently to work with him as a colleague on the College's Academic Board. His courage in taking his own independent line within Anglo-Jewry, his willingness to stick to his principles, and his remarkable breadth and depth of knowledge, all these have been sources of inspiration and encouragement for a younger generation of Rabbis who have sought to combine Rabbinic responsibilities with the imperative to study and teach.

Since it was over issues of revelation within the Hebrew Bible that much of the 'Jacobs controversy' raged, it seems appropriate to examine a subject that relates to his own interest in Jewish law and the text of revelation itself, the laws included in the 'Book of the Covenant' in Exodus. Moreover since another area of his scholarly concern is the structure of Talmudic passages, it is fitting to offer an analysis of the structure of a key passage of the Hebrew Bible.

This study began as an examination of Exod. 23.1-9. The starting point was the occasion of preaching on this passage at an interfaith conference where the striking discontinuity between verses 4-5 and the rest of the section became an interpretative challenge. The transition from a homiletic to a more formally scholarly medium led to an examination of the passage in the wider context of the 'Book of the Covenant' (Exod. 20.22–23.33).

The second point of departure was an earlier study on the structure of Leviticus 19 (Magonet, pp. 151-67), where another text, also an apparent mixture of structured and random components, proved to have some underlying organisational principles.

The Text: Exodus 23.1-9

The passage is generally regarded as a unity, a section lying between a collection of miscellaneous social and cultic laws (22.18-31) and a 'cultic calendar' (23.10-19), the whole belonging to the latter part of the laws of the 'Book of the Covenant' (20.22–23.33). The 'unity' of this passage, as a series of laws about the conduct of justice, is broken by the insertion of two verses (4-5) which deal with behaviour towards one's 'enemy'. Nevertheless compared with the miscellany that immediately precedes it, it is far more homogeneous in theme, and thus similar to the earlier thematic collections, for example, the laws about slavery (21.1-11) or damages (21.18-36).

Yet it is precisely the interruption of the section by verses 4-5 that is intriguing and challenging. Since the text is well attested, scholars have had a number of strategies for explaining this apparent dislocation: misplacement (Driver, p. 237); some contextual significance (Noth, pp. 188-89; Childs, pp. 480-81); linguistic association (Cassuto, pp. 297-98); randomness (Durham, pp. 330-31 following Daube, pp. 74-101 and Carmichael, pp. 19-25). Some of the classical Jewish sources on the passage have been gathered by Leibowitz (pp. 425-36). These either treat the individual laws separately or seek to find a contextual relationship.

What none of these studies examine is the sense of symmetry that inheres in the section as a whole, or at least in certain parts of it. Verses 4 and 5 are located midway between ten distinct commandments, and indeed interrupt an obvious pairing (vv. 3 and 6), both of which deal with legal treatment of the poor[1]—neither favouring their case nor perverting justice to their detriment.

---

1. The suggested amendment of דל to גדל cf. *BHS* and Noth, p. 189 (on the model of Lev. 19.15) has no textual warrant. Similarly, Cassuto's suggestion (p. 289) that אביון is chosen because it is an otherwise unknown synonym of אויב—though possible on the basis of assonance—leads to a dubious thematic linkage (Leibowitz, p. 427; Childs, p. 451).

Another pairing are the two laws in v. 2, with their shared concern about following the majority, difficult though the text of the latter part of the sentence may be.[1]

Verse 7, on the face of it, contains two separate and unrelated components—avoiding something you know to be false and avoiding condemning to death the innocent or guiltless. However the two do belong together if they are seen as representing two polarities: deliberate dishonesty in judgment as opposed to honest but mistaken judgment.

To these pairings one must add the obvious similarity of the two verses that 'intrude'—both concerning behaviour towards animals belonging to someone who is an enemy/hater, both introduced by the same 'if—then' formula, and both employing, the infinitive absolute with the finite verb, in their closing phrase.[2]

Having found these pairings, one is tempted to look at the remaining individual laws to find similar relationships. The two commandments in v. 1 seem less well matched, though it depends on how widely or precisely one interprets the context of the demand that one not 'lift up' a rumour—spread it or accept it. Does this apply in general to society (cf. Lev. 19.16), or specifically to the situation of a legal dispute—'hearsay evidence' (cf. Clements, p. 148)? If the latter, as our context would suggest, then the implication is that a 'rumour', especially a 'false rumour' is something not substantiated by 'evidence' or direct 'testimony', a crucial requirement for the Biblical legal process (Falk, p. 70; de Vaux, p. 156). In this case the contrasting law about not deliberately becoming a 'witness who promotes violence'[3] would point to the unifying concern with 'authentic witness' as being crucial: ignore the insubstantial evidence of a rumour; do not pervert true evidence by becoming a false witness.[4]

Thus four pairs of polarities emerge which reflect matters that need to be addressed within legal procedures:

---

1. See, for example, the long discussion in Rashi, or Childs' textual note (p. 450). The text appears to distinguish between following the majority when you know they are mistaken (cf. Cassuto, p. 296) and joining a deliberate attempt to 'pervert' justice.

2. The sense would appear to be to assert the opposite of what someone might ordinarily be expected to do—in such a case you *must* return it/ you *must* unload it with him. For the meaning 'unload' for עזב see the views of Avraham ben Ha-Rambam, Benno Jacob, and Abraham Ibn Ezra presented by Leibowitz, p. 431.

3. See the discussion on the terminology of עד חמס by Phillips, p. 144.

4. Cf. Cassuto, p. 296.

a. (v. 1) *Evidence*: Insubstantial evidence—false evidence.
b. (v. 2) *Decision by majority*: Do not be swayed if you do not accept the verdict of the majority—do not go along with deliberate injustice perpetrated by the majority.
c. (vv. 3.6) *Abuse of power*: Do not favour the poor—do not use the system to harm the poor.
d. (v. 7) *Wrong verdict*: Deliberate injustice—unintentional wrong verdict.

The four pairs reflect four kinds of abuse, in each of which there appears to be a different degree of culpability. See figure 1, where those above the midline show a relative innocence of intention, while those below represent actual conspiracies or other deliberate action.

a. Rumour Evidence	b. Majority in error	c. Favour the Poor	d. Miscarriage
False Evidence	Majority conspire	Cheat the Poor	Dishonesty

Figure 1

To all the above, v. 8, with its attack upon bribery and its consequences, appears to be a kind of lynchpin, a midpoint between the 'innocent/deliberate' polarities of the previous sections—a deliberate act which distorts the judgment that should be objective and 'innocent'.

Verse 9 (which echoes 22.20) seems to stand apart—perhaps as a bridge to the next section; perhaps as a reminder of the wider context (the Exodus itself and its attendant values); perhaps as an illustration of extremes of injustice to be avoided within the covenant community: one of the most vulnerable in society being the גר and the most powerful term for oppression/ exploitation being לחץ with its associations with the degradation of slavery in Egypt (Exod. 3.9).

The Context (Exodus 20.22–23.33)

The discontinuity between vv. 3-4 and the surrounding verses remains a challenge precisely because of the symmetrical considerations we have discussed. It appears to be too neatly located to be random, but too distinctive in its context to fit comfortably into any obvious thematic link.[1] We could make various conjectures at this point, but without some system of control, they risk being purely 'homiletic'. One

---

1. The symmetrical placing would seem to make it more than just an interpolated 'footnote'—against Paul, p. 110 n. 1.

option, therefore, is to try to broaden our approach by looking at the wider context within which this passage is embedded.

The immediate context, as we have noted, is the latter part of the 'Book of the Covenant' which is itself included within the description of the revelation at Sinai and the establishment of the covenant. For the purposes of this paper, we will restrict ourselves to the legal materials between Exod. 20.22 and 23.19. We shall deal later with the law of the altar (20.22-26) and the cultic calendar and miscellaneous materials (23.10-19) which effectively create a 'cultic' *inclusio* around the intervening civil legislation.

At first glance our passage seems to provide a necessary complement to the preceding sections, detailing some of the principles whereby legal issues are resolved, including the integrity demanded of all participants. However, in order to see if there is any more intrinsic linkage, particularly with regard our problematic verses, some further evaluation of the legal passages is required.

The standard commentaries offer valuable discussions of the various historical-critical and form-critical problems. Some studies attempt an overview of the underlying principles controlling the sequence and content of the laws themselves, but most end up with negative conclusions about determining what they might be. Durham (p. 315) is perhaps typical in his view that the section 'presents a unity only as a composite made necessary by the setting into which it has been placed. . . The many attempts to find unifying motifs in it, or a logical or theological sequence, have been generally unconvincing'. Nevertheless it may be that one can find a very general underlying motif sufficient for our purpose, acknowledging that in a number of places the pattern does not entirely fit.

The following analysis was made before I had access to Shalom Paul's invaluable study of the sequence of laws in 21.2–22.16. Since I have come independently to a similar view of the organising principles behind the sequence of laws (see especially his summary in Appendix 1, pp. 106-11) it is not necessary to go into overmuch detail.

In the broader context of the Book of Exodus, this opening passage on the release of slaves (21.2-11) would seem to relate directly to the narrative of the exodus from Egypt itself. One purpose of the liberation of the Israelite slaves was to create a society in which slavery of the sort practised in Egypt was abolished. How better introduce the laws of the covenant than by setting formal limits on civil bondage.[1] But what underlies this section are crucial issues of independence/autonomy and ownership in the relationship between people, or, more specifically, between male Israelites within the framework of the covenant. This becomes evident already in the question posed in the opening section (vv. 3-4): Does the wife of a bondsman belong to the bondsman himself or to his owner? The answer is made clear: 'to the bondsman' if he brought her in with him; 'to the owner', if the owner gave her to the bondsman. The fact of 'ownership' is taken for granted, what matters in this moment of transition between two states is to clarify who belongs to whom.

The situation of a daughter is analogous to that of a bondsman but different. She is the 'possession' of her father to be sold into service, at which point she is 'owned' by her new master. But she is to be protected from certain forms of abuse. Thus she cannot be sold to a non-Israelite, and her rights to food, clothing and 'conjugal rights' (?) are to be protected.

Both of these passages have at their heart the same issue: who is 'owned' and who is 'free', or, more precisely, they explore the transition points where ownership is transferred or relinquished and freedom and independence might be gained (or refused).[2] In a sense they define who is a 'person; and who is a 'less-than-person' within the covenant community. That they focus on the point of transition, the juncture between two different states, seems to be common to many of the other passages in the 'Book of the Covenant', though the particular issue may differ.

If we ignore for the moment the next group of laws (vv. 12-17), which are linked by the common punishment of the death penalty, there follow four 'cases' (vv. 18-27) dealing with different sorts of damage caused to another person. In each situation the liability of the one who strikes the blow is assessed, but with different consequences in each case. In the first, two men contend, one strikes the other who is consequently confined to bed. If he recovers, the one who struck him is responsible for the loss of earnings of the injured and for the cost of treatment. Each individual is viewed as having a 'value' measured in terms of potential 'work' or 'earning power'. While the injured is unable to work, the one who struck him is responsible for

---

1. Cf. Paul, p. 52.
2. See the discussion in Paul, pp. 46-52.

what he would have earned; in a sense he takes on temporary ownership of the victim's working capacity or 'worth'. This becomes more
evident in the second illustration, the man who injures his bondsman
(vv. 20-21). If the latter dies, the owner is to be 'avenged' or
'requited' in some unspecified way;[1] however if he survives a few
days, there is to be no punishment, because 'he is his wealth'. That is
to say the one who strikes his bondsman is penalised by the financial
loss this entails.

The third case (vv. 22-25) represents a more indirect example of
injury—when two men fight and a bystander is injured, illustrated by
the case of a pregnant woman who miscarries. Here it is her husband,
the 'owner' of the potential child (and 'earner') who is to be recom-
pensed for 'his' loss.

In all three cases, the harm done to another human being is assessed
in terms of the material loss to the 'owner'—be it the injured party
who loses his ability to earn, the owner of a bondsman who penalizes
himself, or the husband whose potential child is lost. They illustrate a
pragmatic way of resolving the problem of a material claim, yet each
in turn also witnesses to an underlying concept: that the Israelites
within the covenant community are independent human beings (male),
in possession of their own lives and earning power. That situation is
illustrated through the *via negativa*, examples of the conflicts with
each other that might arise where their autonomy is challenged or
threatened.

The fourth example in this group (vv. 26-27) takes us a stage further: the bondsman or bondswoman who loses an eye or a tooth
because of a blow from the owner, presumably to discipline him or
her, gains his or her freedom. At this point we go beyond the permitted limit of human 'ownership' of another—the bonded person may be
the 'possession' of the owner, but the owner's freedom to use that person does not permit physical damage or mutilation. There are boundaries that may not be crossed.[2]

The same set of assumptions underlie the following group of cases
where one's property (the goring ox, a pit) causes damage to another
person or his property. The law focuses on the need to make a decision about the liability. The 'goring ox' or other agent is perceived as

---

1. Paul, p. 70 n. 2.
2. Cf. Patrick, p. 37.

an extension of the owner,[1] as is the victim in turn an extension of its owner. Thus two individuals are impinging upon each other's rights to autonomous, unhindered and unimpaired existence, expressed in terms of their personal lives/selves or of the extension of their lives/ selves into their families and their possessions.

The text of Exodus is therefore quite consequent in examining and adjudicating in other ambiguous situations where two 'ownerships' overlap— namely cases of trusteeship (22.6-12) and loans (22.13-14). Who is responsible for damage or loss, the 'owner' or the one in temporary possession? While these are examples of deliberately arranged transferences between the domains of the two principals, similar sorts of issues arise in cases where no such agreed arrangement is present, but 'property' becomes transferred to another's domain, or someone's domain is damaged by the act of another. Examples given are theft (21.37; 22.2-3), grazing violations and damage by fire (22.4-5), and the seduction of a virgin (22.15-16).

In all the above, significant though the individual regulations may be, and challenging in terms of their historical origins and how far they do or do not reflect contemporary or earlier Near Eastern law, in their totality, they are ultimately concerned with the same issue: the points of breakdown of relationship between autonomous individuals, and their extended selves, as an illustration of the potential areas of conflict of interest within the covenant community. By confronting the points of conflict in a pragmatic legal way, the implicit mutual respect expected of members of the community comes into focus, together with the recognition of the reality of conflict and the need for mechanisms for resolution and reconciliation.

There remain a number of individual laws that do not seem to fit so clearly into this scheme. There are four cases that we passed over, 21.12-17, that are linked together by the death penalty. They start with the blunt statement that one who kills another must be put to death (v. 12). In effect this indicates the ultimate limitation on one's individual autonomy—it does not extend to the taking of the life of another member of the covenant community.[2] There is thus a certain

---

1. Cf. Patrick, p. 31.
2. While this goes back to the general prohibition on taking any human life (Gen. 9.5-6), there are circumstances where it is acceptable or required e.g. war, crimes meriting the death penalty. (See the discussion in Haas, pp. 76-85). Since there are exceptions to the general rule, it is legitimate to treat the examples of the death penalty here as relating specifically to other full members of the covenant community, particu-

logic to the immediately following distinction between manslaughter and deliberate murder, because the same need to preserve each individual life allows for the recognition of the distinction between these two situations. By invoking God's intervention in the case of manslaughter, a divine sanction is given to what may have been a new distinction. Moreover the 'external' partner of the covenant, and its guarantor, is invoked.

In this context, the fact that kidnapping (so as to sell into slavery) also calls for the death penalty (21.16), is a logical extension of the same general view—for to do so is to rob the individual Israelite of his autonomy and freedom, and thus effectively, his life.[1]

More problematic are the two related verses about striking or killing one's parents (21.15, 17). The 'honouring' of parents has a high priority in Israelite consciousness, notably in the Ten Commandments, and the death penalty for 'cursing' them is mentioned elsewhere (Lev. 20.19).[2] Nevertheless within our context their special relationship may have a particular significance. They are, in a sense, the personal extension backwards in time of each individual, as one's children are extensions forward. Moreover, they have previously had a relationship of 'ownership' to the individual. Thus they belong to a special category, so that a lesser infringement of their authority or integrity (though the blow or curse may be perceived as potentially lethal) likewise requires the severest penalty.

Our findings so far may be summed up in the following chart:

21.1-11	A may only 'own' B for a limited period.
21.12-16	A may not 'kill' B.
21.18-27	A may not injure B.
21.28-32	A's animals may not injure B.
21.33-34	A's negligence must not injure B.
21.35-36	A's animals must not injure B's animals.
21.37	A may not steal B's animals.
22.3	(If caught stealing [seemingly threatening B's life], A may/may not be killed [22.1-2]).

---

larly as there are cases, such as the bondsman who is killed, where a different penalty ('requited', 'avenged', 21.20) is mentioned. It is of interest that the terminology of 'striking' here echoes the story of Moses' slaying of the Egyptian (Exod. 21.11-16).

1. Cf. Paul, p. 65.
2. Cf. Deut. 21.18ff.

22.4	A's animals must not damage B's property.
22.5	A's actions must not damage B's property.
22.6-8	If A entrusts money or goods to B, B is not responsible if they are stolen.
22.9-12	If A entrusts animals to B, B is not responsible for their death or injury or if carried away. B *is* responsible if they are stolen or attacked by predators.
22.13-14	If A loans an animal to B, B is responsible for death or injury (unless A is present).
22.14b	If A hires an animal to B, it is at A's risk.
22.15-16	If B seduces A's unbetrothed daughter, he must pay the marriage price (and marry her if A agrees).

Figure 2

The above scheme shows the sequence quite clearly. The section probably begins with the laws about slavery because of the Exodus setting and concerns, but also because they highlight the issue of owner and owned, autonomy and dependency: the ideal member of the covenant is a free man, the owner of himself, who does not readily surrender his freedom. After this, the text deals with killing, which expresses the extreme limit set on individual freedom because it negates the individual autonomous existence of another. It continues through lessening degrees of assault on the individual in terms of his ownership of self (physical injury) and possessions (injury to his animals or his property). It then examines varieties of custodianship (where the same property is 'owned' for a time by two different people)— those that are nogotiated (trusteeship, loan, hiring) and those that are not negotiated (theft). It thus moves away from the immediate person of the 'owner' (and likewise of the offender or victim) through their extended selves in terms of their possessions, from direct responsibility for harm that is done to indirect responsibility.

There remain a number of 'miscellaneous' laws (22.17-30) that are more problematic in terms of the overall schema. If all the above laws have been contained within a single organising principle, defining the rights of the autonomous Israelite, it may be necessary to evoke a second such principle to explain how the rest of the laws fit, one which pertains to the broader context of the 'Book of the Covenant' as a whole. For the other 'autonomous partner' in the covenant is God whose overarching concern has created the covenant itself and whose particular demands must also be met. Thus the laws against oppressing the stranger (v. 20), the widow and orphan (vv. 21-23), and the laws against usury and witholding a pledge (vv. 24-26) are all concerned with those most marginal within the society who are not 'owners' or 'owned' like the others and are therefore in need of separate evaluation, and indeed special protection. This special situation may provide a clue to their inclusion here, and indeed the other 'cultic' laws that are interwoven with them. For if these people are not the 'property' of others, they are perceived as being the 'property' of God[1] who will exact punishment if they are abused (vv. 23, 26). Hence the reminder about the exodus from Egypt in this context (v. 20 c.f. 23.9), for God is the other partner in this covenant relationship who brought Israel out of slavery to create a different kind of society. This would also account for the other laws in this group which are specifically concerned with the honour due to God: forbidding the sorceress (v. 17); sacrificing to other gods (v. 19); bestiality (v. 18); cursing 'god/judges' (v. 27); eating forbidden foods (v. 30); and commanding the offering of the firstborn to God. All of these attest to God's 'rights' which must likewise not be infringed. That is to say, if one limitation on the autonomy of the Israelite is that imposed by the autonomy of his fellow Israelite, the second limitation comes from the specific requirements of God: those directly affecting God's 'honour' in the 'cultic' area, and those similarly affecting God's 'honour' in terms of the principles of justice and the protection of the weak—though the two areas are intermingled. Thus the outer frame of the specifically legal part of the 'Book of the Covenant' (the law of the altar [20.22-26] and the cultic calendar and miscellaneous materials [23.10-19]), ensures that the laws concerning the behaviour of Israelites to one another are firmly contained within a set of obligations to God.

We will see in the next section instances where these two principles (honour to fellow Israelite, honour to God) come into conflict

The Text in Context

What are the consequences of this analysis for our understanding of the intrusive verses about animals in the midst of 23.1-9? Some things now emerge quite clearly. Firstly, the two cases here (vv. 4-5) are diametrically opposite to the entire thrust of the legislation about relations between Israelites in the two previous chapters. Whereas the

---

1. I am indebted to Rabbi Sheila Shulman for this suggestion.

former specifically deal with the areas of conflict where two domains overlap, these two examples dramatise the requirement to cross boundaries into another's 'space': to go beyond the limitations of trusteeship (in returning the straying animal) or formal obligation (in offering assistance) to people precisely designated as 'the enemy' or 'one who hates you'. Whether these are in some sense technical terms for opponents in law (Noth, p. 189; Clements, pp. 148-49) or merely general designations for people with whom one comes into conflict (Leibowitz, p. 428), they indicate the positive ideal of the human relationships within the covenant that will allow people to transcend personal differences and be mutually supportive—illustrated in precisely the same area of ownership and the crossing of domains that formed the bulk of the previous legislation.

Secondly, the specific context of vv. 1-9 makes vv. 4-5 in some way a comment upon the immediately surrounding laws. They may serve as a reminder that despite the human conflict (and legal abuses) designated here, there is a need for human solidarity that transcends them—to the extent of offering help to one who appears to be in direct conflict. But the specific regulation to work 'with him' (v. 4) in unloading the ass may well lead to far wider possibilities of reconciliation (cf. Leibowitz, p. 433, quoting *Tanhuma Yashan Mishpatim*). In this sense it is the polar opposite of the bribe that is condemned in v. 8, an act that clouds judgment and objectivity in a negative way. This is an affirmative action that may permit people to transcend preexisting prejudice and conflict.

There is, however, a third consideration that reflects the fuller context of the two 'partners' to the covenant we have already recognized. Thus a number of the laws here explore the area where the individual is challenged by the covenant community as a whole, specifically when he is called to enter into judgment with others, at which point he also confronts the overriding will of God.

Thus the relation of the individual to the majority (23.2) becomes crucial, for here is the place where individual autonomy is threatened by the community of interest. The message is nevertheless clear, and in conformity with all we have already seen, namely that one should maintain one's individual integrity in all circumstances and pursue justice in accordance with God's will.

If this case dramatizes one's relationship with one's peers, the two verses demanding integrity and justice in dealing with the poor, represent a responsibility to those over whom one has actual power but for whom God has a special concern. In fact God's will is the only effective sanction for misbehaviour in this area.

23.7 is a reminder that all who enter into judgment are themselves at risk because God is the ultimate arbiter of truth.

A Closing Observation

What began as a riddle posed by the unexpected placing of two verses has incidentally illustrated a feature of the formulation of laws within the 'Book of the Covenant'. There is a tendency in these passages to place together laws that in some ways represent polarities or extreme or transitional situations: the pairs of innocent/deliberate wrongdoing in judgment in 23.1-9; the point of transition between slavery and freedom (21.2-11); the contrast between the laws in 21.1–22.16 asserting boundaries between people, and 23.4-5 requiring the crossing of such boundaries; examples like the 'pregnant woman harmed when two men struggle' or the 'goring ox' that are either obviously hypothetical or actually belong to the legal illustrative materials common to Ancient Near Eastern law codes;[1] the intermediate state of an unbetrothed girl seduced by a man—what should be paid and what is her subsequent status; the cases where human self-interest conflicts with divine will.

That is to say they express in different ways, either implicitly or by their justaposition with one another (or other structurally determined relationship), different propositions that allow or encourage the exploration of a variety of intermediate positions and resolutions, and the discovery of underlying principles.[2] Despite being brought together as the legal content of the 'Book of the Covenant', in their sum total they are clearly less than a constitution and yet far more than a random sample of ordinances. Like Biblical narrative and poetry, they demand that the reader become engaged with them, filling gaps and seeking resolutions and conclusions. Which in turn raises fascinating questions about who the 'reader' was meant to be, at various stages in the development of these texts into their final form, how these laws were studied and applied, and what function the whole had within Israelite society.

---

1. Patrick, p. 30.
2. This was a view I expressed in my study of Lev. 19 and one argued much more thoroughly by Patrick.

It seems appropriate to end with questions, particularly ones that are unlikely to find ready answers. The one book of Louis Jacobs published by the Leo Baeck College attests to his fascination with unresolved or unresolvable problems—its title, '*Teyku*'.

BIBLIOGRAPHY

Carmichael, C.M., 'A Singular Method of Codification of Law in the *Mishpatim*', *ZAW* 84 (1972), pp. 19-25.

Cassuto, U., *A Commentary on the Book of Exodus* (trans. Israel Abrahams; Jerusalem: The Magnes Press, 1967).

Childs, B.S., *Exodus: A Commentary* (OTL; London: SCM, 1974).

Daube, D., *Studies in Biblical Law* (New York: Ktav, 1969).

de Vaux, R., *Ancient Israel* (McGraw Hill, 1965).

Driver, S.R., *The Book of Exodus* (Cambridge: Cambridge University Press, 1918).

Durham, John I., *Exodus* (WBC 3; Waco: Word Books, 1987).

Falk, Z.W., *Hebrew Law in Biblical Times* (Jerusalem: Wahrmann, 1964).

Haas, P., ' "Die He Shall Surely Die": The Structure of Homicide in Biblical Law', in *Thinking Biblical Law, Semeia* 45 (1989), pp. 67-87.

Leibowitz, N., *Studies in Shemot: The Book of Exodus* (2 vols.; Jerusalem: The World Zionist Organisation, 1976).

Magonet, J., 'The Structure and Meaning of Leviticus 19', *Hebrew Annual Review* (1983), pp. 151-67.

Noth, M., *Exodus: A Commentary* (OTL; London: SCM Press, 1962).

Patrick, D., 'Biblical Law as Humanities', in *Thinking Biblical Law, Semeia* 45 (1989), pp. 27-47.

Paul, S.M., *Studies in the Book of the Covenant in the Light of Cuneiform and Biblical Law* (VTSup, 18; Leiden: Brill, 1970).

Phillips, A., *Ancient Israel's Criminal Law: A New Approach to the Decalogue* (Oxford: Basil Blackwell, 1970).

11

LAW IN REFORM JUDAISM

Dan Cohn-Sherbok

When I was a rabbinical student at the Hebrew Union College in the United States we were assigned a textbook by Louis Jacobs, *Principles of the Jewish Faith*. This was my introduction to Louis Jacobs's work, and I had many oportunities to use this volume during my studies. When I came to England to do research after I was ordained, I was most anxious to meet Dr Jacobs. Over the years I have been fortunate to have many occasions to sit at his feet and join him in theological discussion. For these opportunities I am most grateful. He has been an inspiration to me and to all of those in my generation who are involved in Jewish studies. In his writings one of Louis Jacobs's central concerns has been the nature of Jewish law. This study, of which an earlier version appeared in the *Jewish Law Annual* 8, concerns some of the central difficulties in formulating a Reform code of Jewish law.

Introduction

According to traditional Judaism not only did God give Moses the law recorded in the Pentateuch, but He also revealed the oral law. Thus the ultimate authority for the legal system is God Himself. Very early in the nineteenth century, however, the Reform movement departed from this traditional view, taking an antinomian position. Subsequently various Reform rabbis and synods were concerned with the status of traditional law; yet only recently has there been an attempt to systematize Reform Jewish practice. In this regard Rabbi Solomon Freehof has been the leading figure and his writings have been of seminal importance. As W. Jacobs notes, 'Solomon Freehof has been a leader in this area of Reform Jewish development. He has continued and broadened a tradition rooted in the beginnings of our movement'.[1] The publication of Freehof's study of Reform Jewish observance in the light of its rabbinic background (*Reform Jewish Practice*, I and II) marked the beginning of a scholarly investigation into the sources of Jewish law which has resulted in the publication of six volumes of his responsa. The purpose of this chapter is to evaluate the procedure Freehof adopts in defending Reform Judaism's attitude to traditional law.

Solomon Freehof's Philosophy of Law in Reform Judaism

In various studies[2] Freehof discusses the role of law in the various branches of Judaism. Orthodox Judaism, he writes, is imposing. 'Its self description appeals to all who have reverence for the past. It declares itself to be a system of law, going back consistently and without interruption for thousands of years to the beginning of our history. All the elaborations of the law found in the later Orthodox Codes are held to be not novelties at all but rediscoveries. Whatever the "latest scholar" adduces from a comparison of texts and opinions is really not his own but "was already said on Mt Sinai".'[3]

Yet, according to Freehof, this picture of an eternal, onward-moving legal system breaks down when we face its astonishing shrinkages. Confronted by great areas in Jewish law that have disappeared, Orthodoxy is compelled to explain how such non-observance occurred. Some loses are attributed to the fact that certain laws can only be observed on sacred soil are therefore temporarily suspended. Other laws, however, have practically vanished for no justifiable reason. People, for example, who consider themselves Orthodox have simply ceased to resort to rabbinical courts in a wide variety of areas of life. Thus there is a large gap between the total Orthodox doctrine and system and the limited observance of Jewish law. For Freehof this neglect of the law within Orthodoxy in the face of modern seculariza-

---

1. W. Jacobs in an introduction to S. Freehof, *Reform Responsa for our Time* (Cincinnati: Hebrew Union College Press, 1977), p. xxvii.

2. In particular the introduction to *Reform Jewish Practice* (New York: Union of American Hebrew Congregations, 1963), and *Reform Responsa* (Cincinnati: Hebrew Union College Press, 1960), as well as *Reform Judaism and the Law* (Cincinnati: Hebrew Union College Press, 1967).

3. Freehof, *Reform Responsa*, p. 4.

tion illustrates the incompatibility of traditional Judaism with contemporary life.

The rapidly shrinking area of observance within Orthodoxy is, according to Freehof, the reason for the existence of Conservative Judaism. 'The confidence of conservatism that Judaism can be adjusted to modern life', he writes, 'is rooted in the fact that Orthodoxy itself was never monolithic, that it has always changed. But whereas in the past the people changed and the law reluctantly followed, Conservatism would prefer to make the law itself more flexible so as to provide for change legally'.[1] Yet, Freehof argues, there are two difficulties with this position. First, Conservative Judaism sets too great a task for Jewish law to accomplish nowadays: 'There is no stretching of the law or liberating of it that can enable it to roof over the realities of modern Jewish life'.[2] Second, the Conservative approach is bound to intensify Orthodox bitterness: 'Any liberal interpretation of the law emanating from Conservative circles is met with violent reactions, denunciations of the Conservative rabbis as being no true rabbis, whose evil aim is to lure Israel into sin'.[3]

Given the problems that beset these two movements Freehof advocates a freer approach to Jewish law as embodied within Reform Judaism. Since Reform Jews do not consider the total rabbinic literature to be of Divine origin, it is not authoritative. Nonetheless Freehof believes that Reform Jews should respect traditional law and seek its guidance: 'Some of its provisions have faded from our lives. We do not regret that fact. But as to those laws that we do follow, we wish them to be in harmony with tradition. . . Our concern is more with people than with the legal system. Wherever possible, such interpretations are developed which are feasible and conforming to the needs of life. Sometimes, indeed, a request must be answered in the negative when there is no way in the law for a permissive answer to be given. Generally the law is searched for such opinion as can conform with the realities of life'.[4]

Despite this assertion, Freehof admits that there are considerable difficulties in declaring what role traditional law should play in Reform Judaism.[5] Nevertheless, he contends, it is urgent that Reform

1. Freehof, *Reform Responsa*, pp. 12-13.
2. Freehof, *Reform Responsa*.
3. Freehof, *Reform Responsa*, p. 14.
4. Freehof, *Reform Responsa*, pp. 22-23.
5. Freehof, *Reform Judaism and the Law*, p. 19.

Judaism determine what are legitimate practices: 'The lack of a sense of law in our movement', he writes, 'gives us a feeling of frustration'.[1] It is in response to this situation that Freehof attempts to establish an acceptable outline of Reform Jewish observance. These observances, however, ought not to be regarded as authoritative law; according to Freehof, they are guidelines whose purpose is to give shape to the religious life of the average Jew.

Criteria for Accepting Orthodox Law

Surveying present-day Reform Jewish practices in the light of traditional Judaism in *Reform Jewish Practice*, I and II, Freehof lays down explicitly the various criteria for deciding whether Orthodox laws should be retained. In accordance with his view that traditional Jewish practices should serve as the starting point for determining Reform observance, Freehof asserts that there are a number of traditional laws which should be rigorously followed. Concerning circumcision of Jewish babies, for example, he quotes as authoritative the provision in the *Rabbi's Manual* (Central Conference of American Rabbis, Cincinnati, 1928) which lays down that 'the ancient practice of circumcising a male child at the age of eight days, the first commandment given to Abraham our father (Gen. 17.11) is strictly observed'.[2] Similarly Freehof argues that Reform Judaism should adopt the same position as Orthodoxy regarding intermarriage: 'The attitude of Reform Judaism. . . became exactly the same as that of all of Judaism, namely, that while marriage of a Jew and a converted gentile is considered a perfect marriage in every respect, marriage between a Jew and an unconverted gentile cannot be considered Jewish marriage and a rabbi cannot officiate'.[3]

In these examples Freehof maintains that Reform practice should be in accord with Orthodoxy. In other cases, however, Freehof argues that traditional Jewish law, while providing general guidelines for Reform Judaism should be extended. Concerning autopsy, for example, Freehof points out that, in general, autopsy and dissection are forbidden by Jewish law, but there are some Orthodox authorities who permit autopsy when there is in the same locality a person suffering

---

1. Freehof, *Reform Judaism and the Law*, p. 20.
2. Freehof, *Reform Jewish Practice*, I, p. 113.
3. Freehof, *Reform Jewish Practice*, I, p. 65.

from the same disease. Thus autopsy is permitted if it could save a life (this accords with the Orthodox ruling that in order to save life all the laws of the Torah, except idolatry, incest and murder, may be violated). Extending this principle Freehof goes on to explain, quoting the *Central Conference of American Rabbis Yearbook* 35, that since 'nowadays the discoveries made by one physician are broadcast all over the world and may result in the saving of innumerable lives',[1] it is in line with this Orthodox ruling to allow all autopsies to take place.

Yet it should be noted that Freehof is not always willing to extend Orthodox rulings. For example, in the case of the traditional ruling that marriages are not to be held during the first month of mourning except in certain circumstances, Freehof does not extend this leniency in the law to allow Reform rabbis to perform any marriages during that month.[2]

In other cases Freehof appeals to the spirit as opposed to the letter of the law. For example, concerning seating in the synagogue, the law requires each man to have a regular place. In Reform Judaism, however, this stipulation does not apply; each person can sit wherever he desires. Freehof argues that this free seating system fulfils the spirit of the law in practice 'since people generally as a matter of habit occupy the same seats week after week'.[3]

The preceding examples illustrate Freehof's dependence in one way or another on Orthodox law. Yet Freehof frequently argues that Reform Jewish practice should run counter to Orthodoxy where ordinances are based on custom rather than law. For example, he states that the popular custom to turn mirrors to the wall or to cover them in the room where a corpse lies has no basis in Jewish law and in fact is part of a general folklore.[4] Thus he contends there is no reason to observe it in Reform Judaism. Or again concerning the covering of the head in synagogue Freehof point out that this is an ancient practice, only the result of custom, and therefore it need not be continued.[5]

A legal argument of a different order is occasionally used by Freehof to justify a Reform departure from traditional practice. Freehof asserts that a particular observance should be adopted if it is grounded in Biblical Judaism even if it runs counter to present-day Orthodoxy.

1. Freehof, *Reform Jewish Practice*, I, p. 116.
2. Freehof, *Reform Jewish Practice*, I, p. 80.
3. Freehof, *Reform Jewish Practice*, II, p. 32.
4. Freehof *Reform Jewish Practice*, I, p. 154.
5. Freehof, *Reform Jewish Practice*, I, p. 45.

Reform Judaism, for example, celebrates one day of various festivals rather than two because 'the Reform movement reverted to the biblical observance of the length of the festivals'.[1]

On other occasions Freehof recommends that traditional law should be abandoned for difference reasons altogether. Concerning the equality of the sexes, for example, Freehof declares that 'Reform Judaism. . . proclaimed from the very beginning the religious equality of men and women'.[2] Thus Reform congregations abolished the seclusion of women in the synagogue and provided the family pew in which the entire family sits together in worship.[3] The notion of equality also applies to the religious status of all Jews. In Orthodoxy there is a legal distinction between priests, Levites and Israelites, but this has been abolished in Reform Judaism. Therefore, Freehof notes, 'the special prohibition of the law forbidding a priest to marry a divorced woman. . . seemed contrary to the modern spirit of equality of status'.[4]

Traditional law should also be abandoned, Freehof asserts, if it is not well adapted to modern life. For example, Freehof writes, 'since in modern times it was difficult to obtain the close attention and the uninterrupted decorum of the service during the lengthy reading of the entire weekly portion, the custom arose in Reform congregations to shorten the reading'.[5] Freehof also contends that certain laws should be eliminated on humane grounds. Where a husband has disappeared, for example, Freehof writes that 'there is a tragic hardship involved in Jewish law of divorce which the best rabbinic minds have been unable to remove, namely, the case of the Agunah (the woman "chained" to marriage even though her husband has disappeared). . . in which countless women whose husbands have disappeared have no way of being freed from the bonds of matrimony'. For reasons of humanity, he states, the Reform movement has abolished the traditional laws of divorce.[6]

Unseemly rituals, Freehof contends, should be abandoned as well. This applies to the Orthodox custom of avoiding stones in wedding rings based on the following law: 'If he marries her with an object,

---

1. Freehof, *Reform Jewish Practice*, I, p. 19.
2. Freehof, *Reform Jewish Practice*, I, p. 25.
3. Freehof, *Reform Jewish Practice*, I, pp. 54-55.
4. Freehof, *Reform Jewish Practice*, I, p. 105.
5. Freehof, *Reform Jewish Practice*, I, p. 31.
6. Freehof, *Reform Jewish Practice*, I, pp. 105-106.

with regard to the value of which it is easy to err, such as precious stones, it is necessary to make evaluations. Therefore it is the custom to marry with a ring that has no stones.'[1] The idea of estimating the value of wedding rings, Freehof believes, is out of place in Reform marriages; thus any ring is used whether it is plain or is set with stones.[2]

Furthermore, Freehof states that Orthodox practices which are based on superstitions should be omitted. Freehof declares, for example, that the ritual of breaking a glass at wedding ceremonies is 'of superstitious origin'. Thus, 'the breaking of the glass is entirely omitted from Reform marriage ceremonies'.[3]

There are other instances in *Reform Jewish Practice* where, instead of offering a justification for overturning Orthodox law, Freehof simply asserts that this should be done. For example, concerning the Orthodox custom of leaving some blades of grass or a pebble on the tombstone after visiting the grave, Freehof decrees without explanation: 'The custom of leaving pebbles on tombstones is not observed by Reform Jews'.[4]

There are some instances, however, where Freehof advocates that Jewish law be observed out of respect for the Orthodox and Conservative community even though it goes against Reform convictions. For example, in the case of a Jewish couple (where one partner has been divorced civilly) who ask a Reform rabbi to marry them because they have been refused by their own Orthodox or Conservative rabbi, Freehof writes: 'It would seem that consideration for the religious scruples of Orthodox and Conservative congregations should impel the Reform rabbi to refuse to marry members of other congregations whose rabbis refuses to marry them (because they have not obtained a Jewish divorce)'.[5]

From this brief survey we can see that Freehof has an ambiguous attitude to traditional Jewish law. Sometimes he advises following the letter of the law, and at other times the spirit, while in some instances he advocates observing traditional law merely out of respect for the Orthodox and Conservative community. Frequently, however, he recommends that Orthodox law be abandoned either because it is based on

1. *Shulḥan Aruk Even Ha'ezer*, 31,2.
2. Freehof, *Reform Jewish Practice*, I, p. 91.
3. Freehof, *Reform Jewish Practice*, I, pp. 98-99.
4. Freehof, *Reform Jewish Practice*, I, pp. 98-99.
5. Freehof, *Reform Jewish Practice*, I, pp. 109-10.

custom rather than law, because it is based on a rabbinic rather than Biblical precept, or because it is ill-adapted to modern life. Some laws he regards as discriminatory to women or to groups within Judaism (priests, Levites and Israelites), and others as simply inhumane, unseemly or superstitious. In addition, as a final category there are some laws he recommends discarding without any explanation whatever.

A Critique of Freehof's View

The central difficulty with Freehof's approach is that his recommendations are internally inconsistent. On the one hand, Freehof stipulates without explanation that certain practices in Orthodox Judaism should be adopted by Reform Jews (such as forbidding mixed marriages), while, on the other hand, he regards other practices as unacceptable (such as leaving pebbles on tombstones). Yet there is no obvious criterion established to decide which laws should be abandoned and which retained. Such seemingly arbitrary and contradictory judgments also apply to those cases where Freehof argues that Reform Jews should follow the spirit rather than the letter of the law. Regrettably he does not explain how to determine what the spirit of a particular law is. This is unfortunate since there is inevitably an element of subjectivity involved in attempting to extract the spirit (his justification of the absence of fixed synagogue seats is an eloquent illustration of this), and it is by no means certain that one can preserve the essential point of a law if its provisions are eliminated.

It is equally mysterious why Freehof justifies extending the prescriptions of one law rather than another. For example, it is not easy to understand why all autopsies are permitted in Reform Judaism whereas not all marriages during the first month of mourning are allowed. A similar criticism applies to the distinction he makes between rabbinically-based ordinances and biblical practices (such as celebrating a festival for two days or one day). It is also not at all clear why biblical laws should take precedence. Moreover, in stating that one ought to observe traditional laws out of consideration for the Orthodox on some occasions (such as refusing to marry a couple who had previously been refused by an Orthodox or Conservative rabbi), Freehof offers no explanation why this principle should not apply universally.

Equally problematic is Freehof's stipulation that laws should be changed if they do not adapt to modern life. It is arguable that there are many traditional practices (such as circumcision of Jewish babies) which Freehof encourages Reform Jews to observe which ought to be eliminated on this basis.

Many of these criticisms apply to the several volumes of *responsa* literature in which, while attempting to answer specific questions concerning Jewish practices, he is similarly inconsistent. In some cases, for example, Freehof argues that Reform Jews should follow the spirit rather than the letter of the law, whereas in other cases he contends that the letter of the law is all-important. Thus in answer to the question whether there is any legal justification for the practice of some Reform groups of accepting adult converts without circumcision, Freehof points out that although the Talmud, Maimonides and the Code of Jewish Law have circumcision as a firmly established law, 'it seems contrary to the spiritual and ethical spirit of Judaism to insist upon this ritual'.[1] In other cases, however, he maintains that traditional law should be upheld. In the case of a married gentile couple where the man wishes to convert to Judaism, for example, Freehof argues that if we convert the husband he would become a Jew under the yoke of the law married to a Gentile: 'He was a righteous Christian before we converted him. Now, if he is the head of a gentile family, he becomes a sinful Jew. . . We have no right to convert him.'[2]

Turning to the distinction Freehof draws between those practices based on custom as opposed to those based on law, there are similar difficulties. For example, in response to the question whether one ought to fast if the Torah is dropped, he writes: 'fasting if the Torah is dropped is not a legal requirement. . . since this custom has no real legal status, nothing should be done by the entire congregation'.[3] In other cases, however, he maintains that Jewish customs should be practised by Reform Jews. For example, concerning the question whether a marriage can take place without a rabbi and without Hebrew, Freehof contends that though these customs are not based on legal requirements they should be adhered to.[4]

---

1. Freehof, *Reform Responsa for our Time*, p. 77.
2. Freehof, *Reform Responsa for our Time*, pp. 69-70.
3. S. Freehof, *Contemporary Responsa* (Cincinnati: Hebrew Union College Press, 1974), p. 119.
4. Freehof, *Reform Responsa for our Time*, pp. 204-205.

There are also several occasions in his *responsa* where contrary to his approach in *Reform Jewish Practice* he advocates following rabbinically rather than Biblically based ordinances. Thus in answer to the question whether wearing costumes on Halloween is forbidden by Jewish law, he states, 'There is a biblical basis upon which an objection could well be raised. The Bible, in Deuteronomy 22.5, clearly prohibits men from putting on women's garments and women from putting on men's garments.' Nevertheless Freehof believes that one should follow the ruling of the great Orthodox rabbi Judah Minz who decreed that it was permissible to wear masks and costumes on Purim. Though this decision relates specifically to a Jewish festival, Freehof argues that it should apply as well to Halloween since this holiday has no Christian associations.[1]

Questions concerning religious and sexual equality are also answered in a way inconsistent with the principles outlined in *Reform Jewish Practice*. For example, in reply to the query whether the children of a widow who are adopted by the second husband who is a cohen are to be considered cohenim, Freehof appeals to a number of distinctions made in the law about Jewish status. 'If the woman's first husband was a cohen', he writes, 'then the children remain cohenim. No matter how many times or whom she marries. If her first husband was not a cohen and her second husband is a cohen, this marriage does not affect the status of the children of a previous marriage'.[2] In this instance he completely neglects to mention that the category of cohen has been abolished in Reform Judaism because of the Reform belief in religious equality. In another case Freehof declares that if a Jewish man is living together sexually with a non-Jewish woman who eventually converts to Judaism, he may never marry her. Yet he states that if a gentile man lives together sexually with a Jewish woman 'perhaps it would be right to convert the gentile so that they may be able to marry in accordance with Jewish law and custom'.[3] Here it is clear that Freehof undermines the view he repeatedly expresses that men and women should be treated equally.

There are also instances in the *responsa* where Freehof advocates following laws which are arguably ill-adapted to modern life. For

---

1. S. Freehof, *Current Reform Responsa* (Cincinnati: Hebrew Union College Press, 1969), pp. 93-96.
2. Freehof, *Contemporary Reform Responsa*, pp. 145-46.
3. Freehof, *Reform Responsa for our Time*, pp. 69-70.

example, in response to the question whether anaesthetics should be used for circumcision, Freehof states: 'We should not institute the use of anaesthetics as a regular procedure, but should permit them when the surgeon or the parent asks that they be used'.[1] Yet given that Jewish law does not insist that pain be experienced in circumcision, there is every reason for Reform Judaism to adopt this modern scientific advance.

The same point applies to those laws which are arguably inhumane. For example, discussing the question whether it is in accord with the spirit of the Jewish tradition to encourage the establishment of a congregation of homosexuals, Freehof remarks: 'Homosexuality runs counter to the sancta of Jewish life. There is no sidestepping the fact that from the point of view of Judaism, men who practice homosexuality are to be deemed sinners.'[2] Here Freehof appeals to Orthodox law as a basis for the Reform attitude, but there are significant humane reasons for adopting a more accepting approach to homosexuals particularly since a more humane view is generally justified by modern medical and psychiatric opinion. Another example relates to the question whether a doctor should be permitted to inform a patient that he is dying. In this instance Freehof declares that 'in the light of Jewish law and tradition, it is clearly wrong to tell a patient that his case is hopeless and that he is dying'.[3] Yet there are patients who desire to know the truth about their illness so that they are better able to cope with death; to deny them such information, as Freehof recommends, could be a heartless act. Again, regarding the question whether euthanasia should be permitted in Reform Judaism Freehof declares that it is forbidden in Jewish law to take life; thus 'the act of killing a patient for whatever motive is absolutely forbidden'.[4] On humane grounds, however, it is possible that euthanasia could be a morally defensible act given the mental and physical agony of some patients in the face of a long, useless and incurable illness. Thus it is not clear why Freehof accepts that the law should be modified to be more in tune with modern life and general principles of humanity in some cases, but by no means in all.

1. Freehof, *Current Reform Responsa*, p. 105.
2. Freehof, *Contemporary Reform Responsa*, p. 24.
3. Freehof, *Reform Responsa*, p. 125.
4. Freehof, *Reform Responsa*, p. 118.

Conclusion

In his lecture 'Reform Judaism and the Law' Freehof emphasises that Reform Jews should engage in the study of traditional Jewish law. 'We can begin', he writes, 'by systematizing and indexing the great *responsa* literature, whose approximately three thousand tight-packed volumes are full of treasures of Jewish history, thought, feeling and experience.'[1] Freehof himself has done this admirably in his writings, and in this respect he has made a major contribution to Jewish scholarship. However, as we have seen, when deciding which traditional laws should be retained in Reform Judaism, he frequently does not follow his own principles of selection. Sometimes his judgments seem to be based simply on modern expediency, while at other times they seem motivated by an unjustified prejudice for traditional ways. But whatever the reason, such inconsistency results in uncertainty and confusion about Reform Judaism's relation to traditional Jewish law.

What is clearly needed in Reform Judaism is a coherent and consistent philosophy of law where the criteria for accepting Orthodox practices are clearly delineated and rigorously followed. Indeed there are times when Freehof seems aware of the deficiencies of his approach. For example he states in the same lecture that Reform Judaism should now begin to 'work out the entire philosophy of Jewish law and of our relationship with it. It will have to be a system that will find room for individuality and unity, for obedience and freedom, for recorded tradition and for operative originality. Such a philosophy of Jewish law will require much study, many articles by many thinkers and much debate. It may require a generation or two for its accomplishment'.[2] What a study of Freehof's survey of Reform Jewish practice illustrates is the urgency of this task.[3]

---

1. Freehof, *Reform Judaism and the Law*, p. 22.
2. Freehof, *Reform Judaism and the Law*, p. 20.
3. See further my 'Freedom and Law in Reform Judaism', *Journal of Reform Judaism* (1983), pp. 88-97.

12

MOSES MENDELSSOHN'S CONCEPT OF TOLERANCE

David Patterson

This paper originally appeared in a volume entitled *Between East and West*.[1] It is a pleasure and privilege to re-publish it in a volume honouring Louis Jacobs. I first met Louis Jacobs in Manchester some forty years ago, and I was at once impressed by his scholarly and human qualities. In the following decades, my admiration and affection for him have grown steadily. He is undoubtedly one of the leading scholars in the field of Jewish studies in Great Britain. A highly cultivated and deeply thoughtful man, he combines the finest traditions of Jewish learning with the rigorous criteria of the best of English scholarship. Strictly observant in practice, he maintains a refreshing tolerance and breadth of vision. Like Livy's ideal gentleman, he is aware of his own dignity and the freedom of other people. Hence, the subject of this essay is particularly appropriate.

Since this article was first published, striking advances have been made in the study of Moses Mendelssohn and his environment. Pride of place must be given to the magisterial work of the late Professor Alexander Altmann[2] whose biography of Mendelssohn is surely definitive. Among his numerous scholarly publications, two further works by Altmann are worthy of particular attention, one a volume of essays[3] and the other an introduction and commentary to Allan

---

1. A. Altmann (ed.), *Between East and West. Essays Dedicated to the Memory of Bela Horovitz* (London, 1958).
2. A. Altmann, *Moses Mendelssohn, a Biographical Study* (London, 1973).
3. A. Altmann, *Essays in Jewish Intellectual History* (Hanover and London, 1981).

Arkush's translation of Mendelssohn's *Jerusalem*.[1] An anthology edited by Alfred Jospe is highly informative.[2] Two further volumes, one by Moshe Pelli[3] and the other by David Sorkin[4] shed important light on the intellectual background of German Jewry.

There are four translations of Moses Mendelssohn's *Jerusalem* into English. The earliest, and the one used in this essay, by M. Samuels appeared in London in 1838. Published a little over half a century after the appearance of Mendelssohn's *Jerusalem* in Berlin, 1783, its dignified and elegant prose retains much of the flavour of the original. A second translation by I. Leeser appeared in Philadelphia in 1853 and a third by A. Jospe in New York, 1969. The most recent translation by A. Arkush was published in 1983.[5] The translation is accurate, idiomatic and felicitous. After more than two centuries Mendelssohn's *Jerusalem* remains a fascinating and challenging study.

The difficulties of Moses Mendelssohn's *Jerusalem* stem primarily from the variety of motivations which the author endeavoured to harmonize in this one work. Mendelssohn's standpoint was conditioned by three separate facets of his personality, namely, the loyal Jew, the aspiring German and the confirmed rationalist. The problem consisted in reconciling the first of these facets to the second and third, and resulted inevitably in an attempt to break down the whole structure of religious disabilities as the first step in such a process of integration. But the extreme difficulties of eradicating so deeply rooted a concept necessitated making the means almost an end in itself, so that an attack upon ecclesiastical authority becomes the central theme of the *Jerusalem*, with the defence of Judaism from dogma following naturally as a consequence of having to harmonize Judaism with that pro-

1. Moses Mendelssohn, *Jerusalem or On Religious Power and Judaism* (trans. Allan Arkush; Introduction and Commentary by Alexander Altmann; Hanover and London, 1983).
2. A. Jospe (ed.), *Studies in Jewish Thought, an Anthology of German-Jewish Scholarship* (Detroit, 1981).
3. M. Pelli, *The Age of Haskalah. Studies in Hebrew Literature of the Enlightenment in Germany* (Leiden, 1979).
4. D. Sorkin, *The Transformation of German Jewry 1780–1840* (Oxford, 1987). All these volumes are thoroughly researched and replete with footnotes and bibliographies.
5. See above n. 2.

cess.[1] As the work consists, therefore, of an attempt to solve a socio-logical problem in theological and philosophical terms, it is hardly surprising that the thought-sequence is sometimes strained.

The sociological motivation may be clearly discerned in the sequence of events leading to the composition of the *Jerusalem*. When the persecuted Jews of Alsace turned in despair to Mendelssohn to compose a memorandum to be presented on their behalf to King Louis XVI of France, Mendelssohn enlisted the support and sympathy of the young but highly gifted Christian Wilhelm Dohm. The latter was so moved by his investigations that he finally composed a work of much wider compass, *Upon the Civil Amelioration of the Condition of the Jews* (1871).[2] This great apology by a Christian writer provoked no small stir, and was followed, whether directly or indirectly, by the Emperor Joseph of Austria's famous Patent of Toleration (1781),[3] a few months after its publication.

In the fierce controversy which broke out over the question of civil rights for Jews, Mendelssohn persuaded a young friend, Marcus Herz, to translate into German the famous tract of Menasseh Ben Israel, *Vindiciae Judaeorum*, which more than a century previously, in 1656, had argued the case for the readmittance of the Jews to England, and which aimed at destroying such prejudices as militated against the acceptance of the Jewish people within the pale of humanity.[4] To this

1. Not unlike Maimonides' process of demythologizing Scripture. With respect to Mendelssohn's debt to Maimonides, see Ernst Cassirer, 'Die Idee der Religion bei Lessing und Mendelssohn', in *Festgabe zum zehnjährigen Bestehen der Akademie der Wissenschaft des Judentums*, 1919–1929 (Berlin), p. 40.

2. Among the proposals advanced by Dohm there was a clause advocating that perfect freedom of worship should be granted to the Jewish people, together with the right, enjoyed by other religious communities, of expelling dissenting members either temporarily or permanently. Mendelssohn was rigidly opposed to the latter proposition.

3. Although this loudly acclaimed Patent postulated certain improvements in the educational facilities and range of economic activities permitted to Jews, their basic disabilities, such as closely restricted rights of residence and the subjection to additional taxes, remained unaltered. See M. Grunwald, *Vienna* (Jewish Communities Series; Philadelphia, 1936), pp. 152ff.

4. After refuting the blood libel, Menasseh Ben Israel proceeds to demonstrate that Jews are not idolaters; do not curse Christians three times a day; are not blasphemers; do not proselytize, and that their entrance to England will not damage the trade of the indigenous population. Very indicative of the prevailing mental climate is his argument that the exclusion of the Jews from England is preventing the fulfilment of the prophecy in Dan. 12.7, that the holy people must be scattered!

translation Mendelssohn himself added a preface (1782), in which, after defending the wisdom of permitting unrestricted Jewish partici- pation in all branches of economic life, he proceeded to deny the validity of ecclesiastical jurisdiction for Gentile and Jew alike. The keynote of the preface is a heartfelt plea for liberty both in the physi- cal and the spiritual sense. The first paragraph, in which Mendelssohn expresses his satisfaction with the gradual acceptance of the doctrine of the Rights of Man, illustrates the author's view of tolerance not as a boon to be craved by the weaker party, but as a moral duty incumbent upon the stronger.

> The spirit of conciliation, just like love, demands that the stronger party should take the first steps. He must waive his superiority and make the overture, if the weaker party is to gain sufficient confidence to respond. . . [1]

But the author is at pains to demonstrate the limitations of even the more liberal spirit beginning to find expression.

> Previous writings and arguments about tolerance, however, are concerned only with the three religious denominations favoured in the German empire, at most including some of their offshoots. Pagans, Jews, Mohammedans and Deists are mentioned only with the object of making the arguments in favour of tolerance more debatable. According to your premises, the opponents argue, we must not merely entertain and tolerate Jews and Deists, but even let them participate in all the rights and obliga- tions of mankind. . . [2]

Having embarked at once upon the social aspect of religious dis- abilities, Mendelssohn proceeds to castigate the obstinate refusal of German society to admit the Jews on an equal footing, mercilessly laying bare the calumnies and illogical accusations which served as the pretext for such refusal. Particularly powerful is his exposition of the change in the type of pretext varying with the times.

---

1. Moses Mendelssohn's *Gesammelte Schriften* (Leipzig, 1843), III, p. 179. This lofty conception of tolerance may well be compared with that of Mirabeau voiced before the French National Assembly, 23 August 1789: 'The unrestricted freedom of belief is so sacred in my eyes, that even the word tolerance sounds despotic, because the existence of the authority that is empowered to tolerate injures freedom, in that it tolerates, because it could also do the reverse' (*apud* H. Graetz, *History of the Jews* [English Edition, London, 1892], V, p. 466; cf. S. Rawidowicz, 'Moses Mendelssohn, The German and Jewish Philosopher', in the *Gaster Anniversary Vol- ume* [London, 1936], pp. 474ff.).

2. Mendelssohn, *Gesammelte Schriften*, III, pp. 179-80.

In former superstitious times it was sacred things that we wantonly defiled; crucifixes that we stabbed and made bleed; children that we circumcised in secret and delighted in mutilating; Christian blood that we used at Passover; wells that we poisoned, etc. . . On account of which we were martyred, robbed of our fortunes, driven into exile, if not actually put to death.—Now times have changed, and such slanders no longer have the desired effect. Now we are charged with superstition and stupidity; lack of moral feelings, taste and good manners; an incapacity for the arts, sciences and useful trades, particularly in respect to the military and civil services; an overwhelming inclination towards fraud, usury and evasion of the law. Such charges have replaced those cruder accusations, to exclude us from the ranks of useful citizens, and to eject us from the maternal bosom of the state. . . We are still barred from all the arts, sciences and useful trades and occupations of mankind; every avenue to improvement is blocked, while a lack of culture is made the pretext for our further oppression. They tie our hands and reproach us for not using them.[1]

It is of interest, however, that Mendelssohn is equally forthright in denouncing the spirit of intolerance and persecution to be found within the ranks of his own brethren. In spite of the zeal he displays on behalf of his fellow-Jews, he is not blind to their faults.

Nations are tolerating and countenancing each other, and showing a certain kindness and forbearance even towards you, which with the help of Him, who moulds the hearts of men, may grow to real brotherly love. O, my brethren, follow the example of love, just as formerly you followed that of hatred. Emulate the virtues of nations, whose vices you previously felt constrained to imitate. If you desire protection, toleration and sufferance from others, then protect, tolerate and suffer each other! *Love, and you will be loved.*[2]

1. Mendelssohn, *Gesammelte Schriften*, III, pp. 182-83.
2. Mendelssohn, *Gesammelte Schriften*, III, p. 202. In this respect it is interesting to compare the remarks of Ahad Ha-Am in a letter written from London on 19 May 1914, to A.M.L. Jerusalem: 'I am utterly opposed to every form of boycott. Even in my childhood I detested the Jerusalem *herem*, and the feeling remains to this day. Whether the boycott is pronounced by Rabbis at the Wailing Wall to the sound of the *Shofar*, or by the Teachers' Union in an announcement in *Herut*—it is all one. Nor does the change of name change my attitude. Call it *herem* or call it boycott, I loath it. . . If I were in Palestine, I should fight this abominable practice with all my might. It had almost died out in Jerusalem when it was brought back from Europe under a foreign name, as though to suggest that being approved by non-Jews, it is all right for 'idealists' of European Culture. I do not care if they call me reactionary or even traitor: What I thought ugly thirty years ago I still think ugly. . .'(*Ahad Ha-Am* [trans. and ed. L. Simon; Oxford: East and West Library, 1946], p. 315).

The plea for tolerance in the preface, however, was not the issue on which he was to be challenged, perhaps because it was unanswerable. His critics at once fastened upon another theme, which Mendelssohn had woven into his preface—the argument against ecclesiastical jurisdiction. The author was challenged to explain his religion in the light of his denial to Jewish ecclesiastical power of the right to expel members from the congregation. And it must be admitted that this idea aroused no less astonishment in Jewish than in Christian circles. Mendelssohn's opponents argued that the power of ecclesiastical law constituted the very basis of the Jewish polity, and that in attacking it, Mendelssohn had undermined the whole fabric of Judaism. It was felt that the author of the preface had so far departed from the basic concept of Judaism, that he was openly invited to embrace Christianity.[1] In the face of such direct provocation Mendelssohn was compelled to defend his views, couching his reply in an analysis of Judaism entitled *Jerusalem or Upon Ecclesiastical Power and Judaism* (1783), of which the argument is summarized below.

The first part of the *Jerusalem* is devoted to a definition of the respective function of Church and State towards society, demonstrating that the essential difference between them consists in the fact that the State is invested with powers of compulsion, while the Church must rely solely upon persuasion. To prove his point Mendelssohn uses the theory of the social contract based on the natural rights and duties of mankind. This theory postulated that in entering society there is established a relationship of man to man, whereby every member agrees that a proportion of his natural rights be applied to the benefit of society as a whole. The State is imagined as a moral entity presiding over these rights, deciding cases of conflict, and therefore endowed with jurisdiction over man's goods and actions, with the power to punish or reward. The contract is founded on the mutual assistance which every man requires from his fellow, without which society cannot function. But the Church is concerned with the relationship of man to God, and God has no need of man's assistance, nor can man's rights ever be in conflict with His.[2] Yet all the violence, persecution and dis-

---

1. See Moses Mendelssohn, *Jerusalem* (trans. M. Samuels; London, 1838), I, p. 138.
2. Cf. Milton's 'On His Blindness':

> '. . . God doth not need either man's work, or His own gifts: who best
> bear His mild yoke, they serve Him best. . .'

cord fomented under the cloak of religion have arisen from the insinuation of a conflict between the rights of God and man. But if God needs no assistance from man, and demands no sacrifice of man's rights for His benefit, the Church can under no circumstances presume to have the authority of deciding cases of conflict, where conflict is impossible. There can be no covenant between Church and man, whereby man sacrifices a portion of his rights to the jurisdiction of the Church. Therefore the Church can have no rights over goods or property, nor can she punish, since religious actions admit neither of bribery nor coercion. The function of the Church is to instruct, fortify and console.

The difference between State and Church in the sphere of action is thus sharply defined. But with regard to belief, which cannot be subject to coercion, their standpoint must be the same. Both may instruct and advise, but neither may punish, force or bribe. The slightest preference given publicly to one religion is an indirect bribe, just as the witholding of the smallest privilege from dissenters is an indirect penalty. Moreover, such privilege or restriction once condoned can be so enlarged as to constitute civil happiness on the one hand, or oppression, persecution and exile on the other. Hence the Church may wield no form of government, neither should the State take part in any religious dispute.[1]

It follows that the State cannot compel its public servants to profess any particular creed. 'Let it not be forgotten', Mendelssohn wrote, 'that according to my principles the State is not authorized to attach income, dignity and privilege to certain distinct dogmas.'[2] It follows also that the right of proscription and banishment, which at times the State may think fit to exercise, is contrary to the spirit of religion, which must bind its adherents by lovingkindness. Excommunication cannot be devoid of civil consequences, which the Church has no mandate to engender.

Having defined the scope of ecclesiastical authority Mendelssohn proceeds in the second part of the *Jerusalem* to demonstrate that

---

1. Mendelssohn makes, however, the following proviso: 'Admittedly the State must take care from a distance that no doctrines be propagated, which do not accord with the public welfare, or which, like atheism and epicurism, undermine the foundation, on which the wellbeing of civil society rests' (*Jerusalem*, p. 287). J. Guttman tends to gloss over the proviso; see *Dat u-Mada'* (Jerusalem, 1955), p. 212.

2. Mendelssohn, *Jerusalem*, p. 295.

Judaism is in perfect accord with such a delimitation. Here he faces the question which was raised as the most important objection to his views: 'What are the laws of Moses but a system of religious government, of the power and rights of religion?'[1] The question implies that by denying religion the weapon of excommunication Mendelssohn was undermining the whole structure of Judaism. The problem revolves upon the nature of Judaism, and the author is constrained to expound those aspects which constitute its individuality.

> Judaism does not know of a revealed religion, in the sense in which it is understood by Christians. The Israelites have a divine legislation, laws, commandments, orders, rules of life, instruction about God's will as to how to conduct themselves in order to merit both temporal and eternal happiness; these rules and restrictions were revealed through Moses in a wonderful and supernatural manner; but no dogmas, no saving truths, no general self-evident positions. The Lord always reveals the latter to us, as to the rest of mankind through *nature* and *events*, never through *words* and *written characters*.[2]

Thus ancient Judaism has no articles of faith, nor oaths of creed. It is founded not on theological dogmas, but on religious commandments. The unchangeable truths of God, His government and His providence have no need of revelation in words or writing, but are accessible everywhere and always to every rational creature, and are, therefore, the common property of humanity, Gentile and Jew alike. But in addition to these unchangeable truths Judaism is compounded of two more specific elements. On the one hand it is founded on historical truths, testifying to the national union, which were received on trust and confirmed by miracles. On the other it comprises a system of laws, judgements, commandments, and rules of life peculiar to the Jewish nation. The lawgiver is God Himself, who gave them publicly and in a marvellous manner, to be impressed upon the nation for ever. The object of this ceremonial law is happiness both for the community and for the individual, and by its agency the inquiring reason is guided to the divine truths.

According to the early concepts of Judaism, State and Religion were not united, but identical. There could be no conflict between man's relation to society and to God, because God was both Creator and Administrator. Similarly the State could make no demands contrary to

---

1. Mendelssohn, *Jerusalem*, p. 306.
2. Mendelssohn, *Jerusalem*, p. 311.

the duties of God. Where every law was religious, every service to the public was true divine service. Conversely, every offence against the authority of God was a political offence, and was punished not as *misbelief* but as *misdeed*. That the Mosaic code neither authorizes ecclesiastical law and power, nor attaches temporal punishment to misbelief is clearly shown by the fact that after the civil bonds of the nation were dissolved, religious infractions no longer constituted State offences.

Having proved his main thesis Mendelssohn proceeds to clarify his position with regard to two additional questions of importance. He lays it down as axiomatic that Israel must observe its Law punctiliously until God should change it, and consequently if Jews can obtain civil rights only by departing from the Law, they must regretfully renounce those rights. However he is at pains to demonstrate that such a condition should not be made, but rather that the Christians should help to prepare the ground for emancipation.

> Look upon us, if not as brethren and fellow-citizens, at least as fellow-creatures and countrymen. Show us the way and supply us with the means of becoming better fellow-countrymen. . . [1]

Finally he disposes of the suggestion, popular among the exponents of the *Aufklärung*, that a union of religion provides the shortest way to brotherly love and toleration. He argues that the suggestion may well contain a snare for liberty of conscience, and far from achieving toleration is likely to bring about exactly the opposite of it.

> Nobody thinks and feels exactly like his neighbour; then why should we wish to mislead each other with deceiving words? Alas! we are prone to do so in our everyday transactions and conversations, which are of no special significance: but why, also, in such things as affect our temporal and eternal welfare, our entire destiny? Why in the most important concerns of our life should we make ourselves unknown to one another by disguise, especially when God has deliberately stamped on every man his own particular features?[2]

The concluding paragraph of the *Jerusalem* embodies a great and noble plea:

> Reward and punish no doctrine, offer neither allurement nor bribe for any religious opinion. Let whoever does not disturb the public happiness,

1. Mendelssohn, *Jerusalem*, p. 358.
2. Mendelssohn, *Jerusalem*, pp. 360-61.

whoever complies with civil law and acts righteously towards you and his fellow citizens, be allowed to speak as he thinks, to call upon God after his own fashion or that of his ancestors, and to seek eternal salvation wherever he believes it may be found. Let no-one in your states be a searcher of hearts and a censor of opinions; let no-one arrogate to himself a right which the Omniscient has reserved for himself. If we render unto Caesar that which is Caesar's then you, yourselves, should render unto God that which is God's! Love truth! Love Peace!

The concept of tolerance in the *Jerusalem*, therefore, is founded upon Mendelssohn's demonstration that belief cannot be subject to compulsion. Upon this base the twin pillars of his edifice, one religious and one civil, are erected. In the religious sphere Mendelssohn evolves the principle that the Church may not impose its will by force and that all excommunication, which is a method of exerting such pressure, is unjustifiable. Quite apart from the wider implications of such a principle, it is aimed specifically against external measures detrimental to the Jews on the part of the Christian Church, and against the internal structures of Rabbinical authority. The supreme importance which the author attaches to this principle involves the entire function of religion, which is hereby limited to positive aims, and stripped of negative potentiality. But the full implications of the thesis emerges in the civil sphere. It follows from Mendelssohn's argument that no civil consequences may be attached to the holding of particular beliefs, that no State office can be dependent upon the profession of specific dogmas. Hence Jews should not be excluded from public office, from the professions or from any other branch of economic or social activity because of their refusal to accept certain religious tenets.

The urgent necessity of such demonstration of principle is amply illustrated by the lengthy works written to prove that religious tolerance and the compulsory profession of certain dogmas for public office are quite compatible.[1] The inherent paradox of any such argument was exposed by the *Jerusalem* once and for all. But many years were to elapse before the implications of Mendelssohn's work were to

---

1.   William Warburton in *The Alliance between Church and State* (first published 1736), wrote: 'We shall demonstrate the perfect concord and agreement between *Religious Liberty and a Test-Law*' (*The Works of William Warburton* [London, 1811], VII, p. 23). With regards to the definition of *Test-Law*, he wrote: 'By which I understand some sufficient proof or evidence required from those admitted into the administration of public affairs, that they are members of the religion established by law' (*Works*, p. 242).

be translated into living reality, and before the profession of Judaism ceased to be a stumbling block for the full participation in the life of society.[1] Neither the broad humanitarian concepts of the *Aufklärung*, nor the greater emphasis upon religious tolerance, towards which German Lutheran Protestantism had slowly gravitated,[2] were sufficiently strong to outweigh the deep-rooted prejudice and distrust, which barred the way to Jewish participation in civil rights. But there can be no doubt of the important influence exerted by the *Jerusalem* throughout the whole course of that bitter struggle.

In spite of the vehemence with which Mendelssohn defended Lessing against the charge of being a Spinozist,[3] it is not surprising that the *Jerusalem* bears some striking affinities to Spinoza's *Tractatus Theologico-Politicus* in view of the latter's avowed purpose of demonstrating the importance of freedom of thought and discussion in every well-ordered commonwealth.[4] Mendelssohn bases his defence of Judaism on Spinoza's contention that in the ancient Hebrew state civil polity and religion were one and the same, and that the tenets of Jewish religion were not doctrines, but declared laws and commandments.[5] But whereas Spinoza held the view that such a theocracy was not consonant with philosophic freedom,[6] Mendelssohn, starting from a similar premise that Judaism contains no dogmas but only religious commandments, infers that it cannot hamper freedom of thought. Whereas Spinoza invested the civil power with authority over sacred matters—even though he was careful to distinguish outward religious observance from inner worship and pious contemplation, which latter

---

1. As clearly demonstrated by the 'Verein für Kultur und Wissenschaft der Juden', founded 1819 in Berlin by Leopold Zunz, Edward Gans and Moses Moser, whose members were required to take an oath that they would not convert to Christianity in order to obtain a government position. The subsequent conversion of Gans and Heine becomes even more poignant in the light of such an oath.
2. See W. Zeeden, *The Legacy of Luther* (trans. R.M. Bethell; London, 1954), *passim*.
3. Cf. Guttman, *Dat u-Mada'*, p. 193; Rawidowicz, 'Moses Mendelssohn. . .', p. 475.
4. Spinoza, *Tractatus Theologico-Politicus* (trans. R. Willis; 2nd edn; London, 1868). See title-page and p. 347.
5. Spinoza, *Tractatus*, p. 294, Cf. Guttman, *Dat u-Mada'*, p. 216.
6. See 'Ein ungedruckter Vortrag Hermann Cohen's über Spinoza's Verhältnis zum Judentum', in *Festgabe zum zehnjährigen Bestehen*, pp. 46-49.

are the inalienable rights of all[1]—Mendelssohn believes that both religious thought and practice are outside the sphere of the State's power of coercion.[2]

Such a conclusion is essential for Mendelssohn's social purpose, and in this respect the author of the *Jerusalem* leans heavily upon John Locke.[3] In his exposition of the 'social contract', and the rights and duties of man, Mendelssohn follows the pattern of Locke's *Second Treatise of Civil Government*. He is equally faithful to the delineation of the spheres of religion and civil government which appear in the English philosopher's *Letter Concerning Toleration*. Locke's definitions that 'all the life and power of true religion consists in the inward and full persuasion of the mind',[4] or that the magistrate's power 'consists only in outward force',[5] are closely followed in the *Jerusalem*. Even Locke's denial of tolerance to those 'who deny the being of a God'[6] is echoed by Mendelssohn.

There is, however, one essential difference in the chain of reasoning, which completely alters the emphasis of the *Jerusalem*, and it is in this difference that Mendelssohn's originality may be primarily sought.[7] Although Locke stresses that belief cannot be compelled by external force, he nevertheless assigns to the Church the power of admission or expulsion,[8] the latter representing the sole punishment the Church can administer.[9] According to Locke, tolerance does not demand that a Church retain an offender, although he is careful to add

1. See Spinoza, *Tractatus, pp.* 327ff. and pp. 342ff. Cf. Guttman, *Dat u-Mada'*, p. 211.

2. Cf. Guttman, *Dat u-Mada'*, p. 214.

3. Although the ideas are not always original to Locke; his concept of tolerance, for example, was probably influenced by the Remonstrant congregation in Amsterdam. (See M. Branston's article, 'John Locke, The Exile', in *The Listener*, 3 November, 1954.) Mendelssohn's specific acquaintance with Locke's ideas is shown by his reference to him in the *Jerusalem*, pp. 261ff. But in any case, such concepts as the 'rights of man' and 'equality before the law' had reached the Continent from England via Voltaire's *Letters about the English* (1732), and had been largely absorbed into the prevailing mental climate.

4. John Locke, *The Second Treatise of Civil Government and a Letter concerning Toleration* (ed. J.W. Gough; Oxford, 1946), p. 127.

5. J. Locke, *Second Treatise*, p. 127.

6. J. Locke, *Second Treatise*, p. 156.

7. Guttman notes this difference, *Dat u-Mada'*, p. 212, without developing its significance.

8. J. Locke, *Second Treatise*, pp. 129 and 131.

9. J. Locke, *Second Treatise*, p. 131.

that 'In all such cases care is to be taken that the sentence of excommunication, and the execution thereof, carry with it no rough usage of word or action whereby the ejected person may any wise be damnified in body or estate'.[1] Not only can Mendelssohn not accept this argument, but he proceeds to direct the whole weight of his reasoning in the *Jerusalem* against it. He does so not merely in order to prove that excommunication is inevitably attended by detrimental civil consequences.

> What anathema, what excommunication is entirely without civil consequences, entirely without influence on at least the civil esteem and the reputation of the victim, and on the confidence of his fellow-citizens, without which no-one can follow his calling, be useful to his fellowmen, or in other words, enjoy civil happiness?[2]

Important as this objection is, there is yet an underlying argument of much greater cogency.

Early in the *Jerusalem*[3] Mendelssohn refers to the arguments propounded against Locke's view that the state is a society of men invited to promote their temporal welfare, and should not concern itself with differences of religion. His opponents reasoned that the spiritual life under the guardianship of the Church is more important than the material life under the domination of the State, since the eternal life is of more consequence than the temporal. Hence all secular realms fall under the dominion of the spiritual potentate. In such circumstances the terrible edge of the weapon of excommunication may readily be understood, and it is not surprising, therefore, that Mendelssohn, directs his stoutest shafts against it. That which in Locke is easily conceded becomes the focal point of attack in the *Jerusalem*. Mendelssohn considered ecclesiastical authority to be so dangerous that he sought to clear Judaism entirely of the charge of attachment to it.

From what precedes it may readily be discerned that for all its clarity of thought and persuasiveness of style, the chain of argument in the *Jerusalem* contains a number of weak links. Hamann was not entirely unjustified in reproaching the work with inconsistency, claiming the first part to have been written by Mendelssohn the advocate of enlight-

---

1. J. Locke, *Second Treatise*, p. 132.
2. Mendelssohn, *Jerusalem*, p. 297.
3. Mendelssohn, *Jerusalem*, pp. 261ff.

enment, and the second part by Mendelssohn the Jew.[1] Certainly the attempt to reconcile these separate interests with each other, and with the third interest of the loyal citizen can only be carried out with a good deal of stress and strain. The positive assertion that Judaism has no dogmas is at least subject to question.[2] The separation of the spheres of belief and action makes no adequate allowance for the direct subordination of the latter to the former. The idea of tolerance is made dependent on a theological conception, the burden of whose proofs rests on outmoded sociological concepts. Moreover the definition of Judaism as a revealed legislation gives no more freedom of belief than by leaving it a revealed religion. Indeed, as Guttman has pointed out,[3] the recognition of God as the ruler of the State premises an internal metaphysical consciousness of His existence, and there is no further place for freedom in matters of belief where the citizens of the state are obliged by internal, metaphysical consciousness.

In fact the power of the *Jerusalem* stems not so much from the inexorable logic of the argument as from the dignity of its author and the passion of his plea. Mendelssohn made no apology for his Judaism[4]— indeed, the very idea of apology would have appeared to him absurd. He accepted it with the same naturalness and assurance that a man accepts the fact he is alive. His appeal for tolerance was not the supplication of the weak to the strong, an apology for inferiority and a servile promise of Jewish self-improvement. He demanded tolerance as an elementary human right, as a prerogative due to the dignity of every man. He demanded it not with arrogance, not with remonstrances or threats, but with quiet certainty of absolute conviction, with the knowledge that the right to believe just as the right to live a free, unfettered life is fundamental to that most noble of concepts— brotherly love.

1. See Bamberger, 'Mendelssohn's Begriff vom Judentum', in *Wissenschaft des Judentums in deutsche Sprachbereich* (ed. K. Wilhelm; Tübingen, 1967), II, p. 536.
2. See S. Schecter, 'Dogmas in Judaism', in *Solomon Schecter* (ed. N. Brentwich; Oxford: East and West Library, 1946).
3. Guttman, *Dat u-Mada'*, p. 217.
4. Cf. Rawidowicz, 'Moses Mendelssohn', pp. 482ff.

13

THE QUEST FOR A JEWISH THEOLOGY
AND A NON-FUNDAMENTALIST HALAKHAH

Paul Morris

Rabbi Dr Louis Jacobs, in the first of a series of controversial studies, wrote that one of the great barriers to a contemporary Jewish theology was 'the fact that hardly anybody, nowadays, is thoroughly at home in both modern philosophy and the massive Jewish learning of the past' (1957, p. 11)—I would like to suggest, however, that 'hardly anybody' includes Louis Jacobs himself.[1] Rabbi Jacobs has been, and continues to be, a controversial figure in Anglo-Jewry, but his position in these public 'debates' is founded upon a deep Jewish learning coupled with the desire 'to present a coherent picture of what Jews can believe without subterfuge and with intellectual honesty' (1973a, p. 4). These controversies can be seen as falling under the rubric of *mahloket le-shem shamayim* (controversy in the name of Heaven [*Avot* 5.20]), that is, arguments, based on the tradition, for the sake of Jewry. My intention, in this study, is to examine a number of what I consider to be Rabbi Jacobs's main theological concerns, not in terms of the well-documented and commented on 'Jacobs Affair', but rather as a critical

---

1. For details of Jacobs's education see 1989, pp. 20-81. On the question of Jacobs's mastery of modern philosophy, it is important to note that he was one of the first scholars to apply 'linguistic analysis' to the interpretation of Jewish sources (1957; 1964; 1968; 1985, p. 101), and this represents one of the distinctive features of his work. His engagement with German idealism has been much more limited, e.g. his treatment of Kant; his misreading of Hermann Cohen's notion of 'idea' as employed by Mordecai Kaplan (1957, pp. 18-20); his analysis of the Marxist critique of religion (1968, pp. 126-34); and his obvious difficulties with Leo Baeck, Martin Buber and Franz Rosenzweig, whom he characterizes as 'ponderous' and 'elusive' (1973, p. 13). Further, it might be noted that Jacobs's work is almost devoid of technical philosophical discussion. This is most particularly evident in his work on Maimonides (e.g. the analysis of Maimonides' third principle [1964, pp. 70ff.]).

study of more than thirty years work attempting to create a 'synthesis. . . between the permanent values and truth of tradition and the best thought of the day' (1957, p. 11). In many ways this is a continuation of a long-standing conversation that I have had with Rabbi Jacobs, first as an avid reader of his books and articles, and more recently as one of his students in his challenging textual classes on 'classic' sources, such as Mainomides' *The Guide of the Perplexed*, Cordovero's *The Palm Tree of Deborah*, and *Sefer Ha-Zohar*, during his time as Visiting Professor of Jewish Studies at Lancaster.[1] It is with deep appreciation to Professor Jacobs that I offer this paper, to the great scholar and teacher, who, in response to whatever I have been working on in recent years, has always gently suggested, 'You might look at such-and-such a source', and then immediately cited a totally appropriate text.

There is much truth in the assertion that theology, in the sense of a systematic project, is not indigenous of Jewry, but is the product of the Jewish encounter with the 'Greek' inheritance in its, albeit different, historical guises. The framework for a Jewish theology has proceeded along established lines, including the claim that the divine origin of all knowledge provides the basis for a 'synthesis' of 'Greek' and Jewish thought, and the task of defining the core-beliefs specific to Judaism. Jews have attempted to expound these foundational 'dogmas' in 'Greek', that is, the deliniation of the 'Jewish *logos* (or *logoi*)' in alien language and terms. Jewish theology can be seen in part, at least, as the attempt to create a 'Jewish' thinking to underlie, and be in accord with, traditional Jewish life and practice.

In the modern period Jews have entered into the non-Jewish world in an unprecedented fashion, especially in terms of general education, and it is no longer simply a case of the Jewish communities facing outside challenges. New forms of Judaism have arisen, together with novel ways of understanding Jewish identity. The problem of the gap between Jewish life and general thought have become particularly acute and the need for a Jewish theology correspondingly so. One of

---

1. Every student who has participated in one of Rabbi Jacobs's textual classes will recognize what Eugene Borowitz means when he refers to Jacobs's 'extraordinary perceptiveness to Jewish texts' (*Choices in Modern Jewish Thought* [New York: Behrman, 1983]), p. 268.

the more perceptive among modern Jewish 'theologians', Franz Rosenzweig, asserted that:

> We are Christian in everything. We live in a Christian state, attend Chris-
> tian schools, read Christian books, in short our whole 'culture' rests
> entirely on a Christian foundation. . . today the Jewish religion cannot be
> 'accepted', it has to be grafted on by. . . dietary observances, and *Bar
> Mitzvah* (Rosenzweig, p. 45).

Abraham Joshua Heschel, in his call for 'Jewish theology', wrote:

> Now, we live in a very strange situation today. . . We are essentially
> trained in a non-Jewish world. . . We are inclined to think in non-Jewish
> terms. I am not discouraging exposure to the non-Jewish world. I am
> merely indicating that it is not Biblical, Rabbinic, Hasidic think-
> ing. . . We would like to apply the Bible and *Hazal* and they are often
> incongruent. If you take Biblical passages. . . or Rabbinic statements,
> and submit them to a Greek mind, they often are absurd. They make no
> sense. . . How to think in a Jewish way of thinking? (Heschel, 1969,
> p. 7).

Underlying many of the issues and debates in modern Jewish thought
is this question of how to think in a Jewish way. Jacobs's writings have
been concerned with a number of the most significant of these issues,
and he has always sought to situate his own views in the context of
these contemporary Jewish debates and those of the Jewish past.

Whilst it is true that 'What Jacobs had to tell the world was not particularly new to non-fundamentalist Jews and Christians' (Marmur,
1982, p. 150), his importance as a modern Jewish thinker lies in the
sustained attempt to construct a Jewish theology for contemporary
Jewry, undertaken by the 'most articulate, learned, and prolific exposi-
tor of traditional Judaism for the modern world who is writing in
English today' (Novak, 1985, p. 210). Jacobs offers a Jewish theology
worthy of the most serious consideration by Jewish scholars of all
camps, and he has been a major figure in the recognition of the present
neglect and importance of the theological quest by contemporary Jews
and the range of sources on which such theological efforts can draw.
His mastery of the textual sources allows him a particular perspective
on the present challenges to the tradition, and also the possibility of its
creative re-interpretation.

Underlying Jacob's work is the claim that modern knowledge presents contemporary Jews with an unprecedented challenge. The traditional 'fundamentalist' view of the divine origins of the *Torah* has

been undermined by the 'assured' findings of Biblical scholarship (1960, p. 3), resulting in a separation of the new scholarship from the 'old' Jewish learning. He holds that 'fundamentalism' is 'untenable', and in his writings he attempts to synthesize the insights of the scholar and the believer, to steer a path between a Jewish fundamentalism and a liberal Jewish humanism.

Jacobs describes his theological position as 'liberal supernaturalism' (1989, p. 261), and his theology as a *'true* Jewish apologetic' (1957, p. 11)—a synthesis of tradition and modernity based on a comprehensive examination of each of the two elements. This is vouchsafed by the assumption that *all* knowledge is God-given and the Truth is one (1973a, p. 4; 1960, p. 460). This 'true' apologetic rejects 'religious schizophrenia' or 'compartmentalism', and any 'premature cheap' synthesis.

Before looking at Jacobs's position it will be helpful to consider something of his notions concerning the nature of religion in general, and these in relation to Judaism in particular. Jacobs was greatly influenced by the History of Religions scholarship of the 1950s and 1960s, which tended to emphasis the similarity of religious traditions, usually by stressing their supposed universalistic characteristics. These aspects were held to be more fundamental, at this time, than other divergent elements. This tradition—'liberal apologetics'—based on a creative method of selective proof-texting, made a distinction between lower and higher forms, identifying the latter with contemporary, acceptable liberal positions. Religious traditions were to be evaluated and presented in terms of their 'highest expressions'. These tendencies can be discerned to some extent in Jacobs's writings. He identifies rabbinic and Hasidic doctrines with universalistic,[1] Indian and Chinese positions,[2] and considers Judaism as a form of universal theism;[3] Hasidism as a form of universal mysticism;[4] Jewish ethics as universalistic;[5] and he successfully isolates the 'lower' from the 'higher' elements within the tradition.[6]

---

1. 1960, p. 123; 1957, p. 131; 1968, pp. vii, 62, 173.
2. 1976, pp. 156-57; 1960, pp. 113, 116; 1975, p. 79.
3. 1960, pp. 7, 68; 1964, p. 366; 1968, pp. 127, 173.
4. 1960, p. 114; 1968.
5. 1957, pp. 69, 91, 131; 1978.
6. 1957, pp. 120-21, 131; 1960, pp. 39f., 67f.; 1964, pp. 364, 456, 1968, pp. 83, 176ff.; 1973, x.

A related view concerns the nature of Judaism. Jacobs draws from a wide range of Jewish sources and warns against a narrow interpretation of Judaism,[1] an account which would eliminate some of the greatest Jewish thinkers from the tradition.[2] He stresses the past plethora of Jewish voices, often contradictory, although tending to regard them as secondary to the positions of 'normative Judaism'.[3] However, too frequently, it would seem to me, these are reduced to only two, and Jacobs advocates that the normative position lies in the tension between them.[4] These various Jewish positions additionally require 'demythologizing' and re-interpretation as they are almost all based on notions of *Torah* that are 'fundamentalistic'.[5] Yet Jacobs remains one of the few Jewish liberals, in the above sense, who finds great theological value and inspiration in the thought of the widest variety of past Jewish thinkers.[6]

An examination of Jacobs's conceptual and analytic distinctions—variations of the problematic fact-value distinction—is valuable in understanding his notion of Jewish theology. He clearly distinguishes theology from scholarship. Scholarship has no natural object and is without presuppositions, yielding objective *facts* after the systematic assessment of the available evidence 'in which the truth is followed wherever it may lead' (1960, p. 27). It can equally well be undertaken by believers or unbelievers 'and like the physical sciences is neutral so far as faith is concerned' (1988, p. vii). Scholarship provides the benchmark against which traditionally held *facts* are to be evaluated, and when found wanting must be rejected or subjected to re-interpretation: 'The discovery of what happened in Jewish and world history is a matter of scholarship not faith, for historians, philologists, literary

---

1. Jacobs warns us 'how precarious it is to speak of *the* Jewish attitude to complicated moral, ethical and religious problems, as if there were only one attitude' (1982, p. 300). See also, 1960, pp. 9, 148; 1968, p. 174; 1975, p. 81; 1988a, p. vii.

2. See, 1973, p. 1; and Jacobs's Preface to Lawrence Fine, *Safed Spirituality* (New York: Paulist Press, 1984): ix.

3. Jacobs rejects the idea of an essence of Judaism but considers it to be an 'undeniable fact that for all the variety of moods in Judaism's history there does emerge. . . a kind of consensus of the main issues' (1974, p. 9); see 1966, p. 89; 1984c, p. 89.

4. 1957, p. 20; 1968, pp. 176ff; 1973a, pp. 21, 72, 78-80; 1979, p. 157; 1987b, p. 297.

5. See 1968, p. 167; 1964, pp. 189-90; 1981b, pp. 216, 194; 1988a, p. vii.

6. Cf. 1987b, p. 234.

critics, and anthropologists, not for theologians *qua* theologians' (1987b, p. 237).

Theology, however, does have a particular 'object'—God. And it holds prior suppositions, namely 'that God is' and that He reveals Himself in 'revelation'.[1] 'Jewish theology' is the critical and systematic presentation of Jewish teaching (1973a, p. 1). Theology is subjective in that it is an activity for believers (1973a, p. 1)—'it was never a question of examining the sources of Judaism in an objective manner in order to discover the basic principles of Judaism' (1964, p. 9), rather, it is a response to the challenges of contemporary thought.[2] Jewish theology has its origins in the Middle Ages with the systematization of the tradition by the Jewish medieval philosophers as its definitive model and contemporary Jewish theology is understood to be a continuation of this 'quest', ultimately for beliefs that are 'both Jewish and true' (1973a, p. 8). He insists that theology is concerned solely with *beliefs* and not with practice, although the beliefs that underlie practice are theological (1964, p. 292; 1973a, p. 12).[3]

1. Cf. 'The *given* things are the existence of God and the belief that the Torah contains the revelation of His Will' (1960, p. 25); 1973, p. 16; Also, 'the modern believer *will refuse* to challenge' that God revealed Himself to man (1964, pp. 219, 240).

2. 'Jewish theology differs from other branches of Jewish learning in that practioners are personally committed to the truth they are seeking to explore' (1973a, p. 1). It is important to note that Jacobs (1964; 1968), whilst recognizing a subjective element in theology, at that time understood (linguistic) philosophy as 'objective', and on the basis of his analytical distinction (factual and interpretive beliefs) considered that theology could be pursued 'objectively'. Later, he rejected this view but still considered the distinction to be valuable (1988a, p. vii) and continued to use it (1987b, pp. 235-37). After (1973a) Jacobs tended to stress the subjective element in theology, e.g. when distinguishing theology from halakhic deliberation,. . . but matters of belief in all their complexity demand the free response of the individual human personality' (1974, p. 345). Jacobs defines Jewish philosophy in much the same way as Jewish theology (1969, p. 53), although he often limits 'philosophy' to the Middle Ages. It is not always easy to grasp his criteria for this distinction as he refers to Baeck, Cohen, Buber and Rosenzweig as philosophers (1984d, pp. 84-85).

3. For Jacobs, regarding the details of Jewish observance, or specifics relating to Jewish ethics, 'theology cannot provide detailed practical solutions to the problems facing the Jews (it can only). . . foster certain attitudes which, from the theological point of view, are sounder than others' (1973a, p. 281). For example, concerning the challenges raised by the State of Israel, he argues: against a 'crude interpretation of the notion of "sacred soil" '; that 'Hebrew culture is not *Torah*'; and, that 'Jewish nationhood is no substitute for religion' (1973a, p. 281). In (1982), Jacobs advo-

The most significant aspect of Jacobs's notion of theology, what distinguishes it from earlier modern attempts at formulating a Jewish theology, is a much more explicit understanding of theology as a 'way of speaking'. He is influenced by Christian theological reflections formulated in light of the insights drawn from the then contemporary philosophy of language. Theology is essentially a non-factual 'language', or a 'language-game' for conveying and discussing (religious) values. In this regard, it is important to note Jacobs's frequent use of the rabbinic 'as it were' when 'speaking theologically', and the frequent qualifications, such as, 'in theological language, God really did command Jews' (1984a, pp. 245-46). God's command is not to be understood as a 'fact' of the same order as a 'scientific fact'. The issue here is that the truths expressed theologically are a different order of 'truths', and not merely theological language expressing truths in different ways—theology as a different order of expression. Theology, for Jacobs, is what we might call the non-factual language of belief.

The theologian, guided by scholarship, attempts to formulate what a Jew can believe today, based on 'consistency with the tradition and coherence with the rest of our knowledge' (1973a, p. 14). Jacobs's belief in the objectivity of scholarship paves the way for his theological method. The theologian examines a particular issue. He begins with the Bible and traces its development through the rabbinic, philosophical, mystic and Ḥasidic sources, in the light of contemporary knowledge (1973a, p. 13; 1987b, p. 233). On this basis, Jacobs considers that he can objectively 'describe' the past in terms of its then-contemporary meaning and *subsequently* 'evaluate' this meaning in terms of current concerns (cf. 1978, p. 41).

Jacobs contends that our belief in revelation is not challenged by biblical criticism but only that this belief must be re-interpreted. It is not that 'the Bible itself is revelation' (1964, p. 270) but that it is the 'record of revelation'. This biblical record is a human product but one which 'contains' divine revelation. The Bible consists of both, revelation (the unchanging 'permanent truths', divine in origin and immune to history), and the *human* interpretations of these truths (subject to

cates a non-literal interpretation of the claim that *Eretz Yisrael* is the divinely promised land, understanding it as 'promised' only by historical experiences and association. He also warns against the use of messianic language in the context of present Israel; offers a plea for an 'enriched universalism' as opposed to the dangerous implications of limiting the message of Judaism to the Jews; and questions the elevation of the state as a Jewish ideal.

the historical conditions of their formation and error). If the biblical text is the product of human interpretations, even if the humanly mediated experience of *the divine*, Jacobs asks, what are criteria for distinguishing the divine from the human in the Bible and its interpretation?[1]

The above question is answered, in part, by his analytic distinction between two types of belief that one can hold concerning traditional claims—'factual beliefs' and 'interpretive beliefs'.[2] The former are concerned with the 'material world' and can be contradicted by new factual knowledge, and would include beliefs such as: the Mosaic authorship of the Pentateuch; the age of the world; the unity of the book of Isaiah. These beliefs are based on traditional opinions about facts and when they are contradicted, must be abandoned. The latter cannot be so contradicted and are concerned with 'the meaning of human life' (1964, p. 460), and would include beliefs such as: the belief in God; His self-revelation to Israel; Israel's special role; the immortality of the soul; that man is to be righteous, just and compassionate. Jacobs writes:

> The interpretive beliefs, which are those of most fundamental significance, have not changed and it is here that the continuity of Jewish belief is assured. . . Divine revelation is confined to the interpretive beliefs, which are true for all time, and not the factual beliefs which are always open to revision' (1964, p. 462).

Jacobs characterizes the interpretive belief that God exists as a 'way of looking at the world' (1987b, p. 235) and understands that such beliefs are to be held in light of 'the best possible explanation of the facts as a whole' (1964, p. 460). Past beliefs, which were taken by the tradition to be factual but are subsequently contradicted by 'new facts', are to be rejected (1964, p. 460; 1987b, p. 236), and the traditional interpretation of factual beliefs is to be accepted 'until the application of tried methods of investigation renders the traditional account implausible' (1987b, p. 237). So, for example, Jacobs holds that God

---

1. Jacobs, very much along the lines of Maimonides' 'negative' theology, has little 'positive' to say about God, and considers that the purpose of theology is to 'refine the God concept so that more and more is understood of how God is wholly other' (1973a, p. 3).

2. Jacobs also uses the approach of linguistic philosophy to good effect in his treatment of the goodness of God (1964, p. 67) and in his application to the distinction between 'belief in' and 'belief that' (1968, pp. 3-18).

really did reveal Himself to his servant Moses (an interpretive belief), and that, without factual evidence to the contrary, we can accept the traditional 'factual beliefs' concerning Moses and the Exodus (1964, pp. 210-11; 1987b, p. 235). On this basis, he contends that we can distinguish between which 'traditional formulations about historical events are true to the facts and which are ficticious, mythical or speculative' (1987b, p. 237).[1]

How can we be sure that our interpretive beliefs are divine revelation? Jacobs is certain that 'there can be no Judaism without revelation' (1964, pp. 219, 240, 281)—but what is it that has been revealed? Influenced by Martin Buber, he holds that the Bible is a unique record of the encounter between God and humanity. This 'intensely personal meeting with God' (1973a, p. 208) is in itself essentially contentless. It is 'the Self-disclosure of God Himself' (1973a, p. 214)—'an event'. Jacobs writes, 'We hear the authentic voice of God speaking to us through the pages of the Bible' (1957, p. 82), and he understands the content of revelation to be the human response to this meeting in thought and deed. The uniqueness of the message, recorded in response to the original encounters, appreciated by us in our reading of the Bible, awakens 'our higher natures', in particular, the exercise of our human reason by way of a response. We are, thus, he argues, able to discern the genuine Word of God by reading the Bible in the 'spirit of reverence' demanded by this awakening of our 'higher natures'. In addition, the biblical teachings are unique in a number of ways in that, unlike the now lost texts of other ancient cultures (1968, p. 107), they 'gave rise to the eternal truths by which man [sic] can live' (1964, p. 270); in the extend of their influence as indicated by the acceptance of the Bible as revelation by 'a large proportion of mankind' (1968, pp. 107-108); in their unparalleled 'lofty' message of 'world peace, of holiness, justice and mercy, (and) of freedom' and, in

---

1. In (1973a) he presents his position on the 'record of revelation' a little differently, 'In a sense it (the *Torah*) is *all human* (in that the record was produced by human beings and can be studied and examined by the methods by which other works of human genius are studied). In another sense it is *all divine* (in that it is a unique record of God's encounter with man)' (1973a, p. 215). He also appears less confident, 'Once it is recognised that there is a human element in the the Torah it must be seen that there is no simple method by means of which this can be distinguished, as it were, from the divine element'. However, he continues to employ criteria to make just such judgements, and in these he implicitly utilizes the factual-interpretive distinction, and in later works (1987a; 1988b), he returns to its explicit use.

their 'civilizing influence'. Jacobs considers that these factors are 'impossible to account for. . . unless Israel *really met* with God'. Thus, he argues, we have good reasons for believing that the Bible conveys the divine 'encounter'.

In order to overcome the difficulty of clashes between interpretive beliefs, Jacobs postulates a hierarchy of such beliefs with the 'less significant' giving way to the 'more significant', such as the belief in eternal punishment (incapable of being contradicted by new facts) giving way to the 'more significant interpretive belief in the goodness of God' (1964, p. 464). The less significant are held to be 'human' in origin and 'pass into oblivion' in the tradition. He argues for a sort of dialectic by which exposure to the tradition, based on revelation, shapes the Jewish character (1960, p. 26) and guides the Jew in the discernment of the human from the divine—'Thus the power to discern and its cultivation are themselves part of *Torah*' (1960, p. 26).

Jacobs's model of discernment gives him nine eternal, divinely revealed, biblical truths:

> God is One; there are no other gods; God is a Being who is holy and just and who demands these qualities of man; the people of Israel have a significant role to play in the fulfilment of God's purpose; the Sabbath is His witness, testifying to His creative power; the strong and the fortunately placed must help the weak and unfortunate; God cannot bear the sight of evil and wishes those who serve Him to combat evil; God is constantly at work in human history of which He is Lord; those who trust in him shall be blessed (1964, pp. 271-72).[1]

The encounter with God assumes a particular and central position in Jacobs's theology. As we can no longer be certain of God's existence in the old circular fashion through the details given in scripture, the encounter itself is now the very foundation of Judaism. While he recognizes that belief in God is an interpretive belief and thus cannot be factually demonstrated, he goes to great lengths to argue for the plausibility of the belief by countering objections, and concludes that 'theism makes the (best) sense of the universe and human experience in it' (1964, p. 45). It is almost as if the belief in God is required independently to justify the claims that scripture contains the genuine record of revelation, a reversal of the traditional position—'If a man

---

1. A variant account of the 'principles of contemporary Jewish faith' is found in 1964, pp. 459-60.

believes in God he cannot help but see that it is in *this* book, or better collection of books, that He revealed Himself to man' (1964, p. 271).

Jacobs writes: 'God still speaks to us but through the distortions of the human record' (1973a, p. 214) as recorded in the historical experiences of the Jewish people. Tradition plays a central role as the vehicle for the transmission of the record of the divine–human, and, as revelation is contained in this record, of revelation itself. Our faith in revelation is 'ultimately faith in tradition. . . the faith that men in the past. . . have claimed to have met a Being who endowed their lives with moral worth and signficance' (1968, p. 99). But, Jacobs insists, 'since tradition can be mistaken, it is indeed, never an adequate guide to belief' (1964, p. 460). 'We don't argue that the belief is true because it is in the tradition, but we can appreciate that the belief is in the tradition because it is true' (1968, p. 100). He advocates the formulation of 'a creative Jewish theology. . . built on the idea of a 'command' through man, of God, as it were giving the Torah not so much *to* Israel as *through* Israel' (1973a, p. 206), an idea that he claims is not 'entirely foreign' to the rabbinic tradition. Our approach to tradition, as with the Bible, is by extension, to be a process of sifting the sources in the attempt to distinguish the divine from the human. In the light of modern scholarship, 'the Oral Law has a history' (1964, pp. 281, 291).

While the notion of the divine–human encounter and the historical reflection upon its nature can plausibly provide the foundation for a model for the history of religious belief (theology), such a model may be equally applicable to any religious tradition that is textually ('record of revelation') based. Jewish 'religious practice' presents the Jew with a particular problem. How does one move from an 'intensely personal meeting with God, of which the Bible is the record, to the full acceptance of the detailed laws?' (1973a, p. 208) Here Jacobs departs from Buber's position that 'encounter' does not give rise to 'commandment', and follows a path closer to that of Rosenzweig where revelation as 'event' does entail just such a command. The 'Word of God' is experienced in the form of God's 'command—'they have come down to us pregnant with the imperatives of the divine' (1964, p. 272), and 'is part of the life that man has to lead if the covenant between him and God is to be realized' (1973a, p. 205). He accepts that the practices based on interpretive beliefs, such as 'loving one's neighbour' and those based on justice, compassion, peace, truth, honesty and familial obligations (1964, p. 460) can be accepted as

God's Will. But can we be certain, he asks, that God commands us to keep the dietary laws or to observe the traditional Sabbath (1973a, p. 215), as these are based on the factual belief that the details of the observances were divinely communicated (1964, p. 461)? He rightly sees this move as a 'vast step' to a binding *halakhah* based on a non-fundamentalist approach (1984a, p. 245). The new view of revelation raises an unprecedented question—not the 'why did God tell us to keep certain *mitzvot*?' of the Middle Ages, but, 'Did God tell us to keep certain *mitzvot*?' (1973a, p. 214; 1984a, p. 232).

Although the precise details of Jewish observance are beyond the scope of theology as defined by Jacobs, the basis for Jewish practice is a theological question. He understands the history of Jewish observance as a history of the divine–human encounter and attempts to secure a middle position between the position of the fundamentalist (divinely sanctioned in every detail) and the naturalist (elevating practices sanctioned by Jewish history) by the application of what he calls the 'theological' approach (1968, p. 165; 1973a, p. 224). This approach calls for the theologian to be aware of the scholarly researches into the factual beliefs pertaining to the origins and history of Jewish practices, although the sanction for such practices is not based on scholarship but on faith (1964, pp. 292-93). Jacobs draws a 'fundamental distinction' between 'theory and practice':

> Theories as to the facts obviously require revision when new facts are discovered which demand a revision of the old theory. Practices, however, even when they are based on theories which are later seen to be unsound, may come to possess a value quite independent of the original theories. It can be shown that even those practices based on factual beliefs can and have become (or, at least, many of them have) vehicles for the values expressed in the basic interpretive beliefs. Judaism is an historical religion. The significance of its institutions are due in large measure to the value they have come to express in Jewish life, particularly the religious values through which man is brought nearer to God (1964, pp. 460-61).

Jacobs contends that faith, in the Jewish tradition, is inherently manifest as action, sanctioned, as it were, by the Will of God. The Sabbath, for example, even if based on the 'erroneous' Genesis account of the evolution of the world and whatever its historical origins, still conveys 'the eternal truth that God is the Creator of the Universe'. And to observe the Sabbath is a weekly affirmation and acknowledgment of this truth—'God has commanded Israel to keep the Sabbath' (1968, pp. 168f.). Similarly, the dietary laws are understood as an expression of the recognition of God even in the fulfilment of bodily desires, and circumcision is the 'initiation of new-born males into Israel's dedicatory service of God' (1968, pp. 168f.).

Jacobs also refers to the structure of observances as the 'vocabulary' or 'language of worship'—'the way in which the people of the covenant relives and reaffirms the covenant' (1973a, p. 205), and holds that:

> The precepts of the *Torah* are binding because they provide the vocabulary of worship. . . God did command not by direct communication—as in the traditional view—but through the historical experiences of the Jewish people (1973a, p. 206).

Jewish religious practices have 'evolved' out of Israel's experience, and Jacobs sees the 'hand of God in all this'—'We believe in the God who speaks to us out of Israel's experience. . . God reveals Himself through the community of Israel' (1973a, p. 223). He argues that, 'The sanction for the *mitzvot* is that they succeed in bringing men to God. Because they do this they are commanded by God' (1973a, p. 226). Religious observance as reflected in Israel's history, has, in and through that history, 'become' the Will of God, and is binding on that basis—'The historical experience of the people of Israel . . . serves as (the) source of authority, under God, for Jewish observance' (1964, p. 466).

The most significant element of Jacobs's reinterpretation of the traditional conception of *halakhah* is his contention that it is not the traditional practices themselves but the religious values embedded in these halakhic institutions, that bring humanity closer to God. The 'spiritual power' of an observance is dependent upon its capacity to manifest or convey the underlying religious value. This view not only challenges the traditional sanction for the binding nature of Jewish observance but provides a basis for distinguishing binding practices from those that may no longer be so. A particular practice is binding when the underlying value is promoted, and questionable when this appears not to be the case, when considered in the light of the experience of the people Israel, shaped by their exposure to *Torah*. Jacobs insists, that as the tradition contains both 'truth and error', the *halakhah* is not monolithic, and, therefore, the rejection of a particular practice is not to be understood as a rejection of the whole (1968, p. 167).[1]

Jacobs is the author of a number of studies on the Talmud and halakhic literature which reflect his model of a new Jewish '*lernen*':

> There have undoubtedly emerged two vastly different worlds of Jewish studies, the world of the *Yeshivot* indifferent or even hostile to critical scholarship and the world of modern learning with no formal interest in study as an act of religious work. To date there has been little meeting between these two worlds (1984b, p. 270).

The breach between these two approaches has, he claims, undermined the *Torah* and its study. Jacobs calls for a new type of *talmid ḥakham*, who would synthesize in the new Jewish studies the 'accuracy and objectivity of the critical scholar' (1957, p. 103) and 'the attitude of reverence, commitment, textual understanding and faith' of the traditional scholar (1960, p. 26). On the basis of such a synthesis, he writes:

> The study of *Torah* will once again flourish as one of the most sublime of Jewish values (and) *Torah lishmah* will again be as relevant today as it was in the past (1960, pp. 27-28).

Although he has the highest regard for the depth of insights and reverence displayed in traditional devotional learning, Jacobs argues that its creativity and centrality in Jewish life have been severely compromised by the inability of its practitioners to confront the challenges of contemporary scholarship. There are two aspects to his programme, logic and methodology.

He is concerned, in the former, with the attempt at delineating the 'logic' of Talmudic argument. In a series of innovative, masterful and tantalizingly brief articles, Jacobs seeks to systematically present the

---

1. In (1973a), he categorizes practices in terms of their promotion of underlying Jewish values (1973a, pp. 226-30): the significant (e.g. the dietary laws, Sabbath and festival observance); the meaningless (e.g. the prohibition against shaving with a razor); and, the harmful (where values such as justice are threatened, e.g. the laws relating to *agunah* and *mamzer*). Jacobs's position is similar in a number of important respects to those of Zacharias Frankel (the distinction between God's Will to Israel, and the religious form of the expression of that Will); Louis Ginzberg (the notion of 'faith in action' [Ginzberg, 1958, pp. 195-216]); and, Solomon Schechter (the notions of the secondary sense of scripture, and *Klal Yisrael* (Schechter, 1945, pp. xviiff.); in all these cases, however, Jacobs operates with a quite different notion of theology, and as he quite rightly claims, he is building on their foundations.

indigenous forms of rabbinic thinking. He promisingly compares the Talmudic classification of different procedures of formal argument with established Western forms of logical argument (1961, pp. 3-50). Jacobs extends this comparative and classificatory exercise to attempt a comprehensive enumeration of the rabbinic classification of 'forms of reasoning' as found 'consistently' and in a 'stereotyped' fashion in the Babylonian Talmud, and explicates them by means of the interpretation of textual examples (1974).[1] In *The Talmudic Argument* (1984b), he distinguishes between arguments of 'pure reason' and those of 'factual interpretation', and highlights the range of such arguments, such as those based on the analysis of states of mind (1984b, pp. 1-18).

What is significant about Jacobs's work, and unlike almost all modern scholarship in this area, which tends to follow the post-Talmudic stress on the terms rather than the forms of argument, is his attempt to utilize the 'logical analysis' of materials found in traditional modes of study in the context of modern systematic modes of explanation and classification. These efforts, however, have been restricted to the explication of Talmudic argumentative forms, and are limited in that Jacobs has not sought to develop his analysis beyond an exercise in classification towards a model of 'rationality' (or rationalities), internal, as it were, to Judaism. One can only hope that in future work he will return to the comparative analysis of indigenious Jewish and Western reasoning, for a comprehensive study of the structures of Jewish rationality and Jewish debate is much needed in order for us to have any adequate understanding of Judaism.[2]

Jacobs's concern with methodology is found in his application of the methods of literary analysis and 'higher criticism' to the structure of the Babylonian Talmud in order to discern how the text 'came to its present form' (1984b, p. x). In this way he undermines the traditional portrayal of the Talmud as the 'verbatim reports of discussions which took place in the Babylonian schools' (1961, pp. vii, 132ff.). His examination of the literary style of the *sugya* as an 'artificial' structuring of earlier materials for 'dramatic effect' (1961, p. 127), leads him to conclude that the old view needs to be 'dramatically revised' (1961, p. 54), and that consequently the text as a whole is 'a "contrived" product of great skill in which the older material used has been

---

1. See also, 1971; 1972; 1973c; 1977.
2. I am currently working on this theme for a study, provisionally entitled, *The Jewish Logos: Athens and Jerusalem Revisited.*

reshaped' (1984b, pp. 18-23), and in which a number of 'strata' (1961, p. 70) can be identified. He isolates not only examples of 'editorial amplification' but also the use of 'literary devices' (1961, pp. 53-69). The radical revision that he calls for is not just that the Talmud evidences literary structuring and is the work of 'creative artists'—that the Talmud has a literary framework—but that the 'framework is the Talmud' (1984b, p. 21). He contends further, that this framework shapes not only the verbal form (e.g. 1984b, pp. 50-63) but also the ideas (1984b, p. 203).[1]

The Babylonian Talmud, constructed by the reworking of existing and then contemporary materials, with later additions, along stereo-typific lines with a logical progression of arguments, is a 'unique' literary text which creates the 'sense of immediacy' (1984b, p. 206) that scholars subsequently have entered into. It is this that has given rise to its dominance and centrality in the history of Judaism. Jacobs insists that the new view of the Talmud only enhances its importance as the most creative and unique record of the divine–human encounter in history.

Jacobs has continually emphasised the importance of linking his studies of logic and methodology, particularly in relation to the literary structuring of Talmudic debates and the ways in which the 'logical' traditional Talmudic interpretation is enhanced by an awareness of the text's literary construction. He draws on his *yeshivah* training and its well established tradition of the explication of textual meaning by means of conceptual analysis, and combines this mode of

---

1. One such device, the conclusion that a specific definitional problem cannot be solved by reference to earlier authorities but is 'unsolved' (*teyku*), is explored in his 1981 volume. Jacobs highlights the stereotypic form of these discussions, and that there is no clear evidence that the form in which we find this literary structure is in the form of the original propounder (1981a, p. 292). He concludes that the editors did not merely supply the conclusion (unsolved) as an external device to existing materials (although earlier problems were doubtlessly utilized), but that the *teyku* conclusion is an inherent part of the literary framework of the discussions themselves, that is, it is part of their literary shaping of the text as a whole (1981a, p. 290). Jacobs examines the *Responsa* literature (1975) and amid its legally precise formulations discerns a valuable source of 'theology'. He argues that the same precision, form, methods and sources, are utilized to decide issues of action as are employed in the discussion of matters of belief. Elsewhere (1981d), Jacobs examines an aggadic Talmudic passage and demonstrates that the nature of Talmudic literature shapes both halakhic and aggadic materials in similar ways. On this basis, he cautions against using aggadic materials in any reconstruction of the theological views of the rabbis without due reference to the literary structuring of the material (cf. 1989, p. 263).

analysis and interpretation with the new picture of the evolution of the completed text. Unlike most scholars working on the redaction of the Talmud, he is interested both in the literary form and the 'religious' interpretation or meaning of the text. The importance of his work on the Babylonian Talmud lies in his efforts to combine successfully the two approaches.

In *A Tree of Life* (1984), Jacobs brings together his theological concerns, particularly in relation to the 'theology' of observance, and his critical and historical studies in the literature of the *halakhah*. He writes:

> The central thesis of this book is that the *Halakhah*—the legal side of Judaism—far from being entirely self-sufficient and self-authenticating, is influenced by the attitudes, conscious or unconscious, of its practitioners towards the wider demands and ideas of Judaism and by social, economic, theological and practical conditions that occur when the ostensibly purely legal norms and methodology are developed (1984a, p. 9).

In this study of post-Talmudic *halakhah* the author attacks the view, prevalent among wide sections of Orthodoxy, that the Jewish law is a closed legal system operating solely within its own parameters by a process of deduction based on the infallibility of scripture and of the Talmudic rabbis. Jacobs traces the way, in the Talmud, a literary text, much of which is in the form of 'academic' exercises, became the authoritative source text of halakhic materials and the basis for legal rulings (1984a, p. 25). He selectively traces the extra-legal determinative influences on halakhists—ethical, psychological, philosophical, logical; the influence of the *Kabbalah* and mysticism; the conditions in the gentile world, and socio-economic realities—and highlights the ways in which these influences are expressed in terms of halakhic sources and procedures. He argues that 'Jewish law has the strongest religious dimension' (1984a, p. 182), and that the 'rules and regulations of the *halakhah* became vehicles for the expression of general Jewish values', and we find, *'the reading of such values into the law and details of the law'* (1984a, p. 34). Although the halakhic texts themselves perpetuate the 'myth' of a purely deductive system, the rabbis did not, and do not, approach legal questions in an open fashion but form conclusions based on 'Jewish ideas and ideals' (1984a, p. 11) and *only then* construct their halakhic case.

The 'diversity, flexibility and creativity' of the *halakhah* has been historically ensured by these procedures but is presently under threat from the fundamentalist camp. Jacobs's argument is that, if in the past 'the dynamic Halakhic spirit' was maintained without being dependent upon a fundamentalist view of revelation and inspiration, it can be maintained in the future without such recourse.

A Tree of Life represents Jacobs's most complete statement of his non-fundamentalist 'philosophy of *halakhah*' to date. Unlike his earlier work on this question, here he stresses the notion of 'Oral Law', which he holds has always recognised the human element in revelation (*Torah*), as the foundation for such a non-fundamentalist approach, 'the *Halakhah* has always possessed the vitality to assimilate new knowledge' (1984a, p. 246). The Talmud and halakhic literature as the record of 'the complex divine–human encounter' (1984a, p. 238) represent an 'attempt to bring holiness into the detailed affairs of life in the corporeal world' (1984a, p. 242) and this attempt 'has its roots and expression in the whole life of the community' (1984a, p. 249). Revelation entails a 'command'—'in theological language, God really did command Jews' (1984a, pp. 245-46). For Jacobs, this command is not based on a factual belief but vouchsafed by the history of those who have responded by acting in accordance with the divine imperative, and the command is 'conveyed through the divine human encounter in Jewish history'. In relation to specific commandments he writes:

> The ultimate authority for determining which observances are binding on the faithful Jew is the historical experience of the people of Israel, since historically perceived, this is ultimately the sanction of the *Halakhah* itself, which as we have seen, originated and developed as result of Israel's experiences (1984a, pp. 245-46).

This statement, as it stands, is very close to the position of a number of Conservative thinkers, particularly Ginzberg and Schechter, and his own earlier writings,[1] and as such it is subject to the same criticism in relation to specific decisions concerning specific practices, but it must be considered in the light of Jacobs's view of the *halakhah*. He understands the *halakhah* to be a dynamic, 'theological' system conveyed through legal forms, whose creativity and development have been

---

1. Cf. p. 207 n. 1 above. Jacobs's position can be distinguished from the major Conservative thinkers; see, e.g. Robert Gordis, *A Faith for Moderns* (New York: Bloch, 1960), pp. 136-59; *Judaism for the Modern Age* (New York: Farrar, Straus, Cudahy, 1955), pp. 153-66; 'A Dynamic *Halakhah*: Principles and Procedures of Jewish Law', *Judaism* 28 (1975): 263-82, where Gordis argues that sociology is an integral element in the *Halakhah*.

misunderstood by being conceived in purely legal terms. This is not a claim for the relevance of sociological and other external factors in the making of legal decisions, but rather that a variety of issues beyond the specifically halakhic have always been factors in such rulings. When we understand the nature of the halakhic process, we can rediscover, he argues, the demonstrable creativity and flexibility of the *halakhah*, in order to respond halakhically to changed conditions. In light of his position, the stress in the above quotation should not be on 'the historical experience of the people of Israel' but on 'the sanction of the *Halakhah*'. Jacobs is not advocating that the community of Israel decides that such-and-such a practice is to be re-interpreted, ammended in some fashion, or suspended, but that there is a revival of the traditional way of deciding such issues. The rabbis as halakhists, on recognizing the true nature of the halakhic process as the principal vehicle for the expression of past and contemporary Jewish values, will recover its creativity and flexibility by '*the reading of such values into the law and the details of the law*' (1984a, p. 34).[1]

Unlike his Talmudic studies where the text is 'fixed', here, as with his other 'theological' works, the selection of sources is of paramount importance to the argument as a whole. However, although somewhat problematic on these grounds, *A Tree of Life* represents an inspired and sustained scholarly attempt at a thematic history of the *halakhah*, and on that basis, the formulation of a coherent and cogent foundations for a 'theology of *halakhah*'. Jacobs does not consider it to be a final statement or a 'blueprint for the future' (1984a, p. 246), and recognises that a thorough historical study of Jewish practices is still required, on which such a 'theology' might be based.

Animating Jacobs's work is the notion of 'quest':

> Once the idea is accepted that the quest for *Torah* is itself *Torah*. The Jewish idea of *Torah* study for its own sake is as relevant today as it was in the past and one that is fully compatible with the most objective approach in which the truth is followed wherever it may lead' (1960, p. 27).

This broadening out of the concept of *Torah* to include scholarship and theology combined in the new *lernen*, is fundamental for Jacobs. *Torah* is never fixed, and the quest, endlessly renewed and revived by each Jew and each generation, is not separate from *Torah* but an inte-

---

1. A similar notion is found in the works of the Orthodox thinker, Eliezer Berkovits, *Not in Heaven* (New York: Ktav, 1983).

gral part of it. Judaism is the response of the Jewish people in their quest for *Torah*—the attempt to live and think their tradition in an endless series of contemporary situations. The principal aspect of this quest is its dynamic nature which is ensured by maintaining the broadest view of variety of past Jewish thinking—'modern Jews are heirs to it all and can draw on all these teachings' (1968, p. 174).

The great danger in the history of Judaism has been the attempt to thwart this dynamism and call a halt to the quest. We do not need, Jacobs contends, a system—a 'strong hand'—such as that of Maimonides' Mishneh Torah. Biblical and Talmudic fundamentalism represent the end of the quest and subsequent loss of the inherent dynamism of the tradition as a whole. He contends that the fundamentalist is 'weary of the quest for religious truth', and 'has a deep psychological need to have *found*—to rest secure in uncomplicated doctrine divinely guaranteed to be free from error' (1988b, p. 223). Here, *found* is the very antithesis of *quest*.

On the basis of his historical and theological researches, Jacobs has sought to work out the implications of our new 'factual' knowledge for our understanding of the tradition. His work never loses sight of the texts upon which the Jewish tradition is based, and his expositions of the sources are unparalleled in the current literature. In accord with his views on the nature of the objectivity of scholarship, Jacobs has produced a compelling and plausible portrayal of a dynamic Judaism. His immense learning has been harnessed in the service of the formulation of a powerful, contemporary, defence of traditional Judaism, offering Jews not only a theology (a guide as to what they can believe) but the foundations of a theology of *halakhah* (a guide to practice).

Agreeing with Professor Jacobs, that the events of this century make it difficult to accept the Enlightenment notion of progress, I find it equally hard to accept the notion of objective progress in scholarship. These two notions appear to me to be intimately related. It is not that I want, for example, to argue that Moses *did* receive the *Torah* directly as dictated by God, only that this is a particular historically conditioned way of portraying this event, and the alternative 'historical' account is but another historically conditioned form of portrayal. It is not merely a question of truth or falsity (there are, of course, conditions in which such an either/or does pertain), and even if we do privilege the historical, the issue does not have to be granted the centrality accorded it by Jacobs.

The sociological reality of a vibrant, observant, Orthodox Judaism, may well be indicative of a 'fear of freedom', but more importantly, it suggests a framework of understanding in which the question of the facticity of Mosaic revelation is not a major concern. Indeed, facticity, in a rational, Enlightenment sense, may not be a concern at all. It is significant that in recent Orthodox theologies. where the primary concern is the relationship of Judaism to modernity, this issue is conspicuous by its absence.[1] There is not only one order of beliefs or of truths. And reading back into the tradition anachronisitic notions of facticity may render traditional views based on quite different premises, as Heschel says, 'absurd'. If we do not accept modern rationality as absolute, it becomes much more difficult to discern the 'best thought of the day'. The capitulation of Jewish thinkers to the contemporary 'orthodoxy' of modern rationality precludes the possibility of Jewish thought opposing or offering a critique of modernity, or aspects thereof. Jacobs is correct in that we cannot return to the pre-critical age, but we can at least recognise the possibility that the Jewish tradition can challenge not only the prevailing 'lifestyle' but the foundations of contemporary thinking. What we require is not apologetics, however sophisticated, but Jewish thinking presented in terms of its own categories, or at very least, in Western categories but in the awareness of the underlying indigenous ones.

One might question Jacobs's distinction between theology and scholarship. His assumption that the exponents of *Wissenschaft des Judentums* were objective in the pursuit of their studies is questionable in light of their motivations concerning political emancipation, liturgical reform and so on. One might argue that just as the halakhist works out his ruling, and on that basis presents it in a halakhic form, so the historical scholar provides historical evidence for his insights and in accordance with the *Zeitgeist*. Just as one can marshal evidence for a Judaism largely in accord with the contemporary 'Christian' model of 'higher' religion, one could construct a case that highlighted the differences between Judaism and any such model. It is not that one cannot argue for, or construct, a synthesis of Judaism and modern knowledge, a synthesis most contemporary Jews are already living in one form or

---

1. See, for example, David Hartman, *A Living Covenant* (New York: Free Press, 1985); Jonathan Sacks, *Tradition in an Untraditional Age* (London; Vallentine Mitchell, 1990); and the essay in Rueven Bulka (ed.), *Dimensions of Orthodox Judaism* (New York: Ktav, 1983).

another, but rather that such a synthesis may finally be undesirable by demanding too much, supressing too much, and conceding too much.

Rabbi Dr Louis Jacobs is one of the very few thinkers from the Orthodox camp to have engaged in a sustained encounter with the findings of modern scholarship, bringing his great erudition in both modern and Jewish scholarship to this task. This dual expertise has given him a rare perspective on the possibilities of an accommodation between these two scholarly traditions. His deep understanding of the traditional Jewish sources has allowed him to perceive clearly the fundamental nature of the challenge to traditional Judaism posed by modern studies. This same expertise has opened up the possibility of a 'traditional' Judaism erected upon new historical foundations. The implications of Jacobs's research demand the most serious consideration. The issues raised so forcefully in his works have to be addressed by any scholar concerned with modern challenges to Judaism.

BIBLIOGRAPHY

Ginzberg, L.
1958   *Students, Scholars and Saints* (New York: Meridian).
Heschel, A.J.
1969   'Teaching Jewish Theology in the Solomon Schechter Day School', *The Synagogue School* 28, pp. 4-33.
Jacobs, L.
1957   *We Have Reason to Believe* (London: Vallentine, Mitchell).
1960   *Jewish Values* (London: Vallentine, Mitchell, 1960).
1961   *Studies in Talmudic Logic and Methodology* (London: Vallentine, Mitchell).
1964   *Principles of the Jewish Faith, An Analytical Study* (London: Vallentine, Mitchell).
1968   *Faith* (London: Vallentine, Mitchell).
1969   *Jewish Ethics, Philosophy and Mysticism*, The Chain of Tradition Series, 2 (New York: Behrman House).
1971   'Are There Fictitious Baraitot in the Babylonian Talmud?', *HUCA* 42, pp. 185-96.
1972   'The *qal va-homer* Argument in the Old Testament', *BSOAS* 35, Part 2, pp. 221-27.
1973a   *A Jewish Theology* (London: Darton, Longman and Todd).
1973b   *Hasidic Prayer*, The Littman Library of Jewish Civilization (New York: Schocken Books).
1973c   'The Talmudic *Sugya* as a Literary Unit', *JJS* 24/2, pp. 119-26.
1974   'Hermeneutics', *EJ*, VIII, pp. 366-72.

1975	'Jewish Cosmology', in *Ancient Cosmologies* (ed. C. Blacker and M. Loewe; London: George Allen and Unwin), pp. 66-86.
1975	*Theology in the Responsa*, The Littman Library of Jewish Civilization (London: Routledge and Kegan Paul).
1977	'How much of the Babylonian Talmud is Pseudepigraphic?', *JJS*, 28/1, pp. 46-59.
1978	' The Relationship between Religion and Ethics in Jewish Thought', in M. Kellner (ed.), *Contemporary Jewish Ethics* (New York: Sanhedrin).
1979	'Eating as an Act of Worship in Hasidic Thought', in *Studies in Jewish Religious and Intellectual History Presented to Alexander Altmann* (ed. S.S. Stein and R. Loewe; Alabama: University of Alabama Press), pp. 157-66.
1981a	*TEYKU: The Unsolved Problem in the Babylonian Talmud* (New Jersey: Cornwall Books, Leo Baeck College).
1981b	'Rabbi Aryeh Laib Heller's Theological Introduction to his *Shev Shema'tata'*, *Modern Judaism* 1, pp. 184-216.
1981c	'Zionism after 100 Years', in *Proceedings of the Rabbinical Assembly 1981* 43 (New York), pp. 56-63.
1981d	' The *Sugya* on Sufferings in B. *Berakhot* 5a-b', in *Studies in Memory of Joseph Heinemann* (ed. J.J. Petuchowski and E. Fleischer; Jerusalem), pp. 32-44.
1982	'Praying for the Downfall of the Wicked', *Modern Judaism* 2/3, pp. 297-310.
1984a	*A Tree of Life: Diversity, Flexibility and Creativity in Jewish Law*, The Littman Library of Jewish Civilization (Oxford: Oxford University Press).
1984b	*The Talmudic Argument* (Cambridge: Cambridge University Press).
1984c	*The Book of Jewish Belief* (New York: Behrman House).
1984d	' The Jewish Tradition', in *The World's Religious Traditions. Essays in Honour of Wilfred Cantwell Smith* (ed. F. Whaling; Edinburgh: T. and T. Clark), pp. 72-91.
1985	'Aspects of Scholem's Study of Hasidism', *MJ* 5/1, pp. 95-104.
1987a	'God', in *Contemporary Jewish Religious Thought* (ed. Arthur A. Cohen and Paul Mendes-Flohr; New York: Scribner's), pp. 291-98.
1987b	'Faith', in *Contemporary Jewish Religious Thought*, pp. 233-38.
1988a	*Principles of the Jewish Faith, An Analytical Study* (Northvale, NJ and London: Jason Aronson).
1988b	'World Jewish Fundamentalism', in *Survey of Jewish Affairs 1987* (ed. William Frankel; Associated University Presses), pp. 221-34.
1989	*Helping with Inquiries: An Autobiography* (London: Vallentine, Mitchell).

Marmur, D.

1982	*Beyond Survival* (London: Darton, Longman & Todd).

Novak, D.

1985	Review of L. Jacobs, *A Tree of Life* (1984), *The Journal of Religion*, pp. 210-12.

Rosenzweig, F.

1935	*Briefe* (ed. E. Rosenzweig; Berlin: Schocken).

Schechter, S.

1945	*Studies in Judaism* (Philadelphia: Jewish Publication Society of America).

A BIBLIOGRAPHY OF LOUIS JACOBS

A. Books

1. *Jewish Prayer* (London: Jewish Chronicle Publications, 1955; second edition, 1956; third edition, 1962).
2. *A Guide to Yom Kippur* (London: Jewish Chronicle Publications, 1957; second impression, 1960; third impression, 1966; fourth impression, 1969; fifth impression, 1969; second edition, 1983).
3. *A Guide to Rosh Ha-Shanah* (London: Jewish Chronicle Publications, 1959; second impression, 1962; third impression, 1969; second edition, 1983).
4. *We Have Reason to Believe* (London: Vallentine, Mitchell, 1957; second edition, 1962; third revised edition, 1965).
5. *Jewish Values* (London: Vallentine, Mitchell, 1960). Second edition (Hartford: Hartmore House, 1969). Limited edition reprint, *The Book of Jewish Values* (Chappaqua, New York: Rossell Books 1983).
6. *The Palm Tree of Deborah* by Moses Cordovero, translated from the Hebrew with an Introduction and notes (London: Vallentine, Mitchell, 1960); reprinted in hard cover and paperback (New York: Sepher Hermon Press, 1974).
7. *Studies in Talmudic Logic and Methodology* (London: Vallentine, Mitchell, 1961).
8. *The Jewish Festivals*, a miniature book (Worcester: Achille J. St Onge, 1961).
9. *Tract on Ecstasy* by Dobh Baer of Lubavitch, translated from the Hebrew with an Introduction and notes (London: Vallentine, Mitchell in conjunction with the Society for the Study of Jewish Theology, 1962). Limited reprint edition, *On Ecstasy. A Tract by Dobh Baer* (Chappaqua, New York: Rossell Books). French translation by Georges Levitte, *Lettre aux Hassidim sur l'extase* (Paris: Fayard, 1975).
10. *Principles of the Jewish Faith, An Analytical Study* (London: Vallentine, Mitchell, 1964). First American edition (New York: Basic Books, 1964). Special Commentary Classic edition (New York). Third American edition with a new Preface (Northvale, NJ and London: Jason Aronson, 1988).
11. *Faith* (London: Vallentine, Mitchell, 1968). American edition (New York: Basic Books).
12. *Seeker of Unity: The Life and Works of Aaron of Starosselje* (London: Vallentine, Mitchell, 1966). American edition (New York: Basic Books).
13. *Jewish Law*, The Chain of Tradition Series, 1 (New York: Behrman House, 1968).
14. *Jewish Ethics, Philosophy and Mysticism*, The Chain of Tradition Series, 2 (New York: Behrman House, 1969).
15. *Jewish Thought Today*, The Chain of Tradition Series, 3 (New York: Behrman House, 1970).
16. *Hasidic Prayer*, The Littman Library of Jewish Civilization (London: Routledge and Kegan Paul, 1972). First Schocken edition (New York: Schocken Books, 1973); second Schocken printing, 1973; Schocken paperback, 1975.

17. *The Way of the Jews* (Amersham, Bucks: Hulton Educational Publications, 1972; reprinted, 1975; second edition, 1980; reprinted, 1985).
18. *A Jewish Theology* (London: Darton, Longman and Todd, 1973). American edition in hard cover and paperback (New York: Behrman House, 1973).
19. *Jewish Biblical Exegesis*, The Chain of Tradition Series, 4 (New York: Behrman House, 1973).
20. *What Does Judaism Say About . . . ?* (Jerusalem: Keter, 1973); reprinted (New York: Quadrangle Books, The New York Times, 1973).
21. *Theology in the Responsa*, The Littman Library of Jewish Civilization (London: Routledge and Kegan Paul, 1975).
22. *Hasidic Thought*, The Chain of Tradition Series, 5 (New York: Behrman House, 1976).
23. *Jewish Mystical Testimonies* (Jerusalem: Keter, 1976). American edition in hard cover and paperback (New York: Schocken Books, 1977); latest impression, 1989.
24. *TEYKU: The Unsolved Problem in the Babylonian Talmud* (New Jersey: Cornwall Books, in conjunction with Leo Baeck College, 1981).
25. *A Tree of Life: Diversity, Flexibility and Creativity in Jewish Law*, The Littman Library of Jewish Civilization (Oxford: Oxford University Press, 1984).
26. *The Talmudic Argument* (Cambridge: Cambridge University Press, 1984).
27. *The Book of Jewish Belief* (New York: Behrman House, 1984).
28. *The Book of Jewish Practice* (West Orange, NJ: Behrman House, 1987).
29. *Helping with Inquiries: An Autobiography* (London: Vallentine, Mitchell, 1989).
30. *Holy Living; Saints and Saintliness in Judaism* (Northvale, NJ and London: Jason Aaronson, 1990).
31. *God, Torah, Israel: A Traditional but Non-Fundamentalist View*, The Efrayemson Lecture (Cincinnati: Hebrew Union College Press, 1990).
32. *The Encyclopaedia of Judaism* (ed. Geoffrey Wijoder; Jesuit Publishing House; New York: Macmillan, 1989).

B. *Articles*

1. 'Laws of Marriage and Divorce in Israel', *Jewish Review* (Jan., 1949).
2. 'Halachah and Changing Conditions', *Chayenu* (Jan./Feb., 1950).
3. 'Jewish Attitude to Artificial Insemination', *Journal of Sex Education* (Feb., 1950).
4. 'Modern Problems in the Responsa', *Chayenu* (May/June, 1950).
5. 'The Place of Dogma in Judaism', *JC* (Aug. 18, 1950).
6. 'Jews and Gambling', *JC* (Nov. 17, 1950).
7. 'The Flexibility of Jewish Law', *Chayenu* (Jan. /Feb., 1951).
8. 'Jewish Law in the Modern World: An Orthodox View', *Jewish Monthly* (April, 1951).
9. 'The Sale of Chametz', *JC* (April 13, 1951).
10. 'The Sabbatical Year', *JC* (Sept. 21, 1951).
11. 'Mother or Baby? Jewish View', *Zionist Record* (Nov. 23, 1951).
12. 'Evidence of Literary Device in the Babylonian Talmud', *JJS* 3/4 (1952), pp. 157-63.
13. 'The Spirit of the Din', *Chayenu* (Jan./Feb., 1952).
14. 'Spiritual Healing and Judaism', *JC* (Feb. 8, 1952).
15. 'Slander in Jewish Law', *JC* (April 7, 1952).

16. 'The Days of Awe', *JC* (Sept. 19, 1952).

17. 'Israel Revives Hakhel', *Jewish Review* (Oct. 3, 1952).

18. 'Organic Growth vs. Petrification', *Jewish Spectator* (New York, Nov., 1952).

19. 'Conscription of Women the Halachic Background', *Jewish Review* (Nov. 14, 1952).

20. 'A Matrimonial Problem', *JC* (Nov. 21, 1952).

21. 'The Talmudic Hermeneutic Rule of 'Binyan 'Abh' and John Stuart Mills' Method of Agreement', *JJS* 42 (1953), pp. 59-64.

22. 'The Aristotelian Syllogism and the Qal Wa Homer', *JJS* 4/4 (1953), pp. 154-57.

23. 'Hebraic Elements in the Coronation', *JC* (Jan. 9, 1953).

24. 'The Talmid Hakham', *Jewish Spectator* (New York, April, 1953).

25. 'Jewish Medical Lore', *JC* (May 1, 1953).

26. 'Misplaced Emphases in Present-Day Jewish Life and Thought', *Addresses Given at the Tenth Conference of Anglo-Jewish Preachers* (May 4-7, 1953), pp. 52-62.

27. 'Psycho-Analysis and Faith', *JC* (May 8, 1953).

28. 'Rabbi Israel Salanter A 70th Anniversary', *JC* (June 12, 1953).

29. 'The Plaster on the Wound', *JC* (Sept. 18, 1953).

30. 'Attitudes to the Questioner', *JC* (Jan. 15, 1954).

31. 'This is the Law', *JC* (July 23, 1954).

32. 'Remembering Jerusalem', *Jewish Review* (Sept. 24, 1954).

33. 'The Economic Situation of the Jews in Babylon' (Heb.), *Melilah* (ed. E. Robertson and M. Wallenstein; Manchester University Press), V (1955), pp. 83-100.

34. 'Jewish Faith', *JC* (Feb. 4, 1955).

35. 'The Higher Law', *Liverpool Jewish Gazette* (Sept. 16, 1955).

36. 'To Dwell in Booths', *JC* (Sept. 30, 1955).

37. 'Freud and Judaism', *AJA Quarterly* 2/2 (September, 1955).

38. Review of Abraham Weiss: *le-heqer ha-Talmud*, *JJS* 8/2, 3 (1956), pp. 114-17.

39. 'The Concept of Hasid in the Biblical and Rabbinic Literatures', *JJS* 8/3, 4 (1957), pp. 143-54.

40. Review of Solomon Goldman: *The Ten Commandments, Conservative Judaism* (Summer, 1957), pp. 42-44.

41. 'The Economic Condition of the Jews in Babylon in Talmudic Times Compared with Palestine', *JJS* 2 (4 Oct. 1957), pp. 349-59.

42. 'Greater Love Hath No Man. . . The Jewish Point of View of Self-Sacrifice', *Judaism* 6/1 (Winter, 1957), pp. 41-47.

43. 'The Sources of Jewish Law' and 'Property', in *An Introduction to Jewish Law* (ed. Peter Elman; London: Lincolns-Prager, 1958), pp. 11-17 and 44-55.

44. 'Further Evidence of Literary Device in the Babylonian Talmud', *JJS* 9/3, 4 (1958), pp. 139-47.

45. 'Views of Youth', *JC* (Jan. 10, 1958).

46. 'Our Relations with God', in *The Principles and Practices of Judaism*, ed. Raphael Powell (London, 1959), pp. 84-94.

47. 'What is Kabbalah?', *Jewish Heritage* 2/1 (Spring, 1959), pp. 17-22.

48. 'The God of his Fathers: Herman Wouk's Judaism', *AJA Quarterly* 6/1 (April, 1960), pp. 18-20.

49. 'Jewish Principles and the Eichmann Trial', *JC* (March 17, 1961).

50. 'The Hidden Light: The Religious Philosophy of Rabbi Kook', *JC*, New York Section (Sept. 8), 1961.

51. 'Montefiore and Loewe on the Rabbis', The Claude Montefiore Lecture (London: The Liberal Jewish Synagogue, 1962).
52. ' The Mystical School', in *Jewish Philosophy and Philosophers* (ed. Ramond Goldwater; London: Hillel Foundation, 1962).
53. 'Martyrdom and the Maccabees', *JC* (Dec. 21, 1962).
54. 'Selfishness in Prayer', *JC* (Jan. 18, 1963).
55. ' Torah Wisdom in Modern Diction', *JC*, Supplement (April 12, 1963).
56. ' The Image of God', *JC* New Year Section (Sept. 13, 1963).
57. ' Torah and the Personal Life', in *Great Jewish Ideas* (ed. Abraham Ezra Milligram; Washington: B'nai B'rith Adult Education Series, 1964), pp. 81-94.
58. Review of Max Kadushin: *The Rabbinic Mind, Conservative Judaism* 20/1 (Fall, 1965), pp. 67-69.
59. 'Marriage in Jewish Law', *JC* (Dec. 31, 1965).
60. 'Women and Jewish Law', *JC* (April 29, 1966).
61. 'Problems of Conversion', *World Jewry* (May/June, 1966).
62. Contribution to Symposium 'God Where Art Thou?', *Twentieth Century* (Autumn 1966), pp. 7-10.
63. 'One of the People' (Ahad Ha-Am), *JC* (Dec. 30, 1966).
64. ' The Doctrine of the "Divine Spark" in Man in Jewish Sources', in *Studies in Rationalism, Judaism and Universalism in Memory of Leon Roth* (ed. Raphael Loewe; London: Routledge and Kegan Paul, 1966), pp. 87-117.
65. 'Liberal Supernaturalism', in *Varieties of Jewish Belief* (ed. Ira Eisenstein; New York: Reconstructionist Press, 1966), pp. 109-22.
66. ' The *Via-Negativa* in Jewish Religious Thought', Allan Bronfman Lecture (New York: Judaica Press, 1966).
67. 'Current Theological Literature: Philosophical Theology', *Judaism* 16/1 (Winter, 1967), pp. 84-89.
68. 'Current Theological Literature: Symposia', *Judaism* 16/2 (Spring, 1967), pp. 207-13.
69. 'Freud and Judaism', *World Jewry* (March/April, 1967).
70. 'Current Theological Literature: Theological Responsa', *Judaism* 16/3 (Summer, 1967), pp. 345-52.
71. 'Mysticism in Modern Jewish Life', *European Judaism* 2/2 (Summer, 1967), pp. 32-35.
72. 'Current Theological Literature: Mysticism', *Judaism* 16/4 (Fall, 1967), pp. 475-81.
73. 'God and Man', *World Jewry* (Sept./Oct., 1967).
74. 'God and I', *Nova* (Jan. 1968), pp. 60-61.
75. 'Current Theological Literature: Providence', *Judaism* 17/2 (Spring, 1968), pp. 197-202.
76. 'Current Theological Literature: The Problem of Evil in Our Time', *Judaism* 17/3 (Summer, 1968), pp. 347-51.
77. 'Sin and Forgiveness', *JC* (Sept. 27, 1968).
78. ' "Honour Thy Father": A Study in Hasidic Psychology' (Heb.), in *Hagut 'Ivrit Be'Eyropa* (ed. M. Zohari and Arye Tartakover; Tel-Aviv, 1969), pp. 136-43.
79. ' The Pulpit as an Instrument of Theological Teaching', Proceedings of the Rabbinical Assembly of America (1969), pp. 9-24.
80. 'Current Theological Literature: Jewish Perspectives', *Judaism* 18/1 (Winter, 1969), pp. 78-83.

81. 'Current Theological Literature: Prayer', *Judaism* 18/2 (Spring, 1969), pp. 210-15.
82. 'Current Theological Literature: Hasidism', *Judaism* 18/3 (Summer, 1969), pp. 337-42.
83. 'Current Theological Literature: Time and Eternity', *Judaism* 18/4 (Fall, 1969), pp. 458-63.
84. Review of Max Kadushin: *A Conceptual Approach to the Mekilta*, *Conservative Judaism* 14/1 (Fall, 1969), pp. 93-94.
85. 'Judaism Without God?', *JC* New Year Section (Sept. 12, 1969).
86. Review of Eugene B. Borowitz: *A New Jewish Theology in the Making* and *Can a Jew Speak of Faith Today?*, *Commentary* 48/5 (November, 1969), pp. 80-91.
87. 'Formula for Confession', *JC* (Oct. 9, 1970).
88. 'Halacha and history', *JC* (Oct. 16, 1970).
89. 'Are There Fictitious Baraitot in the Babylonian Talmud?', *HUCA* 42 (1971), pp. 185-96.
90. 'Judaism', in *Man Myth and Magic* 55 (1971), pp. 1529-38.
91. 'The "As-If" Concept', *European Judaism* 6/1 (Winter, 1971/72) pp. 44-49.
92. 'Messianic Ideas', *JC* (Nov. 12, 1971).
93. 'Akedah', *EJ* (Jerusalem: Keter, 1972), II, pp. 480-84.
94. 'Halakhah', *EJ* , VII, pp. 1161-67.
95. 'Halakhah Le-Moshe Misinai', *EJ*, VII, pp. 1167.
96. 'Hasidism Basic Ideas', *EJ* ,VII, pp. 1403-407.
97. 'Hermeneutics', *EJ*, VIII, pp. 366-72.
98. 'Judaism', *EJ*, X, pp. 383-97.
99. 'Messiah in Modern Jewish Thought', *EJ*, XI, pp. 1415-16.
100. 'Moses', *EJ*, XII, pp. 393 and 399-402.
101. 'Passover', *EJ*, XIII, pp. 163-69.
102. 'Purim', *EJ*, XIII, pp. 1390-96.
103. 'Righteousness', *EJ*, XIV, pp. 180-84.
104. 'Sabbath', *EJ* , XIV, pp. 562-67.
105. 'Shavuot', *EJ*, XIV, pp. 1319-22.
106. 'Sin, Rabbinic Views', *EJ*, XIV, pp. 1591-93.
107. 'Study', *EJ*, XV, pp. 453-58.
108. 'Sukkot', *EJ* , XV, pp. 495-502.
109. 'Theology', XV, pp. 1103-10.
110. 'Torah, Reading of', *EJ*, XV, pp. 1246-55.
111. Introduction to reprint German works by David Kaufmann (Farnborough Hants: Gregg International Publications, 1972).
112. Introduction to reprint Don Isaac Abravanel's *Opera Minora* (Farnborough, Hants: Gregg International Publications, 1972).
113. 'Judaism' in *Dictionary of Medical Ethics* (ed. A.S. Duncan, G.R. Duncan and R.B. Welbourne; London: Darton, Longman and Todd, 1977), pp. 191-92.
114. 'The Love of Law and the Law of Love'. Lecture given in the Crypt of St. Paul's Cathedral (London, 1972).
115. 'The *qal va-homer* Argument in the Old Testament', *BSOAS* 35, Part 2 (1972), pp. 221-27.
116. Review of Samuel S. Cohon: *Jewish Theology*, *JJS* 22/2 (Autumn, 1972), pp. 196-97.
117. 'Obituary Abraham J. Heschel', *JC* (Nov. 23, 1972).

118. Introduction to *Modern Jewish Thought Selected Issues* (New York: Arno Press, 1973).
119. Introduction to *Ten Essays on Zionism and Judaism* by Achad Ha-Am (trans. Leon Simon; New York: Arno Press, 1973).
120. 'Judaism and Membership', in *Church Membership and Intercommunion* (ed. J. Kent and R. Murray; London: Darton, Longman and Todd, 1973), pp. 141-54.
121. 'The Relationship between Religion and Ethics in Jewish Thought', in *Religion and Morality* (ed. Gene Outka and John P. Reeder, Jr; Garden City, NY: Anchor Books, 1973), pp. 155-72. (repr. in M. Kellner [ed.], *Contemporary Jewish Ethics* (New York: Sanhedrin, 1978).
122. Review of B.S. Jackson: *Theft in Early Jewish Law*, JJS 24/1 (Spring, 1973), pp. 91-93.
123. 'The Talmudic *Sugya* as a Literary Unit', *JJS* 24/2 (Autumn, 1973), pp. 119-26.
124. 'Face to Faith', *The Guardian* (Sat. July 27, 1974).
125. Review of: Jacob Neusner (ed.), *Soviet Views on Talmudic Judaism*; Roy A. Rosenberg, *The Anatomy of God*; Seymour J. Cohen (ed. and trans.), *Sefer ha-Yashar*; Jacob Neusner (ed.), *Understanding Jewish Theology*; Eliezer Berkovits, *Faith after the Holocaust*; Jeanette Meisel Baron (ed). *Steeled by Adversity*; Eugene B. Borowitz, *The Mask Jews Wear*, JJS 25/2 (Summer, 1974), pp. 342-43, 347-49.
126. 'Face to Faith', *The Guardian* (Sat. Oct. 19, 1974).
127. 'A Study of Four Parallel *Sugyot* in the Babylonian Talmud', *JJS* 25 (Winter, 1974), pp. 398-411.
128. 'Jewish Cosmology', in *Ancient Cosmologies* (ed. Carmen Blacker and Michael Loewe; London: George Allen and Unwin, 1975), pp. 66-86.
129. 'Judaism', in *Family of Man*, 5, Part 69 (1975), pp. 1929-31.
130. 'Prayer in Judaism', *The Month* (June, 1975), pp. 168-70.
131. 'The Lubavich Movement', *EJ* Yearbook, 1975–76, pp. 161-65.
132. 'Meshullam Feivush Heller of Zbarazh', *EJ* Yearbook, 1975–76, pp. 361-62.
133. Review of David E. Powell: *Antireligious Propaganda in the Soviet Union, International Journal for Philosophy of Religion* 7/2, pp. 388-89.
134. Review of Hans Jonas: *Philosophical Essays, International Journal for Philosophy of Religion*, 7/3 (1976), p. 454.
135. Review of Gerald Blidstein: *Honor Thy Father and Mother: Filial Responsibility in Jewish Law and Ethics*, JJSO 18/1 (June, 1976), pp. 67-68.
136. Review of Isaac Breuer: *Concepts of Judaism, Judaism* 25/4 (Fall, 1976), pp. 501-504.
137. 'Spinoza Re-assessed', *JC* (Feb. 18, 1977).
138. 'How much of the Babylonian Talmud is Pseudepigraphic?', *JJS*, 28/1 (Spring, 1977), pp. 46-59.
139. Review of Irving J. Rosenbaum: *The Holocaust and Halakhah*, JJSO 19/2 (June, 1977), pp. 98-99.
140. 'Great Affirmation of Torah: A Guide to the Machzor', *JC* New Year Section (Sept. 9, 1977).
141. Review of J. David Bleich: *Contemporary Halakhic Problems, JJSO* 19/2 (Dec., 1977), pp. 205-207.
142. Review of A. Roy Eckhart: *Your People, My People, International Journal for Philosophy of Religion* 8/1 (1977), p. 72.

143. 'The Responsa of Rabbi Joseph Hayyim of Bagdhad', in *Perspectives on Jews and Judaism: Essays in Honor of Wolfe Kelman* (ed. Arthur A. Chiel; New York, 1978), pp. 189-214.
144. 'The Doctrine of the Zaddik in the Thought of Elimelech of Lizensk', The Rabbi Louis Feinberg Memorial Lecture, University of Cincinnati (Feb. 9, 1978).
145. 'The Bible as History', *JC* (May 18, 1978).
146. Review of Moshe Carmilly-Weinberger: *Censorship and Freedom of Expression in Jewish History*, *JJSO* 20/1 (June 1978), pp. 86-87.
147. Review of Simon Greenberg: *The Ethical in the Jewish and American Heritage*, *JJSO* 20/2 (Dec., 1978), pp.186- 87.
148. 'Rabbi Meir Simhah of Dvinsk'. Second Annual Rabbi Dr. Georg Salzberger Memorial Lecture (London, Dec. 10, 1978).
149. 'Eating as an Act of Worship in Hasidic Thought', in *Studies in Jewish Religious and Intellectual History Presented to Alexander Altmann* (ed. S.S. Stein and R. Loewe; Alabama: University of Alabama Press, 1979), pp. 157-66.
150. 'The Relevance and Irrelevance of Hasidism', *The Solomon Goldman Lectures*, II (ed. Nathaniel Stampfer; Chicago: Spertus College Press, 1979), pp. 19-28.
151. 'Kabbalistic World View', in *Ultimate Reality and Meaning*, University of Toronto Press, II/4 (1979), pp. 321-29.
152. 'Giudaismo' in *Enciclopedia Del Novecento*, Instituto dell' Encliclopedia Italiano (1979), III, pp. 370-79.
153. Review of Bernard S. Jackson (ed.): *The Jewish Law Annual I*, *JJS* (Spring, 1979), pp. 105-107.
154. 'Torah and Physics', *JC* (April 27, 1979).
155. 'The Talmud as the Final Authority', *Judaism* 29/1 (Winter, 1980), pp. 45-48.
156. Review of Robert Goldenberg: *The Sabbath Law of Rabbi Meir* and Samuel Atlas: *Netivim be-Mishpat ha-'Ivir*, *JJS* 31/1 (Spring, 1980), pp. 115-16 and 126-28.
157. 'Sons and Mystics', *JC* Passover Suppl. (March 28, 1980).
158. 'Divine Foreknowledge and Human Free Will', *Conservative Judaism* 24/1 (Sept./Oct. 1980), pp. 4-16.
159. 'Saturn in Jewish Literature', *JC* (Nov. 28, 1980).
160. 'The Concept of Power in the Jewish Tradition', *Conservative Judaism* 33/2 (Winter, 1980), pp. 18-28.
161. 'The *Sugya* on Sufferings in B. *Berakhot* 5a-b', in *Studies in Memory of Joseph Heinemann* (ed. Jakob J. Petuchowski and Ezra Fleischer; Jerusalem, 1981), pp. 32-44.
162. 'The Problem of the Akedah in Jewish Thought', in *Kierkegaard's Fear and Trembling: Critical Approaches* (ed. Robert L. Perkins; Alabama: University of Alabama Press, 1981), pp. 1-9.
163. 'Rabbi Aryeh Laib Heller's Theological Introduction to his *Shev Shema' tata'*, *Modern Judaism* 1 (1981), pp. 184-216.
164. Review of M.B. Margolies: *Samuel David Luzzatto*, *The Heythrop Journal* 22/3 (July, 1981), pp. 327-29.
165. Review of Solomon B. Freehof: *New Reform Responsa* and Alan Unterman: *Jews. Their Religious Beliefs and Practices*, *JJSO* 23/2 (Dec., 1981), pp. 147-48 and 154-57.
166. 'Zionism after 100 Years', in *Proceedings of the Rabbinical Assembly 1981* 43 (New York, 1982), pp. 56-63.

167. 'A Fresh Look at the Torah', *JC* (March 19, 1982).

168. 'From Babylon to Spain', *JC* (March 26, 1982).

169. Review of Jacob Haberman: *Maimonides and Aquinas: A Contemporary Appraisal*, *Judaism* 31 (Spring, 1982), pp. 254-56.

170. Review of F.T. Fisher and D.F. Polish: *The Formation of Social Policy in the Catholic–Jewish Traditions*, *The Heythrop Journal* 23/3 (July 1982), pp. 342-43).

171. 'Mezuzot and other mitzvot', *JC* Suppl. (Oct. 8, 1982).

172. 'Praying for the Downfall of the Wicked', *Modern Judaism* 2/3 (Oct., 1982), pp. 297-310.

173. 'The Numbered Sequence as a Literary Device in the Babylonian Talmud', in *Hebrew Annual Review*, 7: *Biblical and other Studies in honor of Robert Gordis* (ed. Reuben Ahroni; Ohio State University, 1983), pp. 137-50.

174. Review of Emil L. Fackenheim: *To Mend the World: Foundations of Future Jewish Thought* and Chaim Raphael: *The Springs of Jewish Life*, *JJSO* 25/1 (June, 1983), pp. 63 and 68-69.

175. Review of James E. Priest: *Governmental and Judicial Ethics in the Bible and Rabbinic Literature*; Rachel Elior: *Torat ha-Elohut be-Dor ha-Sheni shel Hasidut Habad*; Aaron Kirschenbaum (ed.): *Dine Israel: An Annual of Jewish Law*, *JJS* 24/2 (Autumn, 1983), pp. 216-17 and 226-28.

176. 'A Direct Line to Heaven: On Prayer', *JC* New Year Section (Sept. 2, 1983).

177. 'Two Hasidic Masters and the Problem of Discipleship', *The Melton Journal* 15 (New York, Winter, 1983), pp. 3-4.

178. 'The Jewish Tradition', in *The World's Religious Traditions. Essays in Honour of Wilfred Cantwell Smith* (ed. Frank Whaling; Edinburgh: T. and T. Clark, 1984), pp. 72-91.

179. Preface to *Safed Spirituality* by Lawrence Fine (New York and Toronto: Paulist Press, 1984).

180. 'Symbols for the Divine in the Kabbalah', Friends of Dr Williams's Library 34th Lecture (London, 1984).

181. Review of David B. Ruderman: *The World of the Renaissance Jew*, *The Heythrop Journal* 25/1 (Jan. 1984), pp. 98-99.

182. Review of Mortimer Ostrow (ed.): *Judaism and Psychoanalysis*, *The Heythrop Journal* 25/2 (April, 1984), p. 206.

183. 'Face to Faith', *The Guardian* (Monday, April, 2, 1984).

184. 'Halacha: The Movable Feast', *JC* (May 18, 1984).

185. Review of Reuben P. Bulka: *Dimensions of Orthodox Judaism*, *JJSO* 26/1 (June, 1984), pp. 65-66.

186. 'Human Rights and Human Duties', *JC* (June 22, 1984).

187. 'Holy Places', *Conservative Judaism* 37/3 (Spring, 1984), pp. 4-16.

188. 'Why Don't You Say a Blessing Before Work', *Manna* (Summer, 1984), pp. 9-11.

189. 'The Origin of Torah: A Response', *JC* (Nov. 16, 1984).

190. 'There is No Problem of Descent', *Judaism* 34 (Winter, 1985), pp. 55-59.

191. 'Aspects of Scholem's Study of Hasidism', *Modern Judaism* 5/1 (1985), pp. 95-104.

192. Review of Basil Herring: *Joseph Ibn Kaspi's Gevia' Kesef*, *The Heythrop Journal* 26/3 (July, 1985), pp. 322-23.

193. Review of Eliezer Berkowitz: *Not in Heaven*; Eugene B. Borowitz: *Choices in Modern Jewish Thought*; J. David Bleich: *Judaism and Healing*; Ella Belfer: *Manhigut*

Ruḥanit be-Yisrael; David S. Zubatsky and Irwin M. Besent: *Jewish Genealogies*; Edward Zipperstein: *Business Ethics in Jewish Law*, *JJS* 37.2 (Autumn, 1985), pp. 263-65.

194. Review of Eliezer Schweid: *The Land of Israel*, *JJSO* 26/2 (Dec., 1985), pp. 149-51.

195. 'Judaism', in *the Study of Spirituality*, ed. Cheslyn Jones, Geoffrey Wainwright and Edward Yarnold, S.J. (London: SPCK, 1986), pp. 491-97.

196. Review of H.G. Perelmuter: *David Darshan* in *Polin, A Journal of Polish Jewish Studies*, 1 (Oxford: Basil Blackwell, 1986), pp. 361-62.

197. Review of Walter C. Kaiser: *Toward Old Testament Ethics*, *The Heythrop Journal* 27/1 (Jan., 1986), p. 72.

198. 'For the Sake of Heaven', *JC* (Dec. 19, 1986).

199. ' *Tur*, Preface to *Hoshen Mishpat*', trans. and Commentary, *The Jewish Law Annual* 6 (London, Paris, 1987), pp. 211-29.

200. ' The Jewish Tradition in Today's World', in *Religion in Today's World*, ed. Frank Whaling (Edinburgh: T.& T. Clark, 1987), pp. 211-29.

201. 'Attitudes toward Christianity', in *Gevurat Haromah, Jewish Studies Offered at the Eightieth Birthday of Rabbi Moses Cyrus Weiler* (ed. Ze'ev Falk; Jerusalem: Mesharim, 1987), pp. xxvii-xxxiii.

202. ' The Uplifting of Sparks in Later Jewish Mysticism', in *Jewish Spirituality from the Sixteenth Century Revival to the Present* (ed. Arthur Green; New York: Crossroad, 1987), pp. 99-126.

203. 'Faith', in *Contemporary Jewish Religious Thought* (ed. Arthur A. Cohen and Paul Mendes-Flohr; New York: Scribner's, 1987), pp. 233-38.

204. 'God', in *Contemporary Jewish Religious Thought* (ed. Arthur A. Cohen and Paul Mendes-Flohr; New York: Scribner's, 1987), pp. 291-98.

205. Article: 'Attributes of God: Jewish Concepts' in *ER* (ed. Mircea Eliade; New York: Macmillan, 1987), I, pp. 507-11.

206. 'God in Postbiblical Judaism', *ER*, VI, pp. 11-17.

207. 'Hanukkah', *ER*, VI, pp. 193-94.

208. 'Jewish Religious Year', *ER*, VIII, pp. 41-45.

209. 'Passover', *ER*, XI, pp. 204-205.

210. 'Purim', *ER*, XII, p. 100.

211. 'Rosh Ha-Shanah and Yom Kippur', *ER*, XII, pp. 473-76.

212. 'Shabbat', *ER*, XIII, pp. 189-92.

213. 'Shavu'ot', *ER*, XIII, p. 229.

214. 'Sukkot', *ER*, XIV, pp. 131-32.

215. 'Judaism' in *The Encyclopedia of World Faiths* (ed. Peter Bishop and Michael Darton; London: Macdonald Orbis, 1987), pp. 32-53.

216. Review of Paul Johnson: *A History of the Jews*, *The Tablet* (May 2, 1987).

217. Review of Ronald S. Algin and Gershon D. Hundert (eds.): *Community and the Individual Jew: Essays in Honor of Lucy M. Becker*; Nahum M. Sarna: *Exploring Exodus*; Jonathan Sacks (ed.): *Tradition and Transition: Essays Presented to the Chief Rabbi Sir Immanuel Jakobovits*, *JJSO* 29/1 (June, 1987), pp. 63, 68-69, 69-91.

218. 'Sanctity and Meaning of Human Life in Relation to the Present Situation of Violence', in *Fifteen Years of Catholic–Jewish Dialogue*, Libreria Editriot Vaticana (1988), pp. 191-96.

219. 'World Jewish Fundamentalism', in *Survey of Jewish Affairs 1987* (ed. William Frankel; Associated University Presses, 1988), pp. 221-34.

220. 'Historical Thinking in the Post-Talmudic Period', in *Essays in Jewish Historiography* (ed. Ada Rapoport-Albert; Wesleyan University, 1988), pp. 65-77.

221. Review of David Weiss Halivni: Midrash, Mishnah, and Gemara: The Jewish Predilection for Justified Law', *Judaism* 37/2 (Spring, 1988), pp. 244-47.

222. Review of Basil F. Herring: *Jewish Ethics and Halakhah for Our Time*; Abraham P. Bloch: *The Book of Jewish Ethical Concepts, The Heythrop Journal* 29/2 (April, 1988), pp. 244-45.

223. Review of Mordecai Rottenberg: *Rebiographing and Deviance, JJSO* 30/1 (June, 1988), pp. 65-66.

224. Review of Howard Eilberg-Schwartz, *The Human Will in Judaism*; Samuel S. Cohon: *Essays in Jewish Theology*; Harold M. Schulweiss: *Evil and the Morality of God*; Joseph Dan (ed.): *The Early Kabbalah*; Moshe Ideal: *The Mystical Experience in Abraham Abulafia*; Sheila A. Spector: *Jewish Mysticism, JJS* 29/2 (Autumn, 1988), pp. 279-83.

225. Review of Gershon Weiler: *Jewish Theocracy, JJSO* 30/2 (1988), pp. 138-39.

226. 'Jüdische Theologie', in *Evangelisches Kirchenlexikon* (Göttingen: Vandenhoeck & Ruprecht, 1989), pp. 881-88.

227. 'Eye-to-eye on Vengeance', *The Times* (Wed., Jan. 11, 1989).

228. Review of Judith Hauptman: *Development of the Talmudic Sugya*; Moshe Idel: *Kabbalah New Perspectives*; Moshe Ideal: *Studies in Ecstatic Kabbalah*; Moshe Idel: *Language, Torah and Hermeneutics in Abraham Abulafia*; Joel Roth: *The Halakhic Process*; Simon Greenburg (ed.): *The Ordination of Women as Rabbis*; B.S. Jackson (ed.): *Jewish Law Association Studies*, 1 and 2; Abraham J. Heschel: *The Circle of the Baal Shem Tov*; Dan Cohn-Sherbok: *The Jewish Heritage*; William Zuidema: *God's Partner*; Michael Rosenak: *Commandments and Concerns, JJS* 40/2 (Autumn, 1989), pp. 249-52 and 260-64.

229. 'Israel and the Nations: A Literary Analysis of a Talmudic *Sygya*', *The Tel-Aviv Review* 2 (Fall, 1989–Winter, 1990), pp. 372-83.

230. 'Busse', *TRE* (Berlin and New York: Walter de Gruyter, forthcoming)' VII. 3, pp. 439-46.

231. 'Halacha', *TRE* , IV, 3-4, pp. 384-88.

232. 'Herrschaft Gottes im Judentum', *TRE*, XV, 1-2, pp. 190-96.

233. ' "Woe to me if I say it. Woe to me if I do not say it." The Development of a Talmudic Maxim', *Ish Bi-Gevurot: Studies in Jewish Heritage and History Presented to Rabbi Alexandre Safran* (ed. Moshe Hallamish; Jerusalem, 1990).

CONTRIBUTORS

1. Rabbi Dr Dan Cohn-Sherbok teaches Jewish theology at the University of Kent at Canterbury.
2. Professor Jacob Neusner is Graduate Research Professor of Religious Studies at the University of South Florida and Martin Buber Professor of Judaic Studies at the University of Frankfurt.
3. Professor Eugene Borowitz is Sigmund L. Falk Distinguished Professor of Education and Jewish Religious Thought at the Hebrew Union College–Jewish Institute of Religion.
4. Professor Steven T. Katz is Professor of Jewish Studies at Cornell University.
5. Rabbi Dr Albert Friedlander is Rabbi of the Westminster Synagogue, London and Dean of the Leo Baeck College, London.
6. Professor Byron L. Sherwin is Vice President of Academic Affairs and Professor of Jewish Philosophy and Mysticism at Spertus College of Judaica, Chicago.
7. Rabbi Dr Nicholas de Lange is Lecturer in Rabbinics at Cambridge University.
8. Dr Mark Geller is Reader in Jewish Studies at University College, London.
9. Dr Adrian Cunningham is Chairman of the Department of Religious Studies at Lancaster University.
10. Professor Marc Saperstein is Gloria M. Goldstein Professor of Jewish History and Thought at Washington University, St Louis.
11. Rabbi Dr Jonathan Magonet is Principal of the Leo Baeck College, London.
12. Dr David Patterson is President of the Oxford Centre for Postgraduate Hebrew Studies.
13. Dr Paul Morris is Lecturer in Religious Studies at the University of Lancaster.

INDEX OF REFERENCES

INDEX OF AUTHORS

JOURNAL FOR THE STUDY OF THE OLD TESTAMENT

Supplement Series